D0526476

Human Resource Management
for Hospitality Services

Withdrawn from
Queen Margaret University Library

QUEEN MARGARET UNIVERSITY COLLEGE LIBRARY

Series in Tourism and Hospitality Management

Series Editors:

Professor Roy C. Wood
The Scottish Hotel School, University of Strathclyde, UK

Stephen J. Page
Massey University, New Zealand

Series Consultant:

Professor C. L. Jenkins
The Scottish Hotel School, University of Strathclyde, UK

Textbooks in this series:

Books in this series are available on free inspection for lecturers considering the texts for course adoption. Details of these and any other International Thomson Business Press titles are available by writing to the publishers (Berkshire House, 168–173 High Holborn, London WCIV 7AA) or by telephoning the Promotions Department on 0171 497 1422.

Human Resource Management for Hospitality Services

Alistair L. Goldsmith,
Dennis P. Nickson,
Donald H. Sloan
and Roy C. Wood

INTERNATIONAL THOMSON BUSINESS PRESS
I ⓉP® An International Thomson Publishing Company

London • Bonn • Boston • Johannesburg • Madrid • Melbourne • Mexico City • New York • Paris
Singapore • Tokyo • Toronto • Albany, NY • Belmont, CA • Cincinnati, OH • Detroit, MI

Human Resource Management for Hospitality Services

Copyright ©1997 Alistair P. Goldsmith, Dennis P. Nickson,
Donald H. Sloan, Roy C. Wood

The Thomson Learning logo is a registered trademark used herein under license

All rights reserved. No part of this work which is copyright may be reproduced or used in any form or by any means – graphic, electronic, or mechanical, including photocopying, recording, taping, or information storage and retrieval systems – without the written permission of the Publisher, except in accordance with the provisions of the Copyright Designs and Patents Act 1988.

Whilst the Publisher has taken all reasonable care in the preparation of this book the Publisher makes no representation, express or implied, with regard to the accuracy of the information contained in this book and cannot accept any legal responsibility or liability for any errors or omissions from the book or the consequences thereof.

Products and services that are referred to in this book may be either trademarks and/or registered trademarks of their respective owners. The Publisher/s and Author/s make no claim to these trademarks.

Every effort has been made to trace copyright holders of material reproduced in this book. Any rights not acknowledged here will be acknowledged in subsequent printings if notice is given to the publishers.

British Library Cataloguing-in-Publication Data
A catalogue record for this book is available from the British Library

First edition 1997
Reprinted 2000

Printed in the UK by The Alden Group, Oxford

ISBN 1-86152-095-6

Thomson Learning
Berkshire House
High Holborn
London WC1V 7AA
UK

http://www.thomsonlearning.co.uk

Contents

Figures and Tables

Series Editors' Foreword

The international Thomson Business Press Series in Tourism and Hospitality is dedicated to the publication of high quality textbooks and other volumes that will be of benefit to those engaged in tourism, hotel and hospitality education, especially at degree and postgraduate level. The series has two principal stands: core textbooks on key areas of the curriculum; and the Topics in Tourism and Hospitality series which includes highly focused and shorter texts on particular themes and issues. All the authors in the series are experts in their own fields, actively engaged in teaching, research and consultancy in tourism and hospitality. Each book comprises an authoritative blend of subject-relevant theoretical considerations and practical applications. Furthermore, a unique quality of the series is that it is student oriented, offering accessible texts that take account of the realities of administration, management and operations in tourism and hospitality contexts, being constructively critical without losing sight of the overall goal of providing clear accounts of essential concepts, issues and techniques.

The series is committed to quality, accessibility, relevance and originality in its approach. Quality is ensured as a result of a vigorous referencing process, unusual in the publication of textbooks. Accessibility is achieved through the use of innovative textual design techniques, and the use of discussion points, case studies and exercises within books, all geared to encouraging a comprehensive understanding of the material contained therein. Relevance and originality together result from the experience of authors as key authorities in their fields.

The tourism and hospitality industries are diverse and dynamic industries and it is the intention of the editors to reflect this diversity and dynamism by publishing quality texts that enhance topical subjects without losing sight of enduring themes. the Series Editors and Consultants are greatful to Steven Reed of International Thomson Business Press for his commitment, expertise and support of this philosophy.

Series Editors

Professor Roy C. Wood
The Scottish Hotel School
University of Strathclyde
United Kingdom

Stephen J. Page
Massey University – Albany
Auckland
New Zealand

Series Consultant

Professor C. L. Jenkins
The Scottish Hotel School
University of Strathclyde
United Kingdom

Acknowledgements

The authors are indebted to Jean Finlayson for her great skill and forbearance in dealing with four different working styles and four different types of manuscript. Her efficiency and accuracy were crucial to welding this text into a coherent whole under conditions where even her great patience must, on occasions, have been sorely stretched. We would like to acknowledge the permission of *Economist* newspapers for allowing us to reproduce the article shown in Box 10.4; Professor Tom Baum for the illustrations reproduced in Box 1.2; Sage Publications for the material reproduced from J Hyman and B Mason (1995) *Managing Employee Involvement and Participation* in Box 7.1; and Ms Amanda Scott, General Manager of the Copthorne Hotel Glasgow, for the Employee Appraisal Report reproduced in Box 8.1. As always, errors of all types are the responsibility of the authors.

What is human resource management? | 1

Human resource management has enjoyed much popularity as a 'buzz' term since the 1980s. The objective of this chapter is to set the context for the remainder of this book by outlining some of the key issues relating to human resource and personnel management in the hospitality industry.

HUMAN RESOURCE MANAGEMENT – A TERM IN SEARCH OF A MEANING?

Human resource management (HRM) is not a simple synonym for personnel management. Many people do use these terms interchangeably but human resource management is normally conceived as having a much wider scope than personnel management. Personnel management is only one element of HRM. Singh (1992) identifies three component elements to HRM. These are:

- the activities of traditional personnel management (e.g. recruitment, training, remuneration, discipline);
- a specific managerial and organizational 'philosophy' that views people as (a) the **major** organizational asset; and (b) regards workers as instinctively willing and able to be developed; and
- integration of the personnel management function into the strategic management of the organization.

HRM has its origins in the United States, and especially the innovative practices of companies like International Business Machines (IBM) and Hewlett-Packard (Towers 1992). However, as Singh (1992) notes, there is little evidence that human resource management is at all widespread in United States industries. We must be cautious therefore in establishing to what extent those organizations that claim to have human resource management practices actually do so, as opposed to simply paying lip-service to the concept.

Two issues in the current literature on HRM concerning the **motives** for introducing human resource management policies are worth considering. The first centres on HRM as anti- or non-union. There is some consensus that the evolving pattern of HRM-type approaches in UK industry is in part due to the declining significance of trade unions whose powers have been considerably circumscribed since 1979 as a result of legislative measures by government. One argument is that HRM fills this gap, by providing more authoritarian-paternalistic styles of management which are both highly individualistic in seeking to increase the individual commitment of employees to the organization, whilst at the same time undermining trade unionism or providing a bulwark against unions securing entry into an organization. There are two problems with this view. In respect of the extent to which HRM policies are, first, anti-union, Guest (1992) notes that union derecognition has not been exceptional over the 1980s. Second, in industries with little experience of trade unionism, such as the commercial hospitality industry, the failure of trade unions has had less to do with enlightened human resource management strategies than with outright hostility on the part of employers to union involvement in the industry, and the failure of unions themselves to effectively resource the organization of hospitality trades (Wood 1992; Macaulay and Wood 1992; Aslan and Wood 1993).

A second issue bearing on employer motives to introduce HRM concerns the evolution of the 'mission statement' approach to organizational strategy. While by no means entirely novel, the widespread development or refinement of organizational mission statements has very much been a feature of 1980s' approaches to employee relations, growing out of a concern with the development of a positive organizational culture (see Wood 1994). Such statements frequently contain pronouncements about the key role of human resources in defining how organizational missions are to be realized. Yet as Guest (1992) argues, evidence is suggestive of the fact that more often than not, this is little more than lip-service to the concept.

There are, therefore, some grounds for being sceptical of the very concept of human resource management, in that by its very nature, extending beyond formalized personnel policies to link the management of labour to organizational strategy and culture, HRM can admit a wide range of variants. This is an important point because, in countries like the UK where 'traditional' personnel management has developed under the auspices of a strong professional association (the Institute of Personnel and Development, IPD) and where there is broad acceptance of the personnel function as specialist in nature and requiring appropriately trained people, there has been an evolution of standard practices with wide acceptance across many different types of organization. In this context, human resource management can be seen as a source of potential **instability** as far as the process of employee relations is concerned, since, in linking personnel issues to organizational strategy, much greater flexibility in employee relations policies is facilitated which may, ironically, undermine such policies and their execution because there is greater interference in HRM policies by non-specialists in the human resource/personnel function.

There are two basic objections to this view. The first focuses on the status of the personnel function in organizations. This has arguably always been variable, and even where relatively sophisticated personnel systems have existed, they have sometimes been at best tolerated as a necessary evil. Therefore, the idea that a human resource management approach to labour may undermine the personnel function seems, in these circumstances, to be suspect. A second and more positive view is that HRM approaches allow the personnel function to take 'centre stage', enhancing its importance in the organization. Objections to this view have already been noted in that there is reason to believe that many organizations make little more than a 'nod and a wink' to HRM. Perhaps a more important issue here relates less to the extent to which HRM management is **integrated** into the strategic management function of the organization than to the consequences this integration may have for the nature and quality of personnel techniques and activities. A key feature of some HRM approaches is the creation of highly individual relationships between employees and the employer in which collective representation and action – for example, trade unions – is discouraged and individual employees are instead encouraged to enter into a more 'personal' relationship with their employer. In this and the general HRM context great emphasis is placed on 'quality' in the belief that the quality of the organization and its output is closely related to the quality of staff.

PERSONNEL AND HUMAN RESOURCE MANAGEMENT IN THE HOSPITALITY INDUSTRY

Despite the existence of many textbooks on personnel management designed specifically for hotel and catering students, very little has been researched on personnel practices in the industry. The Commission on Industrial Relations (1971) found that few hotel companies had an industrial relations or personnel policy. Johnson (1978) argues that the personnel function in hotel and catering organizations is frequently marginalized. Often, the responsibility for personnel lies with the unit manager who has little or no training in the field. In most circumstances the unit manager's other responsibilities are so wide as to preclude effectiveness in all of them, and often personnel matters take a lower priority than other management functions. A further difficulty in developing systematic procedures arises from the wide range of advice on personnel matters that managers have to contend with. In many cases, advice from government agencies, professional and business organizations and textbooks appears contradictory, even confusing, and support for systematic personnel strategies from senior management in hospitality organizations is often lacking.

In a study by Kelliher and Johnson (1987) which reports two surveys undertaken by the authors, (the 'Ealing Study' and the 'Leeds Study') less than half (42 per cent) of the establishments surveyed in the Ealing Study employed a full-time personnel manager. The likelihood of finding a member of the hotel management team whose primary responsibility was in personnel was closely related to the size of the unit. Some

96 per cent of hotels with more than 200 bedrooms employed a personnel manager, and this manager often had a team of back-up specialists. In smaller establishments, personnel was delegated to a wide variety of people including the managing director, the head receptionist and, in one case, the general manager's secretary. In medium-sized hotels, responsibility for personnel tended to be devolved to assistant managers who performed the role together with other duties. The Leeds Study of ten hotels revealed that half of all the personnel managers surveyed had never held a personnel position prior to their present job, nor had they had any formal training in personnel. Despite this, many felt confident in the role, often because they were able to rely on corporate instruction manuals established by their companies. Many managers relied very heavily on these manuals, often adhering to them rigorously rather than adapting particular procedures to meet their own circumstances. The result was that personnel management practice was highly simplistic and reactive rather than strategic and systematic. Kelliher and Johnson found that the narrow way in which the personnel function was defined may be partly attributable to the main activities of those employed in hotel personnel management which were found to be recruitment and training, with 71 per cent of all the Ealing Study respondents identifying recruitment as the major personnel function and 63 per cent identifying training as a major activity. Training was seen to be more important by those in larger units. Welfare was considered an important personnel task in both small and large hotels but received less attention in medium-sized units, a fact that the authors attribute to the paternalistic management style of the former and the more sophisticated practices of the latter.

In another study, Croney (1988) found that executive support for personnel management in companies bears no relation to the extent to which personnel management is practised at unit level. The physical and social distance between company HQs and the company units is so great that the latter can often ignore corporate philosophies. Croney studied pay systems, recruitment and selection and employee participation in four hotel groups and in all cases found considerable differences between statements of corporate philosophy and the views of executive managers, and the views and practices of managers at unit level. For example, in the context of recruitment and training, even where formal personnel procedures had been laid down at corporate level, most units followed informal procedures trusting in particular to line managers to operationalize personnel procedures. Personnel managers, where present, were frequently confined to effecting the decisions of hotel departmental heads and the preliminary interviewing of candidates for vacancies. Perhaps more important is the fact that two of the hotel groups studied by Croney did not lay down any formal or systematic procedures for unit personnel management, devolving such responsibility to the units themselves. All but one of the hotel groups expressed positive corporate sentiments about the desirability of employee participation in management decision-making and had schemes for facilitating such involvement therein, but most of these schemes were management initiated and controlled, designed principally to foster a sense of common interest rather than encourage true participatory decision-making.

The Oxford Surveys

Some of the most persuasive data on personnel and human resource practices in commercial hospitality services has been elicited by Liz Price of Oxford Brookes University and reported in at least two key papers (Price 1993; 1994). In respect of her work, Price (1994: 48) notes that actual practices in the hospitality industry are so far removed from either an ideal-type 'personnel' or 'human resource management' model that both have limitations for informing research inquiry. Price takes the view that a useful alternative investigatory approach is to focus on 'good practice' in employment which forms the basis of her survey work. The discussion here focuses on her 1994 paper.

In this survey, 426 hotel and restaurant establishments in Britain, excluding Ireland, were surveyed with a questionnaire instrument. There was a 54 per cent response rate which, when combined with responses from a pilot survey, gave a total of 241 establishments. Price is at pains to indicate that this sample is not a representative one. Rather, it tended to focus on the larger, higher quality and (perceptually) more 'progressive' employers. This is reflected in certain parameters of the sample. For example, the median size of establishments was twenty-five employees, which is rather higher than the national average for the hotel and catering sector where around 87 per cent of all units employ between one and ten persons. Further, whereas in the commercial hospitality sector as a whole some 70 per cent of establishments are owner-managed, some 57 per cent of Price's sample were units of public limited companies and 43 per cent were partnerships or self-proprietorships. Perhaps most telling of all was that in Price's sample, some 17 per cent of establishments had a personnel specialist who dealt with employment matters which is congruent with the national average, also 17 per cent.

Price's key finding was that there was a strong correlation between the size of an establishment and the extent to which an establishment conformed to the dictates of employment law in the introduction of appropriate personnel policies and procedures, a fact to some degree explained by the fact that many of the larger establishments were part of a chain with extensive head office or related personnel support. Thus, in establishments employing thirty or more persons:

- over 80 per cent of all employers used written contracts of employment;
- over 75 per cent of employers had developed grievance procedures; and
- over 40 per cent of employers had equal opportunities policies.

These, then, are the measures of good employment practice that Price regards as (initially) most useful in charting the extent to which hotel and restaurant employers follow both the spirit and the word of employment legislation and recommended personnel procedure. The figure for the extent of equal opportunity policies in the sample are of interest, if only because they are so low. Furthermore, Price (1994: 50–51) qualifies these first observations by noting that:

- The majority of employers using written contracts provided no information on pension arrangements and only half offered information about disciplinary and grievance procedures in this context.
- Even when excluding these two elements only 39 per cent of employers in the sample referred to all of the terms and conditions specified in legislation for inclusion in the written particulars of contracts of employment; some 28 per cent never used job descriptions and 37 per cent never used person specifications, making it difficult, Price points out, to determine the fairness or equity of their employment selection decisions, an especially important element in the maintenance of an equal opportunities policy.

To add to these qualifications, Price notes that only around a quarter of employers included the full range of elements specified by ACAS in their disciplinary procedures (ACAS – the Advisory, Conciliation and Arbitration Service – advises companies on what to include in this respect via its Code of Practice, *Disciplinary Practice and Procedure in Employment*).

Unsurprisingly, like many researchers before her, Price found that for low skill and casual posts, word of mouth was the prevalent method of recruitment (see Macaulay and Wood 1992 for a particularly relevant recent example of this). Similarly, in many of the smaller establishments in Price's sample, personnel procedures were even less developed than was the case with the larger units, relying heavily on informal mechanisms. Price's findings again reinforce those of earlier research to the extent that many such employers tend to emphasize that formal personnel arrangements are unnecessary given their 'caring' approach to people management. Often, what this disguises is the fact that employers do not fulfil either their legal obligations in terms of employment practice (where these exist) or follow any recognizably systematic ethical code of conduct in their dealings with their workers. As Price (1994: 51) notes: 'Benign paternalism is no substitute for the introduction of substantive and procedural arrangements intended to guarantee fair treatment'.

Price (1994: 52) goes on to observe that the development of sound personnel practice is to a degree dependent on how well informed managers and proprietors are about both their legal obligations and recommended procedures. In her survey, there was a positive correlation between the level of perceived knowledge of such obligations and procedures and the extent of good practice in establishments, and between the type of job held by respondents and the perceived level of knowledge of respondents. Thus, in respect of the latter, personnel specialists were best informed about legislation, followed by general managers. More worrying was the fact that amongst proprietors and partners, some 17 per cent of those concerned knew little or nothing of the law with only five per cent considering themselves 'very well informed'. This is a particularly interesting finding in the light of Price's earlier noted observations about the 'benign paternalism' of employers in small establishments, for it suggests that not only is there a certain level of ignorance about employment practices among such employers but that this ignorance might almost be perceived as wilful.

This view is to some extent reinforced by examination of Price's data on the formal management qualifications held by members of her sample. Coincidentally, in the small firms sector of the hospitality industry, low barriers to entry to the industry mean that many unqualified persons may 'set up' business fairly easily. More importantly, many of those that do just this have no prior experience of the hospitality sector, let alone formal management qualifications. In fact, across all her sample, only 30 per cent of Price's respondents held a management qualification that indicated some element of personnel management and only five per cent held an Institute of Personnel Management (IPM) (now the Institute of Personnel and Development – IPD) qualification. The most common form of qualification was a diploma or degree in hotel and catering management. When analysed according to status (personnel specialist, general manager and proprietor/partner) these qualifications were unevenly distributed across Price's sample with the proportion of qualifications held by personnel specialists (55 per cent) and general managers (32 per cent) matching national averages for all industry fairly well. The proportion of proprietors or partners holding such qualifications was 13 per cent which has particular significance given that the commercial hospitality sector is dominated by small firms. Indeed, Price (1994: 53) quotes evidence to suggest that overall, 30 per cent of hotel and catering managers have no qualifications whatsoever compared to 12 per cent in the economy overall (see Box 1.1).

Formal management qualifications are but one way in which knowledge of legal obligations in employment and best practice in personnel matters might be disseminated to those in front-line management positions. Continuing professional development and, more specifically, attendance on appropriate short courses, is another. Price examined this aspect of her respondents' profiles and found that training in recruitment and selection techniques had been made available in only 34 per cent of establishments, and in how to deal with discipline and dismissal cases in only 23 per cent of units – almost all such training being in the larger multi-unit organizations included in her sample. In a follow up survey of 85 of the original 241 members of the sample, Price explored this issue further and found that around 94 per cent of all respondents had received some information on training in the previous year with the majority of such information coming from the Hotel and

Box 1.1

Students desert the industry

It is perhaps surprising that so many hospitality managers lack formal management qualifications. After all, in the UK, around fifty hotel schools turn out dozens of diplomates and graduates each year. In strict 'supply terms' therefore, there are no shortages in the output of qualified management personnel. However, a clear problem exists in industry's inability to encourage some such personnel from college directly into the industry or to retain for any length of time those graduates who do enter the hospitality sector.

In a 1995 study by Jarlath Quinn and Kate Purcell of Oxford Brookes University of 1700 hospitality management graduates who completed their courses in 1989, nearly half had left the industry and a further 10 per cent wanted to leave. Low pay was endemic with only 27 per cent of those still employed in the industry earning more than £14,000. Women graduates did particularly badly in this respect, earning on average £3,000 less than similarly qualified males.

In response to this report, the employment and training secretary of the British Hospitality Association, the employers' representative organization, was quoted as saying that the report failed to recognize that this situation is changing and that many employers were responding to the need to motivate and retain their graduate employees. Reassuring though this may sound, such comments have to be viewed in the light of a long history of platitudinous comments about how the situation of industry employees at all levels is improving made by employers and employers' organizations (Wood 1992).

Sources:

Quinn, J. and Purcell, K. (1995) *Hospitality Management Education and Career Trajectories*, Oxford: Oxford Brookes University.

Huddart, G. (1995) Industry fails to keep top students. *Caterer and Hotelkeeper*, 6 April: 7.

Catering Training Company (HCTC), Training and Enterprise Councils and local colleges. Also, 77 per cent of respondents expressed a desire to participate in further professional development and training related to employment practices. The major barrier to participation in such training was cost, a rather surprising factor perhaps, given that in the smaller second sample some 64 per cent of respondents were in units of public limited companies – chains, therefore. Yet only 19 per cent of respondents were willing to pay more than £100 per day for training and 37 per cent said they would pay no more than £50 a day. This cheapskate tendency is startling but unsurprising, reflecting as it does long-standing research findings about the low value put on training by the hospitality industry to which lip- service only is paid. Perhaps ironic in this context is Price's finding from her first sample that just over one-fifth of limited company units and around 39 per cent of units run by partners/proprietors did not use any source of external advice to keep them abreast of personnel developments and of those that did:

- among units of public limited companies, head office was most relied upon for information and updates, closely followed by Croner's (Croner's is a company that publishes several specialist catering information manuals, usually in loose-leaf form, with subscribers receiving regular, often monthly updates);
- among partners/proprietors the catering trade press was the most common source of advice.

Liz Price's survey of personnel practice in hospitality services is one of the most telling ever conducted and confirms not only the validity of the substance of much earlier research into hotel and catering employment, but adds to the detail of hitherto rather sketchy analyses of the nitty-gritty of personnel practice in the industry. Other contemporary research tends to bear Price's findings out. Roberts (1995) in a survey of 150 hospitality companies found that 85 per cent of respondents had no formal recruitment plan and yet 95 per cent of these identified lack of skilled staff and high labour turnover as a problem. Furthermore, 60 per cent of supervisors and heads of department were found to lack accurate and up-to-date job descriptions and, perhaps most interesting in the light of Price's survey, some 70 per cent of respondents favoured in-house training. In a qualifying survey of training, cost did not appear to be a significant factor in respondents' considerations but this is, perhaps, hardly surprising given the large proportion of respondents overall expressing a preference for the use of in-house methods.

Human resource management

On the basis of the foregoing evidence, to say that the hospitality industry continues to neglect the personnel function is to articulate a near truism. Another compelling study of such practices – this time American in origin – is provided by Umbreit (1987). In a study of hotel managers in three different companies where respondents were required to weight the importance of seven hotel manager performance measures, the lowest weighting in all three firms was in respect of the handling of personnel matters. Umbreit is optimistic that if operational quality is to be sustained in hospitality organizations, then the conventional short-termism that typifies human resource practices in the sector will eventually have to yield to systematic policies. Certainly, if the trade press is to be believed, in large companies at least, human resource management has been positively embraced, but it is still too early to tell whether such companies are paying any more than lip-service to the 'new' concept of human resource management, if only because the development of high quality human resource management strategies appears to have contra-indications for the pursuit of the low wage policies that typify the industry and is reflected in the hiring of large numbers of part-time and casual workers.

In one of the few explicit studies of HRM policies in hospitality organizations to date, Ishak and Murrmann (1990) found that of five key human resource management practices, only four (human resource planning, staffing, appraisal, and training and development) were integrated to any significant extent into the strategies of the restaurant firms studied. One policy, namely compensation, was not viewed by respondents as being integral to business strategy at all. The implications of the authors' analysis are that (a) human resource management strategies in hospitality organizations tend to exclude remuneration from their scope; and (b) that this might be attributable to the discretion allowed to managers – even in chain organizations – in setting remuneration levels.

Whatever the case, even if the majority of hospitality *chains* adopted 'ideal' forms of human resource management strategy, any resulting improvements to employee relations would probably not be felt in the small firms sector. To be contentious, it could be argued that until such a time as hospitality organizations are prepared to offer their employees better pay, then any serious attempts at developing human resource management practices are unlikely to resolve problems of employee motivation.

THE FUTURE OF HUMAN RESOURCE MANAGEMENT IN THE HOSPITALITY INDUSTRY

In this chapter, we have sought to illustrate the differences between 'personnel management' and 'human resource management'. In some respects these differences are 'theoretical' in nature, in that they reflect debates among academics about 'old' personnel management and 'new' human resource management. The distinction is a fair one, however, but it is blurred by the mist of fashion which has dictated that many organizations in both public and private sectors have adopted the term 'human resource management' to describe their personnel practices which have not changed in line with the more sophisticated strategic considerations associated with HRM.

To conclude this discussion, it is worth pointing out that while in the UK case, research evidence broadly supports a pessimistic view of the adoption of HRM practices by the commercial hospitality industry, other commentators tend towards a more optimistic viewpoint. Key among these is Baum (1995) who has surveyed tourism and human resource strategies in a great many countries and argues that human resource management strategies can offer sustainable policies for the commercial development of the tourism and hospitality industry that operators ignore at their peril. Baum differentiates between 'old' HR practice, which we can equate with the hospitality industry's traditional approach to personnel matters, and a 'new', sustainable, human resource paradigm which represents a model of best practice for the industry. The differences between these two approaches is summarized in Box 1.2. Whether Baum's optimism is justified remains to be seen but his model clearly offers a statement of best practice to which the hospitality industry can at least aspire.

Where this book stands

Following from Baum's analysis, this book aspires to be more than simply a 'how to recruit' book. We are, however, perhaps more cynical than Baum and other exponents of the human resources approach and accordingly we seek to chart a path between the demands of good personnel practice and many of the aspirations of the human resource management approach. In terms of personnel practice, we have sought to break down this book into easily accessible topics which describe certain aspects of human resource practice and techniques and procedures available to those concerned with the management of employees. No apologies are made for the somewhat crude simplicity of this approach which is underpinned by two key assumptions, namely:

- that good personnel management can be aided by clarity of procedure (though procedure is never enough on its own); and
- that most of those in the hospitality industry involved in personnel management are not personnel specialists and do not possess specialist knowledge of personnel practice, trends or current legal aspects of personnel practices.

At the same time, we are persuaded of many of the benefits of the human resource management approach which, theoretically at least, links the welfarism of traditional personnel administration to strategic consideration of the value of labour in the organization.

Our approach is, if you like, one of 'constructive naïveté'. We believe that the effective management of personnel or human resources is as much a matter of policy – on equal opportunities, on welfare, on health and safety and so on – as it is of the nitty-gritty of recruitment and day-to-day people management. However, we are not out to change the world, nor do we believe we can. Rather, we take refuge in that rather old-fashioned liberal humanism which puts its faith in people's goodwill, and seek to place this approach within a procedural and policy context which is in essence practical but not deaf or blind to either theory, or social context, or ideology. In using the term 'human resource management' we are not simply glossing over the fact that what this text is really about is 'good old-fashioned' personnel management. Nor do we wish to pretend that this book is entirely consistent with the various human resource management approaches expanded elsewhere. Rather, we do believe in certain commercial realities that pertain to the use of labour in hospitality organizations

Box 1.2

Traditional and sustainable human resource practices

OLD HR PRACTICE	NEW SUSTAINABLE HR PARADIGM
RECRUITMENT AND STAFF TURNOVER	
Recruitment undertaken without reference to local community/labour market	Recruitment based on careful analysis of local community and its labour market
Ad hoc, unplanned recruitment to meet immediate needs	Recruitment of staff based on long-term HR planning
Staff recruited on basis of immediate skills needs	Staff recruited on basis of potential development
Recruitment/'poaching' of staff from other companies	Staff recruited locally from schools/colleges/university
Expatriate staff recruited on long-term basis	Expatriate staff only employed to meet short-term needs and to develop local staff
High staff turnover seen as inevitable/desirable	High staff turnover seen as problematic/undesirable
No measures to reduce staff turnover	Active company policies designed to minimize staff turnover
No interest in why staff leave	Exit interview policy
Continuing high staff turnover	Relatively low staff turnover
PROMOTION AND CAREER DEVELOPMENT	
Few opportunities for promotion/development within company	Career planning/tracking within company
No career ladder/unclear criteria for promotion	Clearly defined career ladder/accessible criteria for promotion
Promotion to 'plug gaps'/no preparatory training	Planned promotion with preparatory training programme
Key staff 'imported' from outside/abroad	Key staff 'grown'/developed within company/locality
Part-time or seasonal staff excluded from training/development/promotion opportunities	Part-time or seasonal staff integrated into training/development/promotion system

No long-term commitment to seasonal staff	Long-term commitment to key seasonal staff
Career mobility seen as disloyal/disruptive	Career mobility recognized as beneficial to the individual
Opportunities limited for women, ethnic minorities, disabled	Genuine equal opportunities in employment

REWARDS AND BENEFITS

Company offers minimum rewards and benefits	Company offers competitive rewards and benefits
Conditions to suit employer needs	Conditions reflect local/individual circumstances and needs
Flexibility demanded to suit employer requirements	Flexibility seen as employer–employee partnership with mutual benefits
Staff attitude to company a matter of indifference	Fostering of commitment and feeling of belonging among employees

EDUCATION, TRAINING AND DEVELOPMENT

Training and development not planned	Planned training and development policies and strategies
Training compartmentalized with specialist department	Training recognized as the responsibility of all supervisors/management
No senior management commitment to training	Full commitment to training from CEO down
Training operates in isolation from other HR practices	Training linked to opportunities for promotion
Gap between industry and education system	Partnership between industry and education system
Education programmes with little industry relevance	Education programmes based on industry research/identified needs
Education/training programmes terminal and not integrated	Education/training courses provide for further development and progression
Industry-developed skills not recognized by education	Industry-developed skills recognized and certified by education

MANAGEMENT CULTURE

Staff seen as short-term expedient	Staff seen as key resource
Staff perceived as a cost	Staff perceived as an asset
Authoritarian, remote management culture	Democratic, participative management culture
Authority vested in management alone	Responsibility delegated to all levels of staff – 'empowerment'
Staff remote from decision-making	Staff consulted/involved with decisions affecting their area of responsibility
Inflexible imposition of corporate culture	Corporate culture responds flexibly to local culture and needs

NATIONAL HR PLANNING FOR TOURISM

Fragmentation of HR planning for tourism	Integrated approach to HR planning for tourism
HR considerations not recognized in tourism policy planning	HR considerations to the fore in tourism planning
Quality in tourism seen in exclusively physical product terms	Human resource contribution to quality recognized and nurtured
Local population detached from/ hostile to tourism	Local population helped and encouraged to recognize their role in tourism

Source:

Baum, T. (1995) *Managing Human Resources in the European Tourism and Hospitality Industry: A Strategic Approach*, London: Chapman and Hall, pp. 12–13.

and in acknowledging this reality, seek to link this belief to another, namely that of the strategic advantages offered by a human resource management approach. What we do not do is believe in this to the extent of ignoring the pragmatic necessities involved in the running of a hospitality business. If this book has one aim above all others, it is to recognize that there are relatively sophisticated responses to these pragmatic necessities that go beyond the crude application of personnel techniques to approach something like a more strategic – and yes, humane – approach than that embodied by the 'new' human resource management.

REVIEW AND DISCUSSION QUESTIONS

1. Consider the differences between 'personnel management' and 'human resource management' outlined in this chapter and consider how you would try to persuade the following people of the benefits of the latter:
   (a) the owner of a seventeen-roomed seasonal boarding house;
   (b) the proprietor of a seventy-five-roomed hotel in a resort area; and
   (c) the franchise of a well-known high street fast food concept restaurant.
2. What arguments would you use to counter the protestations of a proprietor of a small hospitality business that formal personnel practices are unnecessary because of his or her 'caring' approach to employees?
3. Do personnel management techniques offer any cost advantages to the operators of small hospitality businesses?
4. Consider the information contained in Box 1.1 above. With reference to your study or year group identify the factors that attract all the individuals in your set to a career in the hospitality industry and those that discourage such a career route. How many of each type of factor relates explicitly to aspects of personnel practice in the industry? Given that employers often complain that those graduating with diplomas and degrees have 'unrealistic expectations' of the industry, how realistic are your group's expectations? Can you have a highly motivated work-force without relying solely on money as a motivating influence?
5. Sketch the elements you would consider it important to include in a company human resource policy.

2 Principles of recruitment and selection

In this chapter we begin the process of examining various personnel techniques and practices by starting at the commencement of what might be termed the 'personnel cycle' – namely the decision to recruit. Before advancing towards issues of procedure and technique however, we consider the strategic context in which any recruitment process takes place – the labour market.

WHAT ARE LABOUR MARKETS?

Recruitment can be undertaken without even an elementary knowledge of the nature of labour markets but it can be more effective if something is understood about the particular labour markets in which an industry, sector or even individual unit, operates. Sociologists, economists and industrial relations specialists have devoted much time to elaborating theoretical models of labour markets. One such model of use in understanding the recruitment issue in hospitality services is so-called dual labour market theory. As the name suggests, dual labour market theory conceives of available human resources as comprising two distinct but related groups or markets – primary labour markets and secondary labour markets. The differences between these are summarized in Box 2.1.

We can see from this that primary labour markets closely approximate in their characteristics to what has come to be regarded as the human resource management philosophy in employee relations. However, secondary labour markets do not, by the same token, approximate in their characteristics to 'traditional' personnel management in general although they may share some features of this approach. Secondary labour markets do, however, approximate pretty closely in *their* characteristics to much of what happens in the hospitality industry in terms of the behaviour of employees and their treatment by employers.

Now, this is interesting because labour markets are not vast centrally planned and co-ordinated machines. Rather, as Riley (1996) points out, the movement of employees in and out of jobs is the product of thousands of individual decisions by employers and employees which,

Box 2.1

Differences between primary and secondary labour markets

Dual labour market theory proposes that the total market for labour divides broadly in two. The key differences are as follows.

PRIMARY LABOUR MARKETS	SECONDARY LABOUR MARKETS
• Jobs are supplied by large, highly profitable firms	• Jobs are supplied by mainly small firms where profitability is not easily assured
• There is a high capital to labour ratio in these firms, and high productivity	• There is a low capital to labour ratio and productivity tends to be low
• Production is usually large-scale in nature and based on substantial proactive investment in technology	• Production is usually small-scale and intensive in nature and, in commercial personal service industries at least, technological requirements are based on clearly defined needs
• There is a stable demand for products arising from national and international markets	• Demand for products and services is subject to irregular and/or seasonal fluctuations rooted in local and regional markets
• Wages and skill levels are relatively high	• Wages and skill levels are relatively low
• Opportunities exist for training and advancement	• Training opportunities are limited as are opportunities for advancement
• Employment is stable	• Employment is unstable
• Unionization is often high	• Unionization is low or non-existent

superficially at least, are taken independently. We say superficially because, quite obviously, in a particular industry or sector common patterns of employment practice emerge over time. These patterns arise because of the specific features of these industries and sectors, features which include the economics of business operation, the shared ideology of employers and employees and the nature of prevailing economic circumstances. Still, however, employment decisions are taken independently but they are informed by shared cultural values and by distinct patterns of movement by employees over time in any individual sector. For example, the hospitality industry has a reputation for high rates of labour turnover relative to other industries and research evidence shows that many industry managers feel that they have no control over these rates of leaving. This latter belief is a widely shared cultural value which has implications for patterns of movement by employees for, in believing they cannot control labour turnover, managers pursue particular courses of action (or do not pursue such courses) which contribute to the maintenance of the rates of leaving. Thus, managers do not pursue policies that might lead to the retention of staff (because they think 'What's the point? The industry is known for high turnover and there's nothing I can do about it') but in order to minimize the cost of substantial labour turnover they recruit cheap labour from external labour markets. In not pursing policies that might help retain staff – paying more money, training employees and so on – employers are responding pragmatically to their perceptions of how the labour market works. But this pragmatic approach, because it is shared across much of the industry, amounts to a generalized strategy which feeds back into the culture of employment practice, for example, the failure to invest heavily in extensive employee training is justified on the grounds that **strategically**, such investment would be costly and wasteful because of high rates of labour turnover. Such is the stuff of which vicious circles are made.

Of course, we have somewhat exaggerated our labour turnover example in order to make a point – namely that an employment or human resource 'strategy' can grow as much from the perceptions and culture of an industry as it can be the product of deliberate planning by individual organizations. We have seen that the hospitality industry operates broadly in a secondary labour market – mainly because the industry employs several different categories of person differentiated according to skill, and relatedly, status. Thus, within certain occupations – for example cooking – some chefs and cooks are more skilled and experienced than others and skill is a major determinant of occupational hierarchy and hence status. Hotel and catering industry labour markets are further complicated in nature in that the level of skill a person possesses is not necessarily the level of skill a person practices. Thus, chefs and cooks are trained to fairly high skills standards if they attend a college course but not all will be able to practise these skills in their subsequent career. The market position of a hotel or restaurant to a very large extent determines what levels of skills may be practised and what further skills may be acquired. Chefs are not the only category of employee affected in this way. For school-leavers commencing their first jobs in a fast-food operation, the opportunity to acquire food service skills that can be deployed in more 'up-market' establishments (e.g. silver service skills) is extremely limited.

A further point to note about hotel and catering labour markets is that for many occupations and for many status levels within these occupations, the market for labour is essentially a local market. Only for the most senior positions is a hospitality organization likely to recruit beyond local geographical boundaries. For most supervisory, semi-skilled and operative jobs, the majority of employees will be recruited locally. An understanding of the nature of the local labour market in which a unit operates is thus important to any analysis of employee resourcing. For example, in the (today fairly rare) situation where local employment is high, there are obvious logical implications for remuneration strategy if the right quality of personnel are to be attracted and retained. Local competition from other hospitality industry employers in such circumstances is also an important consideration, although for most hourly-paid operative positions there is sufficient mutual interest among employers for them to operate effectively as a cartel, 'pricing' labour at similar rates to reduce the motivation to 'poach' employees while discouraging employees from wanting to move. Interestingly, while there is much to be gained from understanding the nature of, and constraints between, local labour markets on the one hand and regional/national labour markets on the other, it remains a remarkable fact that in an industry known for the flexible use of labour, employers and managers can be fairly inflexible in responding to the operation of such labour markets, a phenomenon reflected in the very high proportion of 'hard to fill' vacancies that continue to be reported by hospitality industry employers (see Box 2.2)

Finally in this discussion, we have said that hospitality organizations for the most part operate in secondary labour markets. We saw in Chapter 1 that, in some cases at least, some management workers are

---

Box 2.2

Hard-to-fill vacancies

Despite the flexibility of labour practices in the hospitality industry and employers' belief in a necessary reliance upon secondary labour markets, the industry still has difficulty filling many jobs, largely because of a failure to offer both competitive remuneration, and acceptable terms and conditions of employment. The percentage of hospitality industry employers reporting hard-to-fill vacancies in the six years to 1995 is as follows:

| **1990** 26% | **1992** 19% | **1994** 27% |
| **1991** 17% | **1993** 21% | **1995** 37% |

These figures are all the more remarkable given that for much of the period, the economy was in recession and, at such times, jobs are at a premium.

Source:
Skills and Enterprise Network (1996) *Briefing*, issue 1/96, February, p.2.

treated as if they 'belong' to what we have identified here as secondary labour markets. This is not true of all higher grade workers however, though it is a worrying trend in much of the industry. One characteristic of **primary** labour markets (and for **some** occupational groups in secondary labour markets) is that organizations tend to have strong internal labour markets. The defining characteristics of strong and weak internal labour markets are shown in Box 2.3 and, once again, it can be seen that strong internal labour markets do not at first sight approximate to employment conditions within the bulk of the commercial hospitality sector, whereas weak labour markets do. An employer who does not pursue strategies designed to develop strong internal labour markets is forced to rely on external labour markets.

As Riley (1996: 140) notes there is nothing **inherently** superior about strong internal labour markets relative to external ones (although one could argue for their moral superiority). The point is that the decision to build strong internal labour markets or to rely on external ones is just

---

Box 2.3

Characteristics of internal labour markets

The concept of internal labour markets mirrors that of the dual labour market in that two principal types are proposed – strong and weak – each with the undernoted characteristics.

STRONG	WEAK
• Hiring standards are precise and unambiguous	• Hiring standards are vague or absent altogether
• Recruitment is formalized and centralized	• Recruitment is often informal and diffused through a unit or organization
• Skill requirements are high	• Skill requirements are low
• There is extensive in-house training available to employees of the unit or organization	• In-house training is often absent or confined to the induction phase of a post
• Criteria for promotion and transfer are clearly stated and often meritocratic	• Criteria for promotion are often vague and dependent on factors other than qualifications, experience and skill
• Pay structures are visible and generally well-known, being bureaucratically regulated	• Pay structures are often invisible or obscured, frequently being the subject of personal negotiation

that – a decision, a **choice**, and it is the role of choice in labour strategy that needs to be emphasized at this point. To do this, let us summarize the five key themes to emerge from the discussion in this section. These are as follows.

- At one level at least, labour markets can be classified according to whether they are primary and secondary and, in this model, it appears that the commercial hospitality industry operates for the most part in secondary labour markets.
- There are good reasons why the hospitality industry operates in secondary labour markets. The most important of these relate to the cultural beliefs of employers and managers in respect of the behaviour of employees, beliefs which reinforce reliance upon secondary labour markets.
- Culture and beliefs are not the whole story, however. These are closely related to perceptions of the economic cost of labour and of labour (personnel) practices relative to the markets in which units operate.
- For the majority of occupations and skill levels, the market position of a unit will dictate that it recruits the majority of its staff from local labour markets and the nature of local labour markets in turn exerts some influence on the behaviour of employers.
- This behaviour is, overall, the result of decisions or choices by employers about what serves their best interests.

We would conclude by emphasizing that contrary to the image of hospitality industry employers often promulgated in academic research, there is a strategic rationality to industry employment practices that works well for employers. This strategic rationality is the product to a large degree of employer choices about how best to staff their operations. Often, over time, these choices have been reactive, resulting from employers' perceptions of the 'reality' of labour markets. Now, however, they possess the systematic regularities that one associates with 'strategy' in that reliance upon secondary, local, labour markets is the defining feature of employment practices in commercial hospitality services and one can no more pretend this is not the case than one can say that it never rains in Scotland! It is the reality of employment strategies which we take to be the basis for all aspects of employment practice in the industry. Rather than offer idealized models of personnel practice (as many personnel texts for the hospitality industry do) it is necessary to outline how effective personnel practices can be operationalized in the light of the realities of overall strategy. At the same time, and remaining true to the spirit of our approach outlined in Chapter 1, we believe that these realities can effectively embrace a (cost) effective approach to human resource management which is much broader in scope than would be suggested by the current limited application of personnel procedures within the hospitality industry.

RECRUITMENT

The first stage in the personnel cycle is the decision to recruit. In the light of what we have learnt about labour markets above and what we know from other research (Wood 1992) it is perhaps unsurprising to find that the hospitality industry, particularly at grass roots operational level, tends to operate on the basis of a system of crisis management. The minute a 'leaver' is signalled, no matter the department or specialism, panic buttons are activated and questions posed. How is the job to be done? Who is to cover the duties? How is the shift system affected? And so the recruitment process gets under way. The first thing to say here is that the fact that a vacancy (or vacancies) exists is the ideal time to take stock of human resource needs. Clearly this is easier when setting standards in a new, as yet to be opened operation, but it can be especially important in long-established operations. Irrespective of the level of employment, senior management or unskilled operative, and the degree of authority to be obtained for replacement, it is useful to consider a number of questions. First of these is 'Does the job exist in the first place?'. Many 'jobs' have evolved as a function of custom and practice in organizations and/or have been serviced admirably for many years by a long-serving member of staff. Much has been the anxiety when the person has retired. Much has been the incredulity when the operation did not grind to a halt without this stalwart.

Second, one can ask if the job for which a vacancy has arisen has become obsolete as a result of technological change or structural reorganization. Gone are the days of vast typing pools, due to the march of sophisticated information technology systems. Modern, computerized stocktaking has seen the end of battalions of hotel and restaurant stores clerks. New management structures, that have flattened or inverted the classic pyramid system of responsibility, have eliminated the need for many traditional supervisory and operative roles.

Third, if it is established that there is work to be done, does the job represent a coherent whole or can components of the job be logically redistributed and added to other jobs, at the same time enhancing the work roles of those other job holders? Furthermore, with the recent trend for subcontracting (or 'outsourcing' as it is often known) set to continue, can a case be argued for passing the responsibility for a particular operation on to an outside operative? This is an obvious solution with service facilities including, for example, gardening, laundry and floral displays, but is not totally unknown in the more esoteric areas of finance, control and housekeeping. Whatever the minutiae of the immediate situation, human resource needs are closely related to the market in which the business operates, and as such are bound to change with time at all levels of employment. As a result it is vital that a clear picture of the requirements of each position within the organization as a part of the whole is maintained and reviewed regularly as the business changes.

Job analysis, job descriptions and job specification

A useful technique in arriving at some conclusions about the relevance of a particular job to the organization is job analysis. The sinister connotations that have been attached to job analysis since time immemorial, as a vehicle for criticism, inquisition, and even dismissal are not easy to dispel. However, by encouraging input by as many people as possible (including those currently involved) coupled with positive communication skills, meaningful participation and realistic results can be obtained from job analysis. The primary purpose of job analysis is to collect, analyse and hypothesize information about a job (not a job holder) in order to establish job content and in turn the construction of a job description. Any job, including that of a leaver, should be examined very simply and honestly in terms of:

- what is done
- how it is done
- why it is done
- where it is done
- when it is done
- who does it

This is a reporting of a status quo. The important thing is to be brutally candid in this work, faithfully describing the components of a job and their interrelationship. If this information is collected for all jobs in the operation/unit/company then any vacancy can trigger a comparative analysis. Even if such analysis is localized to comparison of the job of a single leaver relative to their peers it should still be possible to identify:

- overlap in job function;
- irrelevance in operation;
- obsolete practices contained within the job; and
- duplication of job responsibilities.

The information derived from job analysis can be matched to the human resource needs of the company in the short, medium and long term and may be used as a basis for constructing job descriptions that coincide with these needs. Many may be a reaffirmation of what has been the 'norm' for many a long year, others will set new standards, indicate new responsibilities, and set new and coherent challenges.

Job descriptions themselves should avoid at all costs the propensity to be:

- too long
- too boring
- too turgid
- too full of jargon
- too task-oriented
- too detailed

It is important to remember that a job description is as much a marketing document for the job as it is an internal operational device for formalizing responsibilities. Job descriptions need regular review, renewal, rejection, reconstruction, upgrading, and even repair. Rather than being in letters of stone, they must be seen as transient, vulnerable to proactive change. If this is not done, they can become a crutch for outdated conventions. Nevertheless, job descriptions need to be clear and unambiguous. They should clearly state the main functional aspects of a job. This could be anything from maintaining a constant supply of clean pots for the kitchen to constructing the final accounts at the end of the financial year. It is important to avoid listing those tasks which can either be farmed out elsewhere, or can be interpreted in varying ways. Indicating key objectives of a job canalizes common effort, although such objectives should be understandable and attainable by the operative who then uses initiative in the desired direction. Job descriptions need not be lengthy documents but they are useful in even the smallest operations where there may be a considerable degree of job overlap expected of employees. This use value derives from the fact that, at the very least, job descriptions serve as an *aide-mémoire* to both employer/ manager and employee of the range of duties that have to be performed. Job descriptions should remove any ambiguity over a person's proper role in the operation. A typical job description appropriate to a medium-sized organization is shown in Box 2.4.

The hard work expended in constructing the job description should be used as a benchmark when creating the job specification which is nothing more than a description of the 'ideal' person for a job. This model of perfection does not exist of course – we are all of us human, but the job specification will set a standard to be adhered to in recruitment. The job specification should not demand the unattainable of a potential recruit; it should not value the job either too cheaply (such that nobody applies) or overprice itself. However, it should lay the ground rules with respect to the 'right' person for the job including physical characteristics (being careful of the legal constraints on discrimination), educational attainment, special skills or abilities (not necessarily related to the job) and character traits. Similarly, the ideal should not be too divorced from the minimum with the result that good candidates may see themselves as overqualified. In the same vein if some kind of below-par compromise is suggested, underqualified applicants are attracted. The results of both scenarios are not difficult to deduce. Box 2.5 shows an example of a job specification.

RECRUITMENT SOURCES AND METHODS

The crucial point to remember with recruitment is that it can be very expensive. Obviously the quantifiable elements in terms of advertising, telephoning, correspondence, fees to agencies and the like are not difficult to tally. Nevertheless, less easy to calculate expense is incurred in:

- paying somebody to do the job of the leaver during the interim of the leaver leaving and a replacement commencing work;
- the cost of training a new starter;
- the loss of income as a new employee strives for optimum efficiency; and

---

Box 2.4

Typical job specification

Job title: Storekeeper.
Knowledge: Receiving, storing, issuing and inventorying methods. Quality and grades of foods, beverages and equipment.
Skills and abilities: follow both verbal and written instructions. Perform basic arithmetical calculations. Apply company policies and procedures for this area. Perform heavy physical work.
Personality and related characteristics: Must have strong safety awareness; be able to show initiative and work well with others; must be organized and able to respond effectively to the demands of others.
Work history: A minimum of two years' experience as storekeeper is preferred.
Education: Well-qualifed school leaver with competence in literacy and arithmetical skills.

Prepared by: _____   Date: _____
Approved by: _____   Date: _____

- the cost of the new employee leaving within a few weeks of joining – and the whole recruitment process having to be repeated.

Such costs strengthen the case for considering recruitment within a unit or organization (i.e. utilizing the internal labour market). This credo can be applied to:

- persons in need of job development (i.e. the 'sideways' transfer) in order to broaden their experience in preparation for future promotion or the acquisition of additional responsibility;
- persons in need of promotion to further their potential; and
- persons serving notice as a result of redundancy.

As a matter of policy, many companies require vacancies to be disseminated to existing employees either before or concurrently with external advertising. Recruiting 'in-house' has the advantage of ease of transfer, (usually) limited need for attainment of peak training efficiency sooner than work with 'new' applicants, comfortable availability of the person concerned via negotiation with the relevant line managers, as well as a more latent boost to morale not only of the individual but also the peer group who see the potential within the organization for their own advancement. In addition to this, flaws can be easily diagnosed and rectified – often before the move takes place. This is something that cannot be done with an external candidate who is (generally) going to present the best side possible to the recruiter at interview.

On the down side, internal recruitment can have several disadvantages. Internal jealousies are to be avoided at all costs, weaknesses of

Box 2.5

Ideal job description

JOB INFORMATION
Job title: Storekeeper
Reports to: Head Chef
Department: Food and Beverage (Kitchen)

SUMMARY OF MAIN DUTIES
Storekeeper receives, stores, issues, and inventories food, beverages and equipment used by the kitchen staff.

PRINCIPAL TASKS
1. Receive and check incoming stock for accuracy of amount, price, and quality, using supplier's invoice and departmental purchase order, which includes written specifications. Follows defined receiving procedures to ensure receipt of appropriate quality and quantity of products.
2. Unpack supplies and remove redundant packaging to refuse area to avoid pest problems.
3. Date and store all stock in proper storage area (including dry, refrigerated, and freezer storage). Rotate stock appropriately to ensure freshness.
4. Issue stock using stock requisition forms.
5. Clean and maintain storage areas according to cleaning schedule.
6. Take physical inventory on a weekly basis, using inventory book to ensure accurate food costing and purchasing.
7. Other duties as may from time to time be requested by the management.

EQUIPMENT USED
Refrigeration and freezing equipment; as required; appropriate training will be given.

JOB CONTEXT
Contacts: Frequent contact with both suppliers' drivers and kitchen staff.
Level of supervision: Minimal
Physical conditions and demands: Goods receiving area is outdoors but enclosed; stores area is temperature regulated; kitchen is noisy and crowded at peak times. Work hazards: strenuous job requires frequent heavy lifting: where appropriate, candidates will attend appropriate training in lifting and handling.

Prepared by: _____   Date: _____
Approved by: _____   Date: _____

candidates must be recognized as potential blocks on promotion and training needs must be identified early. Furthermore, internal recruiting without an external trawl of those available for employment could debar many excellent candidates. However, some innovative practices in internal recruitment can help avoid this problem as the concept of Forte's 'Job Shop' shows (see Box 2.6).

GOING OUTSIDE

The information regarding a vacancy can be made known to the external labour market in many ways. Obviously, choosing the appropriate medium is largely dependent on the nature of the job and the supposed availability of suitable candidates. Generally speaking, as we saw in Chapter 1, hospitality industry practice is that the more modest the appointment, the more local the publicity. In other words, semi- or unskilled workers tend to be recruited within a few miles, or easy travelling distance of the place of employment, although, conversely, seasonally employed workers (students for example) may be sourced on a national or even international basis. Similarly, in some more traditional hotels, where accommodation is provided, national recruitment remains a possibility. Many sources of staff exist, both informal and formal. Informally useful (and inexpensive) sources include:

- word of mouth – the grapevine (which several research studies have demonstrated to be one of the most common methods of recruiting operational staff in the hospitality industry – see Macaulay and Wood 1992a);
- casual callers;

Box 2.6

Forte's 'Job Shop'

Opened in London in 1995, Forte's 'Job Shop' liaised with line managers who needed new staff and screened unsolicited applications initially sent to units. The singular advantage of the 'Job Shop' was that it eliminated the need for individual hotels to run their own costly and time-consuming selection process. It also allowed telephone screening in response to press advertisements for staff and thus a more rapid determination of likely suitable candidates for available posts. The 'Job Shop' also ran on-site recruitment sessions involving departmental managers in order to ensure the participation of 'end users' in the selection procedure.

Source:
Tarpey, D. (1995) Job Shop. *Caterer and Hotelkeeper*, 28 September, pp. 60–2.

- past employees;
- past applicants (where previously discarded applications have been kept on file);
- informal acquaintances;
- waiting list; and
- introductions from current members of staff (which may prove a useful means of motivating existing staff).

On the more formal side, key sources of external recruitment include the following.

- School or college/university 'milk rounds'. Currently enjoying a dip in popularity with employers in that they can be hugely expensive and involve considerable commitment of time and resources (albeit they are first rate as a public relations exercise). When economic times are good and graduates in high demand, they can be a necessity.
- Employment agencies – for temporary *or* permanent positions. Employment agencies are useful for the initial weeding of candidates, they can save a lot of time – as long as the agency has the right information – and are especially useful for applicants from operative to supervisory level. Although employment agencies charge a fee, when offset against the internal cost of recruiting this can be money well spent, resulting in savings to the unit or operation.
- Government agencies including local Job Centres, and Job Shops; other self-help groups can provide a rich source of candidates. The Services Employment Network provides a liaison with employers on the market for erstwhile armed forces personnel. All levels of candidate are available.
- Selection consultants take much of the bureaucratic pain out of recruiting. They are valuable when recruiting specialist or relatively senior managerial staff and when time is limited and a pre-selection of candidates is needed. Specialist consultants often have wide experience of finding candidates with particular skills or abilities. In addition to this, since they operate under their own name, the ultimate employer can be kept confidential in the first instance. Selection consultants can provide selection, screening and interviewing techniques that are not always available either to the generalist human resource or personnel manager or to a non-personnel specialist with recruitment responsibility within the organization. There is a fee, but the costs can be justified if the job is well done.
- Search consultants operate in the perceived glamorous world of the 'headhunter'. Geared to seek out top executives and specialist senior management where the numbers of potential recruits are small and the rewards high, they operate in the realms of international executive recruitment. Discretion being their watchword, since the target is often employed by a rival company, many potential candidates may register while still employed, or be sought out by the representatives of the consultancy. Search consultants can act on behalf of the employer, discreetly making contact. Alternatively the consultant

can suggest potential recruits to the customer. Big fees are levied by consultants, and big results expected by the user.

If none of the above has worked or is suitable, it is time to go back to basics.

ADVERTISING THE POST

The risk of making the wrong decision here is great. Advertise in the wrong place at the wrong time and the result is a poor response by unsuitable candidates or a large response by irrelevant candidates! The result can be a readvertising of the position which can give the wrong impression to the right people who should have applied in the first place, as well as being financially very costly. The general rules of job advertising are:

- get the media right;
- get the verbiage right;
- get the timing right; and
- get the frequency right.

. . . and the right applicants will apply. Some suggestions of the best use of certain media are shown in Box 2.7.

Box 2.7 is intended to give a rough guide of the expected effectiveness of a given type of advertising with reference to the type of applicant sought. Nevertheless it is important to bear in mind one or two other factors when evolving a strategy.

Take risks by all means and advertise for a managing director in the evening paper – it has been known to work – but the use of proven sources can be best, in light of the expense. There is no harm in

---

Box 2.7

Likely efficiency of advertising media for different levels of post

MEDIA	SEMI-SKILLED	CLERICAL	MANAGEMENT
Posters/handbills	OK	occasionally	rarely
Evening papers	OK	occasionally	rarely
Local weeklies	OK	OK	rarely
Local dailies	OK	OK	rarely
National dailies	rarely	OK	OK
National Sundays	rarely	OK	OK
Specialist journals	rarely	OK	OK
Local radio	OK	occasionally	no
Local TV	OK	occasionally	no

spreading the net as widely as possible by using a variety of specialist and general publications. Timing is vital. All publications have deadlines, but some specialize in running employment advertising on certain days. Saturdays and public holidays are often considered to be bad days, particularly the latter, when sales of papers can be low. When economic times are good it is said that the employment market is slow. This is something of a moot point. Repeating the advertisement can be good to get additional applicants who were missed the first time around, but regular repetition can suggest to applicants that there is some element of desperation on the part of the employer and give the opposite signal to that intended. Depending on the form of the advert (size, typeface and so on) it can also be expensive.

Using the advertisement to communicate and select

The impression given by the advertisement should be one that attracts the attention of the most suitable applicants, and motivates a response. On the more practical side, it should make it clear how to reply within the required timescale. The advertisement is a selection tool in its own right and should be used as such. The use of company logos and/or easily identifiable 'house styles' can draw the reader's eye. Make the content to-the-point and clear. Set the scene by giving the title of the job and making sure that it is identifiable to the applicant, avoiding meaningless jargon. Give details of the type, size and location of the organization or unit. Be absolutely clear as to the requirements encompassed by qualifications be they academic, skill-oriented, physical attributes, ideal age limits and so on, taking care to observe that no legal strictures including those on sex or race are violated. Pay is important, as are other benefits, for example, the company car, removal expenses and accommodation – they should be exploited as selling points.

Avoid being too oriented towards the company rather than the candidate. By all means, give the reader some idea of what you are all about, but keep the priority the job and its requirements. Similarly, have no hesitation in putting elements of the 'down side' of the job, for example the shift system and working over public holidays. Starting with a deceit or fudging of information ultimately leads only to discontent and high labour turnover. Saving money on the quality of printing and layout in advertising is false economy. Advertisements compete with each other on the page and are usually grouped like with like. Make the advertisement stand out in its own right.

APPLICATION FORMS AND CVS

The curriculum vitae (CV) is increasingly being solicited from applicants encompassing many grades of employment. Indeed, specialist advisers make a living from helping job seekers in their construction. Hitherto, the ubiquitous application form was the order of the day and is still widely used. The advantage of the second of these two formats is that potential employers can guide the applicant along the path of what they want to know, rather than what the applicant is prepared to give – no matter how slick the presentation.

Apart from the obvious details of name, age, date of birth, nationality, address and contact point for mail, education, qualifications and previous employment are vital pieces of information. Applicants often leave unaccounted for 'gaps' in a career on their documentation that are more interesting than that which they purport to have done. Details of progression through previous jobs, promotion therein, why they left (they say) and length of stay in any one position can be telling features. Also, a progression in a career is clearly defined. Many application forms include a section indicating that applicants should declare any criminal convictions. Sceptics declare that few would openly admit to a nefarious past but, in the event of some misdemeanour coming to light, false declarations at the application stage have certain obvious legal implications. Ancillary information on the state of cleanliness of a driving licence, whether the applicant is registered as disabled and the period of notice required by a current employer, require to be clearly stated. Most application forms have some facility for recording the applicant's social interests. Selectors should take heed of these declared interests. Apart from providing opportunities for useful 'ice breakers' at interview, they give a fuller picture of the whole personality and can indicate potentials in directions which are not manifest in the employment record.

Referees (usually two are adequate) are drawn, more often than not, from previous employers or an academic establishment. Character references offered by candidates who have been out of work for some time can be equally viable, but obviously cannot give an opinion of the candidate's abilities in a work situation. Consideration of when references are taken up is important. Contacting a current employer could cause problems, so the candidate must be fully aware of company policy and/or be asked if certain references can be pursued.

SELECTING INTERVIEWEES FROM THE APPLICATIONS: SHORT-LISTING

Depending on the level of the position to be filled in the organization, the trawl of applications is circulated or considered by the persons closely involved. The human resource specialist, where there is one, becomes a crossroads for circulating the information, a role also fulfilled by the person responsible for human resources in smaller organizations. Others involved in assessing the calibre of applicants will include the immediate supervisor of the new recruit and possibly the next above again in the management hierarchy. Where appropriate, specialists will also make judgements on qualifications offered and the depth of previous experience.

The obvious use of the application as the initial selection instrument requires little elaboration. Candidates who do not satisfy the criteria on the grounds of qualification, relevant experience or age can be relatively easily eliminated. However, careful wording of the advertisement should reduce this exercise to a minimum. Choosing those to be selected for final interview is more difficult and, if numbers are high, could involve some kind of intermediary competitive batch testing system. Alternatively, particularly if recruitment at supervisory or managerial level is involved, a group selection process or assessment centres may be appropriate.

In the first of these, large numbers of candidates can be assessed using tests designed to indicate individual skills in numeracy, literacy, spatial awareness and logical problem solving. From the results obtained a ranking of candidates can be obtained and those satisfying the required grades progress to the next stage of the recruitment process – usually 'the interview'. Administration of the tests and calculation of scores requires a degree of skill, involving specialist training. Tests themselves are often 'bought in' by employers. Personnel trained in these skills are often used as part of the package. Clearly this is expensive, so to get best value for the investment careful organization of the sessions to maximize the number of candidates is essential. The session to complete the run of tests could be over two or three hours.

Assessment centres involve groups of candidates working together, usually over a period of two days, where each group is set tasks which simulate work experience. These 'analogous tests' involve committee-type exercises when a problem is set and a solution sought within a fixed timescale. A panel of trained assessors observes the activities of the group and the interaction of the members as each takes a turn at chairing the group. Courses are residential and social interaction is observed by the assessors. In addition to group work, each candidate will undertake cognitive tests at an individual level, similar in intent to those used in batch testing. Finally, each candidate will be interviewed by the panel.

Assessment centres are a first-rate method of selection for those aspiring to supervisory level and above. They are superb for recruiting at head office level when a quantity of recruits is required for distribution to units on a national basis. They set uniform standards and eliminate much personal bias on the part of selectors. However, they require the careful training of assessors, judicious selection of tests and considerable financial investment. Nevertheless, the effectiveness of the assessment centre is not disputed as a means of selecting employees based on the broadest spectrum of examination, although the increased use of various forms of test and testing is a cause for controversy (see Box 2.8).

THE INTERVIEW

Whatever the selection process, like it or not, sooner or later the prospective employee is going to be interviewed by some person or

Box 2.8

Psychometric tests

The term 'psychometric tests' is a generic label for a wide variety of supposedly **psychological** tests that **measure** certain abilities. Increasingly, such tests are being used in employee selection, and in appraisal, promotion and redundancy decisions. Psychometric tests include personality, intelligence and aptitude tests. The current fashionability of psychometric tests has raised some worrying issues about their use. These include:

- the fact that such tests are often 'bought in' by employers from employment consultants: the organization using the tests thus has little real knowledge or control of them or their application;
- many tests are culture bound - that is, they are constructed on the basis of assumptions about the dominant ethnic and cultural group (the so-called WASP – White, Anglo-Saxon, Protestant – effect in our society);
- some tests – particularly personality tests – appear to elicit gender differences in responses in people aged over 30, raising questions about the validity of such tests; and
- wider questions about tests' validity particularly in respect of whether tests actually measure real phenomenon and whether, by extrapolation, these phenomenon are in some way relevant to the aspect of the employment process tests are being used to support.

To the above we can add the observation that where tests are used, there is a danger that because of their aura of objectivity, employers place too great a reliance on test results to the exclusion of other, more traditional, appraisal and evaluation criteria and methods. Within the UK hospitality industry, key users of psychometric tests include or have included Quadrant and Compass (contract caterers), Pizza Hut and Forte's Roadside Division.

persons. Although much valid criticism has been levelled at the interview as a selection technique, as a part of the process, in conjunction (or not) with other means of assessing candidates it is hard to avoid as a final interaction between recruiter and potential employee.

As with the above techniques, considerable skill is required which is only acquired as a combination of specialist training and experience over time. This communication, for recruitment purposes in this instance, is a means not only of eliciting information from the candidate, but also giving information and creating a positive attitude in applicants about the company – even though not all applicants will get the job!

Planning ahead is vital. Constructing the content of the interview, and who is involved, must be meticulous. Each member of the interview list can come in contact with as many as half a dozen people during the course of the 'interview'. Each, in his or her way can affect the behaviour of the interviewee and consequently the impression given. Accepting the criticisms that interviews can be too subjective and biased on one hand, and there is the danger of specious behaviour by the candidate on the other, the more the candidate is put at ease and encouraged to give as honest a performance (because that it is what it is) as possible under the circumstances, the more likely the success of the procedure. Standards of quality management, which should be inherent in any case, must be applied.

Each applicant will be passed through the 'interview' from the receptionist as the point of first contact via possibly a member of the secretarial staff to the formal interview itself. A panel interview could comprise four members. Thereafter, if the interview is continued on an informal basis with a stroll around the unit, where a question and answer session is the order of the day, another new face might be presented. Each member of this team needs to be thoroughly primed as to their function and have an input to the subsequent reporting process.

Creating the setting

The formality of the interview situation is impossible to avoid, but increasingly the single chair in front of the long table with one or more inquisitors in the opposite camp is becoming less favoured. At higher levels of recruitment, for example at junior management and above, part of the formalities could include each candidate giving a presentation on a topic as a means of establishing research and communication skills. A boardroom format could be ideal for this purpose. Less formal arrangements involving comfortable chairs and low tables, ostensibly to relax the candidate, could be favoured. No amount of contrived comfort will eliminate the candidate's butterflies – it could be argued that modest lepidopteral activity is not necessarily a bad thing! However, aggravation of nervousness by the recruiter is not desirable in any circumstance.

Scripting the dialogue

Planning the content of the interview is vital. By covering the same topics with each candidate a valid comparison of the potential recruits is possible. Similarly, a common assessment method is vital.

If the interview situation involves a panel, a chairperson must control the proceedings. Each member will have predetermined questions to ask, with or without supplementary input. In the one-to-one set-up, the interview plan of topics to be covered and their relative weight is just as important. Areas to cover include: past experience, qualifications, current employment, future ambitions, reasons for seeking a new job, reasons for leaving job(s), length of stay at each job, attitudes to authority and peer groups, opinions on promotion, knowledge of the latest technology, knowledge of the latest legal regulations, knowledge of modern working practices or hierarchical structures, knowledge of the company to which the applicant is making an approach – and why?

In light of the timescale – half an hour? An hour? More? Less? – control of the time must be exact. Skilful interviewing involves being able to adjust to the responses of the candidate. Key points to bear in mind include the following.

1. Be aware of the different types of questions that may be asked (see Box 2.9). Keep the questions open and worded in such a way that the response cannot be a simple 'yes' or 'no'. For example: 'Do you think that guéridon service is a good thing?' would probably result in 'yes'. The candidate assumes you want a positive response and gives it. He or she may (or may not) have an understanding of the jargon and may have an opinion at odds with the perceived response he or she thinks should be given.

   Using the traditional 'what, where, when, why, how, who' suitably inveigled into the question elicits a response that cannot be 'yes' or 'no'. Start with anodyne questions, even small talk about the weather or how the candidate found the travelling situation. Going straight for the jugular generates hostility and the guarded answer. Draw the candidate out gently from the shell!

2. Interviews are an opportunity for the candidate to impart knowledge – 20 per cent interviewer talking and 80 per cent interviewee is an ideal bias. By the same token, do not allow the candidate to dominate the ongoings.

3. Do not be afraid of silence. Allow the candidate time to think and consider an answer and use pauses to allow candidates to open up.

4. Be conscious of the mannerisms adopted by the candidate. Doctorates have been gained in the study of body language but the basics of evidence of nervousness, avoiding eye contact, fidgeting should be noticed.

5. Never argue with the candidate. Your views may not coincide but the job of the interviewer is to find out how the candidate thinks, not to influence their opinions. In the panel interview situation, the chairperson must know their job!

6. Keep the interview under control by a combination of flexibility and awareness that a certain amount has to be covered in a finite time.

7. Ask supplementary probing questions. The candidate may not have fully understood the question and the answer may show this. Silence could mean incomprehension rather than ignorance.

8. Allow time for the candidate to ask questions – even if it is about the salary and pension scheme.

9. **Always** tell the candidate when a decision will be reached as to the success or not of the application – and stick to it.

10. Ask when the candidate would be available for employment in the event of the application being successful.

11. On the more practical side:

(a) time arrivals at convenient intervals;
(b) provide comfortable waiting facilities;
(c) keep to the schedule;
(d) take notes openly during the conversation so that vital information is recorded for later reference; and
(e) be a good listener.

Box 2.9

Types of interview questions

TYPE	OBJECTIVE(S)/ FEATURES	EXAMPLE(S)
Open	• Draw the candidates out • Allow the candidates to display their eloquence or reticence	• Did you enjoy life at college? • How do you get along with other people?
Closed	• To check facts • Generally permits of yes/no or limited answer	• You have worked for 5 years in your current job?
Direct	• Tests candidates' responsiveness • Requires clarity of candidate	• How much do you expect us to pay for this job? • Why did you leave your last-but-one job after only two months?
Episodic	• Assess candidates' ability to adapt and, to some degree, how they live their lives	• What has been the best moment in your career to date? • How did your family cope with your last relocation? • When and where do you usually do your paperwork?
Hypothetical	• Tests problem solving ability of candidates	• What do you do if a guest dies in the bath? • What do you do if someone complains of a fly in their soup?

Note: None of the categories are, evidently, mutually exclusive.

Allow time **between** interviews to write up the notes and familiarize yourself with the application of the next interviewee.

Assessing the candidates' performance

Use a common grading system that has been agreed beforehand. Clearly this will vary from job to job, but the tried and tested alternatives of the 'seven-point plan' and 'five-fold grading' take a lot of beating as a basis. They are illustrated in Table 2.1.

MAKING THE DECISION AND TAKING UP REFERENCES

The candidates have been seen, the tests, assessment centre, interviews, showing round the unit have all been done. Now it is time to consider the reference.

The reference

First things first: many companies require written references on the in-house form dated from the time of recruitment, covering standard criteria to be applied to the applicant including; length of service, reasons for leaving, time-keeping, attendance, skill, attitude to others,

Table 2.1 Examples of five and seven point interview grading plan

CONVERSION TABLE OF FIVE-FOLD GRADING AND SEVEN-POINT PLAN		
Five-fold grading	**Human attributes**	**Seven-point plan**
1. First impressions and physique	Physical appearance, health and fitness, speech, bearing with other people	1. Physique
2. Qualifications and experience	Cultural background, knowledge and education, working experience, pay expectations, reflected by lifestyle and responsibilities	2. Attainments
		3. Intelligence
3. Overall intelligence	Ability to absorb and interpret information, speed in learning various kinds of subject matter and potential for training	4. Special aptitudes
		5. Interests
4. Motivation	Personal work interests, levels of achievement set by candidate, degree of success in life so far	6. Disposition
5. Adjustment	Emotional side of life, stability and control, tolerance of stress and ability to adjust, compatibility with others.	7. Circumstances

Source: Adapted from Rodger, A. (1970) *The Seven Point Plan*, 3rd edn., Guildford: National Foundation for Educational Research and Fraser, J.M. (1978) *Employment Interviewing* 5th edn., London: Macdonald and Evans.

honesty, reliability, reason for leaving and so on. Invariably there is a clear question as to the opinion of the referee on the person's honesty with money and/or any known criminal convictions. Insurance companies insist on this, so that in the event of some financial anomaly resulting in a claim being made to the insurer, it is demonstrable that the claimant has made every reasonable effort to ascertain the integrity of the miscreant. Care should be taken in the wording of the appropriate section, and advice sought from the insurers.

On the more practical side, the whole issue of the validity of references as a guide to the potential of a candidate has been debated for many years. Nevertheless, it is still accepted practice that some kind of validation of a candidate's personal integrity, in addition to formal confirmation of past employment or certificated education, is established. It is generally accepted in the UK that the dog-eared testimonial on the letterhead of some hotel dated some years since and signed by 'squiggle' should be treated with the utmost suspicion. However, many recruits from overseas carry with them a dossier of certificates, which is guarded jealously and displayed proudly, awarded by past employers as evidence of excellence while with them. These can be used as an indication, indeed the absence of a certificate in the sequence of employment could be questioned, but a follow up letter/form to the past employer should be sent.

Timing the contacting of referees is important. In the ideal situation an approach is made to a referee in advance of the interview, asking for information, in confidence. For obvious diplomatic reasons, permission should always be sought from the applicant to approach a current employer and a timescale indicated for reply in order that references are available **before** the 'interview' date. A standard form is often used, particularly for unskilled, semi-skilled and supervisory grades, which is sent with a covering letter and a stamped, addressed, envelope for the reply. Graduate recruits and managerial appointments employ the use of a covering letter with, perhaps, details of the job applied for and an indication of the areas to be covered in the more voluble reply couched in the prose of the referee.

Depending on the importance of the position, and/or any questions that were left unanswered, the telephonic solution is not unknown. Tact and skill in the art of sensitive conversation is required in this event. Telephone reference requests are now quite common as they can be cost effective and more likely to elicit a response than the mailed alternative which can find its way into a referee's in-tray where it stays unanswered. Box 2.10 shows a typical format for a telephone interview in pursuit of a reference. Typically, whoever is delegated to obtain the reference would use a pro-forma, each question having a space in which the information is written.

References have the weakness of extremes. Few employers are willing to give a 'bad' reference. The result is either impossibly glowing or obviously anodyne. At the other end of the scale those who are 'out to get' a previous employee are not usually given as referees. However,

---

Box 2.10

Example structure of questions for a telephone reference request form

1. What are the dates of employment with your organization?
2. Please advise on the start and end job title and start and end salary of the applicant when they worked for you.
3. Could you please indicate the core duties performed by the applicant when working for you?
4. How do you rate the applicant's performance when compared to other of your employees?
5. When employed by you, how often was the applicant late for work and how was his/her general attendance?
6. How was the applicant's relationship with others?
7. Did the applicant function in a team?
8. How motivated and enthusiastic was the applicant when employed by you?
9. Why did the applicant leave your employment?
10. Would you or would you not rehire the applicant?
11. Would you recommend the applicant to other employers?
12. Would you like to add anything else?

Note: For many of the questions, a pro forma may allow for multiple choice answers, thus allowing the person soliciting the reference to offer the referee a simple choice of responses. This may speed up the time in which the reference can be taken but lose certain details and qualitative information which the referee may be prepared to give.

---

the piqued employer who is about to lose a good member of staff can often display negative traits. Use references for reassurance and confirmation. Use references for insurance and legal purposes. Use references for diagnostic purposes. But always keep them in their proper perspective.

On occasion, when the need to replace a leaver is urgent, the offer of employment can be made 'subject to satisfactory references' – the let out if the performance at interview belies the performance at work.

The decision

This is usually a consensus involving the interested parties – those superior in the hierarchy and specialist colleagues. Further sanction may be required at higher levels involving a second interview – as could be the case if two candidates were of equal merit and a decision was not made.

Taking into consideration all sources of information, i.e. the initial application, the results of testing, performance at interview, referees' comments and the opinions of work colleagues, a weeding process is carried out. Candidates without the necessary qualifications and experience can be eliminated early. Those whose performance in the testing/ assessment centre exercises falls short of the mark may be next to be set aside. Performance at interview displaying lack of knowledge and inability to communicate are next. Referee reactions should have an influence to confirm the views developed – positive or negative.

Assuming no second interview, and the choice is made, communication with the successful applicant can now take place. If the group of applicants is small and they have been plied with coffee and magazines in an anteroom, the 'winner' may be offered the job there and then. Fine, it is done – but can cause a certain embarrassment all round. Telephoning 'the choice' is perhaps more discreet as a possible alternative. The letter of offer is essential as a vehicle of communication whether preceded by a verbal offer or not.

This document will give details not only of the appointment and the conditions attached thereto, as well as salary, pension and other benefits, but also the more mundane details of when, where and to whom the new applicant should report on the first day of work. An opportunity to formally welcome the new recruit to the company and indicate that a written acceptance of the offer is required – usually giving a timescale. In this book we are not, for the most part, concerned with the detailed legalistic aspects of the employment relationship. However, in Box 2.11, we have outlined certain aspects of such relationships once the decision to employ has been made.

Do not forget the rejects. It is often a good idea **not** to send letters of regret to those who have not been chosen until **after** the acceptance of the 'first choice'. If the preferred candidate says 'no', the first reserve can be called in without undue squirming on the behalf of the employer. At any event, always notify the unsuccessful candidates as soon as possible. It lets them know where they stand and is good public relations. Keep those who were 'near misses' on file for future consideration – but clear the file every few months!

A DIFFERENT TYPE OF INTERVIEW: LEAVING THE ORGANIZATION

To conclude our discussion of recruitment we return to the point made at its start, namely that the recruitment process is triggered by a leaver or leavers. It is common practice in many organizations, though still comparatively rare in hospitality services, to conduct an exit interview with those leaving the organization. Where the leaver is departing in less than amicable circumstances, for example through dismissal (see Chapter 11) this may not be possible or necessary. For those who leave voluntarily however, it is useful for managers and proprietors to keep a record of the reasons for departure. In order for the exit interview to be successful it must be conducted without recriminations and thus there

Box 2.11

The Contract of Employment

Ignorance of the workings of the contract of employment requirements is no defence in law. Failure to observe the fundamental
principles can result, *in extremis*, in expensive, time consummg
and traumatic litigation.

THE STARTING POINT

All workers have a contract of employment, which may be either
verbally agreed, or more explicitly delineated in writing. Both verbal
and written contracts of employment carry the same status, although
in reality it may be hard to prove elements of a verbal contract if any
dispute were to reach an industrial tribunal or the courts. Within the
contract of employment, Kibling and Lewis (1996: 3-12) describe
three distinct types of 'terms'. They can be identified as 'express',
'implied' and 'statutory'.

EXPRESS TERMS

These have been discussed by the worker and employer and accepted
by both parties. They are usually put in writing, often at the letter of
appointment stage and/or in a staff handbook. Good examples
include; rate and frequency of payment, hours of work, holiday
and sick pay; periods of notice by either party; discipline and grievance.

IMPLIED TERMS

This is a more abstract concept, but if in the event of a legal contest,
tribunals tend to apply a test of 'custom and practice' to a point in
question. This could include harassment of some kind – physical,
verbal or sexual; unwarranted disciplining without following laid
down procedures; arbitrary or inequitable action – giving a pay raise
to others and not the employee in question without good reason .
Similarly the employer would be expected to employ a competent
work-force, provide a safe working environment (although this is
covered extensively by its own legislation), and deal promptly with
discipline and grievance matters. From the employee's point of view
'custom and practice' implies that a worker would not deliberately
set out to damage the business or disclose trade secrets, but would be
expected to take reasonable care of artefacts belonging to the business under their control and obey reasonable orders.

STATUTORY TERMS

These are set down by government legislation to protect workers
during and on the termination of employment. Rights on notice given
and received, redundancy and dismissal, maternity rights, protection
against unfair dismissal and discrimination on the grounds of race or

sex are laid down by statute. Workers qualify for these rights after given periods of continuous employment, and once these qualification periods are satisfied, the statutory rights become part of the contract.

Determining if a person is an employee at law is established by application of a number of tests that have been developed by the courts. Boella *et al.* (1996) list them as including the following.

- **The control test** whereby the extent of control of the employer over the employee is used to establish contractual circumstance. Clearly reception and restaurant staff fall under the definition. Greyer areas include gardeners, window cleaners or the piano player in the tea room.
- **A business integration test** is applied to the worker's contribution to the activities of the business itself. Obviously, the chef is an integral part of the business, whereas, again, the poor old window cleaner is on less solid ground!
- **The multiple test** by definition, applies a catholic approach, applying criteria that include the concepts that, (a) the worker agrees to provide his/her work for a wage; (b) the worker will be subject to the employer's control; and (more vaguely) (c) the rest of the contract is consistent with the accepted format.
- The advent of the **Employment Protection (Part-time Employees) Regulations 1995** gives *pro rata* benefits to those working less than the 30–45 hours per week generally supposed to be the full-time qualifying minimum.

THE RIGHT TO WRITTEN STATEMENT OF PARTICULARS OF EMPLOYMENT

Under the Employment Rights Act (ERA) 1996, most workers are entitled to receive within two months of the start of their employment a written statement of particulars of their employment. Although it should be noted that the particulars do not in themselves constitute a written contract of employment, it is likely that they will, in any disputes, offer strong evidence as to what is the contract. The particulars must include the following.

- The employer's name, which may be an individual(s) or a company. Details of the place of work are normally included at this point.
- The date the statement was issued.
- The employee's name and address.
- The date the employment commenced with the business. If there has been a take-over of the business, employment under the direction of the previous owner(s) should be included, with appropriate dates.
- The job title, but a provision regarding other duties when required could be added here if considered necessary.

- Pay details; rate of pay per annum/week; overtime rates (if any); payment by week/month in arrears; and method of payment. Obviously this will change over time – so amendments to a contract are needed when these occur.
- Hours of work. The total number should be stated clearly, and the days of the week involved are a vital component of this section. Shift workers whose hours can vary must have suitable reference made to this in the contract. For businesses whose demand can vary over time, guaranteed payment/lay off conditions could be included.
- Holiday entitlement must be stated, and the conditions invoked when an employee works during a holiday in terms of time off in lieu or payment. From the employer's point of view, notice of intention to take holidays (in writing) should be specified. A month in advance, minimum, should give ample time for employers to organise rotas accordingly.
- Termination conditions apply to both sides of the arrangement. A sliding scale is used by employers. After one month - one week's notice. After two years, two weeks, no matter how many hours are worked. Thereafter a week is added per year of employment up to 12 weeks after twelve years. Obviously, employers can increase this period at their discretion. Similar employee's notice should be built into the contract.
- Sickness and injury benefits via any company scheme, but certainly the state entitlements should be clear in the contract, as well as requirements for contact when sick and submission of sick notes.
- Retirement details stating when employees are expected to retire are often included in the section that embodies pension rights and any company arrangements to that end.
- Discipline and grievance procedures must be covered in the contract of employment. Similarly, any trade union agreement and entitlement must be stated.

Contracts of employment cover a wide range of topics, and the above guide can be little more than representative of the essentials. Finer details can be provided in attendant documentation, rather than be included in the contract itself. For example, a company health insurance policy, pension scheme details, discipline procedures, holiday entitlements could all be detailed in supplementary documentation issued to the employee, and updated as the occasion demands.

must exist a state of considerable trust between operators and their employees, otherwise candour on the part of the latter will be at a premium. At the same time, those conducting exit interviews need to be on their guard against employees who, having nothing to lose, give misleading reasons for their departure. A helpful compromise is to give each leaver a form to complete and return either prior to or on the day of their departure. If employees are aware from the practices and procedures of the organization that they can, if they wish, discuss the form with the responsible person, then the former applies. If, however, the leaver is nervous of their comments, the latter submission date is appropriate, the point being that even such information is useful to the manager/operator than having no information at all. Box 2.12 shows a specimen 'leaver's form' that can be readily adapted to a variety of circumstances.

Box 2.12

Example exit interview questionnaire form

Name: _____   Department: _____
Hire Date: _____   Supervisor: _____
Termination Date: _____   Full-time/part-time: _____
Start Position: _____   Male/Female: _____
End Position: _____

A. Reasons for leaving

    If leaving voluntarily please number the three most important reasons for your decision where 1 = most important

Voluntary (resignation)   Involuntary

- Moving to new _____   • Temporary position
  position (write in   at an end _____
  name of company)
- Moving away from _____   • Laid off/
  area   redundant _____
- Going to University/ _____   • Dismissed* _____
  College
- Health reasons _____   • Student on
                                     placement _____
- Transport difficulties _____
- Home/family reasons _____   *Write in reason for dismissal
                                     here:
- Personal reasons _____   _____
                                     _____
- Dissatisfied with type _____   _____
  of work   _____
                                     _____
- Dissatisfied with lack _____
  of promotion

- Dissatisfied with pay _____
- Dislike working _____
  conditions
- Other (write in) _____
- Retirement _____
- Internal transfer _____

B. Your experience with the company.

In strict confidentiality, how would you rate on a scale 1 to 5 (1 = Outstanding, 5 = Poor) the following aspects of your employment with the company.

1	Pay	1 2 3 4 5
2	Holiday entitlement	1 2 3 4 5
3	Bonuses	1 2 3 4 5
4	Perks	1 2 3 4 5
5	Physical environment and working conditions	1 2 3 4 5
6	Amount and quality of training	1 2 3 4 5
7	Recognition of your contribution by supervisors/ managers	1 2 3 4 5
8	Promotion opportunities	1 2 3 4 5

C. Your feelings about the company

1. Write in this space what you most liked about the company and your job:

   _____
   _____

2. Write in this space what you least liked about the company and your job:

   _____
   _____

3. What could we have done to make your job more pleasant and help you stay with us?

   _____
   _____

4. Would you work for this company again if the opportunity arose?

   _____
   _____

Please sign below

Employee: _____   Interviewer: _____

Note: For involuntary leavers, part of the form under 'A' can serve as a straightforward addendum to any other documentation used as part of the severance process.

REVIEW AND DISCUSSION QUESTIONS

1. Consider the relevance of primary, secondary and internal labour markets for an understanding of recruitment in the hospitality industry.
2. Select a job typically found in a hospitality organization and an establishment in which the job may be located (e.g. a five-star hotel). Produce an idealized job analysis, job description and job (hiring) specification for this post. What difficulties did you have in undertaking this task? Why?
3. Devise an advert for the job chosen in (2) above and include design and typographic elements. What are the current costs of placing that advertisement in various media? At what point does advertising a post become prohibitively expensive?
4. Assess the relative merits of the job selection interview and psychological testing as recruitment tools.
5. Examine the information in Box 2.13. Why have maternity rights?

Box 2.13

Pregnancy and Maternity

Since the emergence of statutory maternity provisions in the 1970s, it is widely agreed that they have become increasingly complicated and complex. A number of changes in the law have added to this complexity and can make understanding of statutory maternity provision difficult for both employers and employees. Lucas (1995: 225-6) has suggested that the primary reason for this complexity lies in what she calls, the 'Great British Compromise' which, in attempting to strike a balance between employees' rights and possible employer inconvenience, has merely served to cloud the issue in confusion.

As a result it is important that both employers and employees have a sound grasp of the law relating to maternity and pregnancy and indeed this is particularly so for employees. For example, Susan Harris, the then employment secretary for the British Hospitality Association, felt that 'Employees may need to be very au fait with their rights in order to get them' (cited in Williams 1994: 53). Notwithstanding that, good organizational practice would support the production of a simple guide for employees to enable staff to understand the provisions. To develop such a policy statement, companies can utilize support from a range of organizations who can offer comprehensive advice to both employers and employees. Usually free advice can be obtained from: the Department of Social Security (DSS), which offers guidelines on maternity benefits, via the booklet, Statutory Maternity Pay - manual for employers; the Department of Trade and Industry which issues a booklet entitled, Maternity

Rights, which is also available in Citizens Advice Bureaux, libraries and Job Centres; and the London based pressure group, Maternity Alliance.

Within this context, to make the current maternity provisions as understandable and as simplified as possible we will outline a sequential approach to pregnancy, which will cover antenatal care through to the return to work after maternity leave. There will also be a brief discussion of related issues in areas like dismissal, discrimination and health and safety (For a much fuller discussion of maternity provisions see, Boella *et al.* 1996; Kibling *et al.* 1996).

ANTENATAL CARE

It is important for employers to be aware that under the Employment Act 1980, all pregnant employees, regardless of length of service or hours worked, are entitled to a reasonable amount of paid time off work for antenatal care (which may also include relaxation classes).

MATERNITY LEAVE

In response to the EC Pregnant Workers Directive (92/85/EEC), the government included provisions in the Trade Union Reform and Employment Rights Act (TURERA) 1993 (which itself has recently been superseded by the Employment Rights Act 1996), to substantially extend maternity leave coverage. This means that all pregnant employees, regardless of length of service or hours worked, have a right to 14 weeks' maternity leave, commencing at any point during the 11 weeks prior to the expected date of childbirth. At the end of this period, they also have the right to return to the same or a similar job – as long as a number of procedural steps are taken both before and after the birth of the child. Further to this, those women who have worked for the same employer for the two year qualifying period have the additional right to maternity absence (up to 40 weeks in total), which means they may return to work any time up to 29 weeks after the birth of the baby – although in relation to the extended absence, employers with five or less employees may be allowed to disallow the extended maternity absence, and may also be exempt from allowing a woman to return to work if it is 'not reasonably practicable'. The right to return is particularly important when we recognize that the Equal Opportunities Commission estimates that around two-thirds of women who have a baby want to come back to work within nine months. Women who are only entitled to the 14-week maternity period do not have to give written notification to the employer of their intention to return. Women on extended maternity absence have to ensure they notify the employer in writing and within applicable time limits of their intent to return, failure to do this is likely to deprive the woman of her right to return.

MATERNITY PAY

Like maternity leave there are two levels of maternity pay. The first is **Statutory Maternity Pay** (SMP), which is payable to all employees who have 26 weeks of continuous service, earnings of more than £57 per week and were employed at the fifteenth week before the expected date of childbirth. SMP is paid by employers, although 92 per cent is recoverable, and employers who pay £20,000 or less annually in gross national insurance contributions (NICs) qualify for Small Employers Relief and may recover 100 per cent of SMP. Currently, SMP stands at 90 per cent of average weekly salary for six weeks and £54.55 for 12 weeks. The same rate is also available for 18 weeks as a **Maternity Allowance** (MA) which is paid by the DSS to those employees who do not have 26 weeks of continuous service. Self-employed and unemployed women can also claim an allowance of up to £47.35 depending on the amount of NICs paid. Much of the debate which surrounds maternity pay is concerned with its value, particularly when compared against similar provisions within other EU countries, where it is consistently higher.

DISMISSAL AND DISCRIMINATION

One of the biggest changes in TURERA was the removal of the two-year qualifying period for unfair dismissal claims. As the law currently stands it is automatically unfair to dismiss a woman due to pregnancy or maternity, relatedly there is also the possibility that women could make claims under the Sex Discrimination Act 1975. Claims for discrimination could also extend to other areas such as promotion opportunities, pay or fringe benefits if the courts felt such discrimination was on the basis of pregnancy.

HEALTH AND SAFETY

Under The Management of Health and Safety at Work (Amendment) Regulations 1994, organizations have to also implement health and safety aspects of the Pregnant Workers Directive. This is particularly in regard to the notion of risk assessment, wherein there is a need to assess the risk to mother and baby, and if necessary, if an employer cannot alter conditions which may be too dangerous for a pregnant employee, they may be entitled to a paid health and safety suspension. Examples of this may include issues such as excessive nightworking, and physical, biological or chemical agents which carry a risk to expectant mothers.

With the increasing number of women in the labour market it is crucial that both employers and employees are fully informed of developments in the field of maternity provisions to ensure that good practice is being followed by organizations. Ultimately such good practice may extend to a more equitable approach which could mean the eventual introduction of paternity leave to compliment maternity leave. As yet there are no statutory provisions, although it could be argued that responsible employers should already be offering such provisions. Nonetheless there is a very good chance that the fairly widespread statutory paternity leave available in a number of European countries could be extended to all EU countries if initiatives such as the parental leave directive of the Maastricht protocol were to be implemented throughout the EU.

Source:
Williams, M. (1994) Pregnant pause. *Caterer and Hotelkeeper*, 15 September, pp.52–54.

3 Equal opportunities

By the mid 1970s the nature of the UK labour market had changed noticeably to include an increased number of females and those from ethnic minorities. It became clear that the employment and career development prospects of those from certain groups within society were being hindered due to the ingrained prejudices of management. Discrimination in employment can manifest itself in two ways.

- **Direct discrimination**. Whereby an individual is treated less favourably than others specifically because of a characteristic such as race, gender or sexual preference.
- **Indirect discrimination**. This is less explicit and therefore more difficult to prove. It occurs when management creates requirements that may on face value appear entirely sensible, yet which in practice have discriminatory consequences. An example of indirect discrimination would be a hotel manager stating that all employees must live within a two mile radius of the hotel, knowing that this excludes applicants from a nearby area that has a concentration of those from an ethnic minority.

A survey by recruitment agency Austin Knight with over 1,000 responses by people working for eight major employers found that (MacLachlan 1996: 11):

- 36.6 per cent believed they had experienced age discrimination during the course of their careers (for those respondents over 40 years of age this proportion increased to 39.4 per cent);
- nearly two-thirds of respondents from ethnic minorities said they had experienced racism in employment; and
- 37.4 per cent of women said they had experienced sexism at work.

The Government introduced defensive legislation in the form of the Equal Pay Act 1970, the Sex Discrimination Act 1975 and the Race Relations Act 1976 as the vulnerability of workers from these emerging groups became apparent. These Acts of Parliament were an attempt to force employers to guarantee equality of opportunity and freedom from discrimination and harassment, irrespective of gender or racial origin. The legislation encouraged employers to display their commitment to equality by implementing equal opportunities policies. Such legislation undoubtedly gave credibility to the cause of equality. However, it was designed to give individuals the power of redress over discriminatory behaviour and this in itself does not tackle the wider problem that discrimination is a result of the application of misguided stereotypical ideas. Despite the stated intentions of the Acts therefore, corporate strategies created in their wake have often been narrow and ineffective.

Successful human resource management rests upon a belief that all employees have the potential for development and that all should be encouraged to make a significant contribution to the organization. This is only possible in a work environment that is free from unnecessary discrimination and harassment. Despite the diverse nature of the hospitality industry work-force, or possibly because of this diversity, companies have largely failed to implement successful equal opportunities procedures. As this chapter shows, the challenges relating to equality that face managers in the hospitality industry are intense. The situation is further complicated by changing laws regarding disabled workers, ever increasing numbers of workers from ethnic minorities and the emergence of topics not covered by legislation, such as discrimination against employees who are gay or lesbian.

Both the failure of companies to successfully implement equal opportunities strategies and the complex nature of the work-force in the hospitality industry should encourage us to find new and effective means of guaranteeing equality for all employees. In recent years the concept of 'managing diversity' has developed, in part as a reaction to past failures, yet also as an accompaniment to progressive human resource management. Kandola and Fullerton (1994: 47) provide a broad definition of this concept as follows:

> . . . managing diversity accepts that the work-force consists of a diverse population of people. The diversity consists of visible and non-visible differences which include factors such as sex, age, background, race, disability, personality, work style. It is founded on the premise that harnessing these differences will create a productive environment in which everybody feels valued, where their talents are being fully utilized and in which organizational goals are met.

The aim of diversity management therefore is to create a non-discriminatory workplace culture so as to maximize the potential of every employee. Kandola and Fullerton argue that by creating specific equal opportunities programmes that are designed to encourage the prospects of particular groups then those that are excluded will suffer. They also suggest that the creation of gender or ethnic targets may encourage management to employ workers simply because of their membership of particular groups, thus perpetuating rather than tackling discrimination.

However, there is a realistic concern that broad diversity management strategies may be too vague to recognize and remedy discriminatory practices that can occur. It may appear admirable to publish idealistic statements about encouraging the creation of a diverse work-force, yet without an understanding of the type of problems that can arise, and comprehensive and well-resourced policies to counteract these problems, such statements are pointless. A survey by the

QUEEN MARGARET UNIVERSITY COLLEGE LIBRARY

Commission for Racial Equality (1995) revealed that despite having written statements relating to equal opportunities few companies actually implement effective measures.

There are examples of companies that have embraced the new doctrine of diversity management and have successfully encouraged the growth of a diverse work-force. Grand Metropolitan's successful bid for the American company Pillsbury Inc. in 1988 brought with it brand names such as Burger King and Häagen Daas. It also brought Grand Metropolitan's first encounter with diversity management. Malcolm Greenslade, the company's employment policy director stated that:

> Cultural diversity creates an environment in which individual differences are evident, different means to an end are respected and the talents and attributes of people from different backgrounds and heritages are fully valued, utilized and developed. Such an environment, we believe, can achieve superior business results.
>
> (*Personnel Management*, December 1991)

Grand Metropolitan's first practical step was to reinforce this commitment through the appointment of a Vice-President of Cultural Diversity. The most important aspect of their strategy was the training of staff and management to break stereotypical notions and to highlight the value of having workers with different characteristics, whether these be of race, gender, age, sexual preference, education or personality. The company also created a Cultural Diversity Council which contained staff from all areas and levels of the business and which was responsible for monitoring progress and making recommendations to management on an ongoing basis. Grand Metropolitan believed that greater business results could be achieved by creating a diverse work-force that more accurately reflected their diverse customer base.

At this point, it is worth distilling the essential components of an equal opportunities/diversity management policy. These are as follows.

- **Commitment**. Without the written commitment of senior management any policy will lack credibility and will be doomed to failure.
- **Identification of potential problems**. Before training can begin it is essential to gain an understanding of the discriminatory problems that can arise and the effects that these can have on individuals and productivity.
- **Diversity awareness training**. Staff must be trained to realize that not only are equal opportunities necessary, but that diversity is to be celebrated. The benefits of a diverse work-force should be communicated.
- **Monitoring**. This should be done in a qualitative sense by encouraging feedback from employees and management. It is inadvisable to set employment and promotion targets for specific minority groups as this is likely to run counter to the inclusive philosophy of diversity management.

While accepting the merits of diversity management it is essential not to disregard specific areas in which problems are most likely to occur (see Box 3.1). What follows in this chapter is therefore an examination of those areas in which problems relating to inequality in employment may arise. The complexity of the labour-force is such that no examination of problem areas can be exhaustive, yet certain topics do merit special consideration, especially in the context of the modern hospitality industry.

SEX DISCRIMINATION

The characteristics of the gender segregated UK work-force are well documented. There is generally a concentration of women in low-paid, low-status and part-time occupations and under-representation of women in managerial positions. Such segregation, both in the type and level of job, stems in part from persistent assumptions about the different roles of men and women in society. Traditionally women have taken prime responsibility for household tasks and child rearing, both of which have limited their ability to maintain long-term, full-time employment. As more women enter the labour market this traditional division of labour can no longer be the norm, yet it still represents a powerful set of stereotypes which in themselves help to perpetuate organizational segregation based on sex.

Theorists have suggested that in reality, men and women operate in different labour-markets, the first for primary occupations with job security and promotional prospects, the latter for secondary, low status occupations (see Chapter 2). Whether or not this is true, it is undoubtedly the case that men and women compete in the work-force on different terms. Due to occupational segregation there still exists what are regarded as 'women's jobs' and 'men's jobs'. It is therefore the case that to secure promotion women do not simply have to prove that they are able, but they must also fight to gain entry to a predominantly male arena.

To a large extent these characteristics of the UK labour market are reflected in the UK hotel and catering industry. A report published by the Hotel and Catering Training Board (1987) showed that women made up 75 per cent of the work-force of the hotel and catering industry and that the majority of women were concentrated in operative jobs. Some 64 per cent of women worked as either kitchen or counter-hands, bar staff, domestic staff, hotel porters or stewards. Only 15 per cent of men worked in such occupations. Women held 47 per cent of managerial positions, which despite being a better ratio than in any other industry, did not represent the proportion of women in the entire hospitality work-force. The report also revealed that women are likely to progress less rapidly through hospitality organizations and that once in management positions will generally be channelled into 'front-of-house' occupations. There is no evidence to suggest that the situation

Box 3.1

Equal opportunities

The emergence of the concept of diversity management has given rise to a debate about the possible decline of the more traditional equal opportunities approach. The controversy centres on the shift in emphasis from encouraging particular groups which are underachieving in the workplace, to encouraging the individual, irrespective of social or cultural background. Some proponents of diversity management believe that to focus attention on particular groups may actually perpetuate discrimination.

However, such tensions need not exist. It is possible to reconcile the broad aim of encouraging diversity with the more specific objectives of certain groups, such as women and those from ethnic minorities. Highlighting the concept of diversity is a useful means of promoting a company's belief that all members of the work-force should be given the same opportunities to contribute and progress and that individual differences strengthen the workplace culture. The success of equal opportunities policies has always rested on the belief that such policies are necessary. Educating management on the benefits that will be gained from achieving a diverse work-force will hopefully ease the implementation of equal opportunities policies.

Despite organisations in the UK being forced to comply with EO legislation, it is clear that workplace discrimination still exists. By promoting diversity companies may be able to bring about the change in attitude that is required if equality of opportunity is to be achieved. Diversity management and equal opportunities can therefore be viewed as being interdependent.

To promote good practice on equality and diversity companies must ensure that any remedial policies which they introduce relate to their specific work environments. It is difficult to find examples of hospitality organizations which have faced this challenge in an effective manner. However, examples of good practice do exist in other industries and could be adopted by hospitality organizations.

For example, Smithkline Beecham surveyed its staff in order to assess how best to use resources to promote equality and diversity. The survey covered areas such as 'workforce composition, working patterns, work and lifestyle, personal opportunity and valuing people's differences'. The results displayed, '. . . gaps in family friendly policies, workplace flexibility, communication, training opportunities and career guidance', all of which are central to equal opportunities. By identifying such problems solutions can be proposed. The Smithkline Beecham staff survey provided useful qualitative information. Any subsequent survey will display the changes in attitude that have occurred on matters relating to diversity.

There is a risk that the concept of diversity can be communicated in a manner that does not convey the benefits which it can bring. As noted by Vikki Ford, managing partner of Kingshill Management Consultants, 'Whatever definition your organization uses for equality and diversity, the important fact is that, by adopting such a strategy, you are working for commercial success'.

Source:
Ford, V. (1996) Partnership is the secret of progress. *People Management*, 8 February, pp. 34–6.

---

for women has improved since the HCTB published its report in 1987. Indeed it may have worsened, for hotel and catering companies tend to favour the labour flexibility and cost reductions that come from employing staff on a part-time basis.

Discrimination on the basis of gender was not outlawed in the UK until the 1970s with the introduction of the Equal Pay Act 1970 and the Sex Discrimination Act 1975. The Equal Pay Act states that men and women must receive the same pay and be subject to the same contractual terms if they are doing similar work or work of equal value. In relation to employment, the Sex Discrimination Act 1975 covers advertising, recruitment, training, promotion, transfer, disciplinary procedures and dismissal. Many occupations in the hospitality industry have strong associations with specific genders. For example, chefs are most often men, whereas room cleaning staff are almost always women. It is unclear whether such gender segregation is maintained because women do not apply for traditionally male occupations and vice versa, or whether it is as result of direct sex discrimination. Managers must be aware that perpetuating such segregation works against the ethos of diversity management. It is also essential to consider whether any employment requirements or conditions that are applied may have indirect sex discriminatory consequences. For example, stipulating that job applicants must be at least six feet tall is likely to adversely affect the chances of more women than men (see Box 3.2).

The Government was twice forced to amend legislation due to the efforts of one woman. Miss Marshall went to the Southampton Industrial Tribunal to protest about the different statutory retirement ages that existed for men and women because she was required to retire at 60. Her claim was successful and the Government was therefore forced to introduce the Sex Discrimination Act 1986, which outlawed different retirement ages. Her second case was about the level of compensation to which she should be entitled considering her forced retirement. The European Court of Justice confirmed that the Government's limit on compensation levels was in breach of European Law. This resulted in introduction of the Sex Discrimination and Equal Pay (Remedies) Regulations 1993 which abolished the limit on compensation payments relating to sex discrimination (Peters 1995: 28).

Box 3.2

Sex discrimination – women managers and women workers in the hospitality industry.

Discrimination often occurs against women in hospitality. The EOC has a code of practice for the elimination of discrimination on grounds of sex and marriage and recommends that questions on marital status, number and age of children should not be included in the selection procedure. Example of questions that should **not** be asked include:

BACKGROUND, FAMILY AND HUSBAND

- Marital status
- Husband's employment (women only)
- Do you live with parents/relatives/boyfriend, etc?
- Parents' occupation
- Are your parents happily married?
- Do you have a boyfriend?
- Are you planning to get engaged or married?

MEDICAL (WOMEN ONLY)

- Any time off work owing to period pains?
- Any time off work owing to 'female ailments'?
- Any gynaecological abnormalities?
- Are you pregnant?/do you intend to become pregnant?
- Do you suffer from menstrual disorders?
- Are your periods regular?
- Are you on the pill?
- Do you intend to start a family?
- Have you ever had a baby?
- Have you ever suffered a miscarriage?
- Are you able to carry on your duties during your periods?

All of the above questions are indications of sex-bias and should be avoided. They are also likely to be against the law.

Many (male) beliefs about women's abilities often intrude unnecessarily into the selection process. For example:

- women with children are unreliable;
- married women or women of child-bearing age are likely to have babies and leave or become unreliable;
- women are more likely to have time off work owing to illness (particularly 'women's' problems);
- women are not mobile, or may have to move because their husband's job has priority; and
- women of marriageable age are interested primarily in short-term employment.

Source:
Jones, W. (1992) Jobs for the boys. *Caterer and Hotelkeeper*, 24 September, pp. 46–8.

It would be inadvisable for companies to rely on the law alone as a means of preventing sex discrimination. Legislation simply gives individuals the right of redress over discriminatory behaviour, rather than tackling the root problem. It is unlikely that any policy, however effective, could change entrenched attitudes about the roles of men and women in society. However, a rigorously enforced policy may limit the potential for discrimination. Such a policy should embrace the following elements.

1. A statement from senior management expressing the company's determination to defeat sex discrimination.
2. A member of the management team should be appointed to take specific responsibility for the implementation of the policy.
3. When composing an advertisement for a new appointment, avoidance of the use of language that displays an intent to discriminate, for example by using gender specific terms such as 'waiter' or 'stewardess' should be observed.
4. Avoidance of informal recruitment methods that may limit applicants to one sex, such as allowing existing male employees to inform their friends of vacant positions.
5. Legitimate guidelines on dress and appearance of employees should not be allowed to degenerate into a beauty contest.
6. Efforts should be made to ensure that female employees are not assessed to be less geographically mobile than their male colleagues and therefore less suitable for promotion.
7. There should be provision of training for management designed at breaking down existing gender stereotypes.
8. Any policy should contain clauses that guarantee access to work, training and promotion on the basis of ability alone.

It is essential to monitor the effectiveness of any policy. This can show whether members of one sex only are applying for positions, being employed and securing promotion. Shortfalls in any areas can be targeted for special attention.

It is also worth aligning the company with external schemes that are intended to promote equality of opportunity. In October 1991 John Major launched 'Opportunity 2000', a programme designed to improve the position of women in the UK work-force. Members pledge to be committed to the representation of women at all levels of the promotional hierarchy. Opportunity 2000 had 275 members at the time of the publication of its third annual report in 1994. Of these, 92 per cent offered training for part-time staff, 71 per cent provided maternity arrangements above the minimum legal requirements and 31 per cent offered initiatives providing paths out of 'non-career jobs'. Becoming part of such a scheme may help companies to create an atmosphere in which discrimination is regarded as unacceptable.

It should be clear that to prevent access to certain occupations for a huge proportion of the labour market is both bad business practice and morally indefensible. The avoidance of sex discrimination must therefore be treated as being of strategic importance, rather than being a marginal issue.

SEXUAL HARASSMENT

Sexual harassment can be a humiliating and destructive experience which can adversely affect confidence and job performance. Harassment of this nature, whether it be a simple show of male (or sometimes female) machismo or a more serious incident, has little to do with sexual desire and much to do with displaying power over others. Where men are the perpetrators, it is a means of reasserting the traditionally dominant role played by men over women. Obviously such behaviour in the workplace is undesirable, for as well as being immoral it limits the ability of people at work to fulfil their potential. An Industrial Society survey of 1993 (cited in Collier 1995: 12) lists how sexual harassment can affect communication, concentration, productivity, absenteeism, sleep patterns and levels of depression.

There are no precise definitions of what constitutes sexual harassment, as what is regarded as unacceptable behaviour by one employee may be acceptable to another. A widely used definition is that of Rubenstein (cited in Collier 1995: 3) who states that sexual harassment is, 'unwanted conduct of a sexual nature or conduct based on sex which is offensive to the recipient'. Such conduct may take various forms, possibly repeated demands for dates, comments about looks or clothing or suggestions that promotional prospects will be damaged if sexual favours are not granted. It is necessary to make employees sensitive to the fact that each individual's perception of behaviour involving sexual innuendo is different and that comments or actions of this nature should therefore be avoided. It is often the case that sexual harassment is more noticeable in work areas which are single sex dominated such as in hotel kitchens, where a woman may be expected to behave as 'one of the lads'. However, relatively visible behaviour in an open setting like a kitchen should not detract from the possibility that more private and damaging harassment may be occurring elsewhere in the workplace.

Incidents of sexual harassment against women may be prosecuted under the Sex Discrimination Act 1975, on the basis of the clause in the Act which states, 'on the grounds of her sex he treats her less favourably than he treats or would treat a man', where 'he' is constituted as being the harasser. It is not only the perpetrators of sexual harassment that are liable for prosecution. Employers can be held responsible and prosecuted due to the actions of their employees, even if they were unaware that sexual harassment was taking place. Employers can only avoid prosecution if they can prove that they took reasonable action to prevent sexual harassment, such as the implementation of a related equal opportunities policy. The Act also offers protection to complainants and those giving evidence from any subsequent victimization.

The Employment Protection (Consolidation) Act 1978 can also have a bearing on cases of sexual harassment. If an employee is dismissed after making a complaint against a colleague then they may be able to claim unfair dismissal. Similarly, if they are forced to resign then constructive dismissal can be claimed. Complaints are only considered valid if they are lodged with the Central Office of Industrial Tribunals within three months of an incident having taken place. It is unlikely that workers in most sectors of the hospitality industry will have trade union representation, guidance and support can therefore be sought from organizations such as Citizens' Advice, The Equal Opportunities Commission and Women Against Sexual Harassment (WASH).

To rely on the law alone as a means of combating sexual harassment in the workplace would be naïve in the extreme. Inclusion of sexual harassment in an integrated equal opportunities policy is essential for a number of reasons:

- as a display of commitment to the welfare and equal opportunities of all staff for without such a commitment, staff may not feel confident enough to approach management with a complaint;
- to show that reasonable action to prevent sexual harassment has been taken, so as to avoid prosecution should a case be taken to an industrial tribunal (see Box 3.3);
- to avoid the adverse publicity that can result from cases of sexual harassment; and
- to avoid the demoralizing effect that a case of sexual harassment may have on the work-force.

Any policy must contain a broad statement which defines sexual harassment and asserts that it will not be tolerated. This should be followed by details of the possible effects of such behaviour, external organizations

---

Box 3.3

Sexual harassment and industrial tribunals

- Until 1994/5 there was a limit of £11,000 on compensation payable as a result of a successful industrial tribunal hearing for cases of sexual harassment. This has now been removed.
- The EU code of practice defines sexual harassment as any unwanted conduct of a sexual nature which is offensive to the recipient and includes: leering and gesturing; the display of offensive materials; suggestive remarks; 'jokes' or personal comments; sexual propositions; threats or personal comments; and physical contact – from touching to rape.

Source:
Merdsley, B. (1995) Tribunals take a tougher line on sexual harassment. *People Management*, 23 March, p. 62.

that can offer advice and the complaints procedure, including information on time scale restrictions. According to Hawkins (1994: 26) effective harassment policies in organizations must be based on the need to overcome victims' reluctance to complain. To do this, organizations must:

- create a climate in which people are confident enough to raise problems;
- ensure people have access to effective procedures and support for resolving claims;
- establish a commitment to eliminating all forms of harassment;
- gain management acceptance that harassment is a problem in their organization (eliminating tendency of male managers to legitimize harassment by trivializing it as 'harmless fun'); and
- ensure policy on harassment comes from the top of the organization, is unequivocal and firm in its commitment not to tolerate harassment.

Also, policies may have to take on board several broad areas of harassment including sexual harassment and that owing to race, religion, disability and sexual orientation.

It may be helpful to appoint one member of staff who is responsible for overseeing policy implementation and staff training. Training should be aimed at creating a culture of intolerance of sexual harassment and at empowering staff to complain and support others should incidents occur. While training management it is useful to emphasize the effect that sexual harassment may have on areas such as productivity and absenteeism. Holding single sex training sessions, especially for female members of staff, is an effective way of encouraging workers to respond to the policy, share their experiences and develop their confidence.

RACIAL DISCRIMINATION AND RACIAL HARASSMENT

The extent to which racism is a problem in the UK hotel and catering industry is unclear, yet its existence is undeniable. Research published by the Commission for Racial Equality (1991) highlighted the nature of the problem. Employees from ethnic minorities are disproportionately concentrated in unskilled occupations and those seeking supervisory or management positions are only likely to be successful if they are not competing against white applicants. On a more positive note, the research also displayed that people from ethnic minorities are more likely to be recruited or promoted in firms where employers take action to destroy the barriers to equality that often exist. Such employers demonstrated an understanding of the connection between equal opportunities and sound business practice. They found a clear improvement in the quality of staff emerging from the recruitment and selection process and reported better staff relationships.

The economic arguments in favour of the implementation of workplace racial equality programmes are well documented. Racial discrimination represents an immense waste of human resource potential resulting in low rates of productivity. What receives less attention in human resource textbooks is the devastating personal effect that such discrimination can have on the recipient. Reflecting on the effect that racial discrimination has had on her life, Agnes Ridley, a well-qualified Malawian immigrant wrote recently in *People Management* (23rd February 1995: 30), 'I see a life of wasted potential and steadily growing frustration characterized by one theme: discrimination in employment'. She reported that there are ways of dealing with the day-to-day racism that she encountered out of work, but that the most profound damage is that of missed career opportunities caused by the racial discrimination of employers. An understanding of both the personal devastation and economic implications of racial discrimination may help to motivate managers into tackling the problem. As was noted earlier, demographic changes in the UK are likely to lead to an increased proportion of the hospitality industry work-force coming from ethnic minority groups. This being the case, senior management must be aware of the potential difficulties and develop strategies to combat them should they arise.

Racial discrimination and harassment were outlawed by the Race Relations Act 1976. The Commission for Racial Equality (1989: 7) has outlined several common forms of discriminatory behaviour that can occur including:

- unjustified refusal to interview, appoint, offer training or work experience or to promote;
- providing different terms of employment, benefits or access to facilities;
- unfair allocation of work, overtime, bonuses or unfair transfer; and
- unfair disciplinary action, dismissal or selection for redundancy.

There is less dubiety about what constitutes racial harassment than exists for other forms of harassment. What is important is the perception of the recipient. If the recipient finds offensive any comment or action by a colleague that is specifically related to race then it can be considered racial harassment.

As noted earlier, in law discrimination can be manifested in two ways. In respect of race, 'direct' discrimination occurs when a person is treated less favourably by colleagues than they would treat someone else, purely on the grounds of race. 'Indirect' discrimination is less obvious. It occurs as a result of regulations or practices that have a detrimental effect, specifically on those from certain racial groups. As noted earlier, an example of indirect discrimination would be a hotel manager stating that all employees must live within a two mile radius of the hotel, knowing that this excludes applicants from a nearby area that has a concentration of ethnic minority citizens.

The Commission for Racial Equality (1991) makes a number of recommendations designed to improve racial equality in hospitality organizations. These should begin, they suggest, with the composition of a policy statement outlining senior management's commitment to creating a non-discriminatory environment. This may seem obvious, yet the Commission's research showed that almost all hotel companies disregard this important first step. This should be followed by a number of practical measures that can be summarized as follows.

1. **Company image**. Publicity material should contain positive images of workers from different racial backgrounds.
2. **Monitor recruitment methods**. Monitoring the wording of advertisements; avoiding word of mouth referrals as this may perpetuate a single race work-force when there exists a multi-racial labour market; not on internal promotion.
3. **Lack of applicants from ethnic minorities**. This can be overcome by: establishing links with representative organizations; instigating work experience programmes; recruiting from schools/colleges that have a concentration of ethnic minority students.
4. **Avoid racial stereotyping**. By adhering to the principles of 'managing diversity'.
5. **Devise and implement effective training programmes**. There can be no model of a standard training programme as the nature of each will be dependent on the size of the organization and the extent of the problem.
6. **Monitor the effectiveness of both the policy and training**. It is dangerous to set achievements in terms of having certain numbers of employees from racial minorities in particular occupational grades as this is likely to run counter to diversity management. However, qualitative research can display if employees feel that opportunities are improving and discrimination is being eroded.

In 1995 the Commission for Racial Equality (CRE) published *Large Companies and Racial Equality*, the results of a survey of the racial equality policies and practices of 168 UK companies, each of which had over 7,000 employees. The survey was carried out throughout 1993 and 1994. Its aims were 'to find out what large private sector companies had done to ensure racial equality in employment; to ask what factors had influenced the companies' decisions to take action (or not) in this area; and to examine the outcomes of action taken' (CRE 1995: 3). The results were poor in respect of hotel, catering and leisure organizations. Of the ten main companies in this sector only 40 per cent claimed to have implemented a racial equality action programme, 30 per cent issued a statement on the topic but had no policy, while 30 per cent were decentralized companies in which management of equal opportunities was presumably devolved to individual trading units. In most industries it is usually the largest companies that are most likely to have structured staff welfare programmes. This being the case we can assume that in the hospitality industry as a whole the proportion of companies that have developed racial equality action programmes is less than the 40 per cent of large companies overall cited in the CRE survey. This problem is compounded by the fact that a high proportion of the hospitality industry work-force comes from ethnic minorities.

The CRE has, in the past, concentrated much of its efforts on providing legal support for individuals who have suffered racial discrimination or harassment. While this remains a priority, it is now placing more emphasis on communicating that the implementation of racial equality action programmes provides direct benefits to business. The starting point of this campaign was the publication in 1995 of a new standard for racial equality for employers entitled *Racial Equality Means Business*. This standard was published in conjunction with the results of the survey of large organizations. It is designed to be a means of transforming the aforementioned Race Relations Code of Practice in to action. The standard is composed of the following three sections (Ollerearnshaw and Waldeck 1995: 24–29).

1. Information relating to the close relationship between running an organization in an effective manner and implementing fair employment practices.
2. Details of how to plan and implement a racial equality action programme. This is basically a checklist of questions that management should address. These range from 'Does the organization have a written racial equality policy clearly linked to the organization's aims and objectives?', to an examination of the desired outcomes of such a programme.
3. The third, and most significant, section of the standard is entitled 'Measure of Progress'. This provides a detailed means of measuring companies' achievement in relation to racial equality. The areas covered are policy and planning; selecting, developing and retaining staff; communication and corporate image; corporate citizenship; and auditing for racial equality.

A more contentious area of racial equality management is that of 'positive action'. The Race Relations Act 1976 allows for positive action policies to increase the number of applicants from ethnic minorities to areas or grades of employment in which they have been traditionally underrepresented. The Commission for Racial Equality (1991) advises hotel companies to encourage applications from individuals in racial minority groups by providing training which will allow them to compete for vacant posts on an equal basis. However, as noted by Kandola and Fullerton (1994), it may be more effective to provide such training for any employee who feels that it would be beneficial. To target particular groups in this way may actually cause resentment, defeating the intended purpose of the action.

Whatever measures are undertaken it will not be possible to totally eradicate racial discrimination and harassment in the workplace. It is therefore essential to define and clearly communicate an appropriate procedure for redress. If diversity management is proving effective then employees should feel empowered to complain should the need arise. It is important to offer a confidential, informal complaints procedure for those who wish to settle the matter in-house, or in cases where an incident is of a relatively minor order. Advice may also be offered on how to make a formal complaint and take a case to industrial tribunal.

MULTICULTURAL AWARENESS

The hotel and catering industry is, in all respects, be it unit locality, clientele or labour-market, probably the most international of all industries. The international nature of the labour market presents problems relating to the effective management of workers with many different cultural backgrounds. Culture, as defined by Hofstede (1984: 21), is 'collective programming of the mind which distinguishes the members of one human group from another'. Organizational difficulties can occur through the inability of workers from one culture to accept the characteristics of those from another. Demographic forecasts suggest that the UK population is ageing, yet the age structure in ethnic minority groups is younger than that of the country as a whole. This being the case the Commission for Racial Equality predicts that the work-force of the UK hotel and catering industry will soon contain a higher proportion of those from ethnic minorities (CRE 1991). This will intensify the need for human resource managers to gain an understanding of the difficulties and opportunities that can arise in a multi-cultural work environment.

It is first essential to develop awareness of the characteristics of the corporate culture in which you are operating. This is displayed in a number of ways that may be conveniently categorized as follows.

1. Physical signs: dress; work space layout; noise levels; building design.
2. Ways of life of dominant group: ethics; management styles; communication of ideas and emotions; workplace practices; language.
3. Published aspects: company mission statement; staff handbook; job evaluation procedures.
4. Underlying assumptions: what is acceptable behaviour; how much individualism is acceptable.

For those in the dominant group in any organization such corporate culture signifiers can strengthen their sense of belonging. The aim must be to create a corporate culture in which those of different races, nationalities or religions do not feel excluded and are able to thrive.

It is worth establishing criteria by which it is possible to analyse the cultural characteristics of others so that the potential for difficulties can be assessed. The research of Geert Hofstede (1984: 37) provides us with such criteria. Hofstede's four 'dimensions' of culture enable detailed examination of the likely effect that a worker's cultural background will have on the work environment and are therefore useful tools for the creation of policies related to racial equality. These dimensions are as follows.

1. **Power distance**. Inequality of authority is essential in any organization if order is to be maintained. Those who come from very formalized, hierarchical cultures tend to have more deference for managers and may be more willing to accept regulations without question. Those from the UK and many other Western countries may feel more free to make their opinions known to management in an attempt to influence the decision-making process.
2. **Uncertainty avoidance**. In cultures that have developed a powerful way of dealing with the uncertainties of life, often through religion, individuals may frequently prefer to operate within prescribed guidelines. This is not always possible within hotel and catering occupations as employees are often required to think 'on their feet' and deal with unusual situations.
3. **Individualism**. The extent to which people feel free to act as individuals and indulge in self-expression varies between cultures. Although individualism is generally linked with ambition and confidence, there is a risk that strong individuals may lack the teamwork skills and company loyalty that are required in hospitality units.
4. **Masculinity**. Hofstede believes that the assumed masculine characteristics of 'assertiveness, advancement, freedom, recognition and independence' are required as essential leadership qualities in many cultures. Women who come from cultures in which male and female roles are clearly defined may find it difficult to condition themselves to the UK where opportunities for advancement into management may be more apparent.

It is essential to avoid making assumptions that everybody from a particular nation will display the same cultural characteristics. Criteria such as those provided by Hofstede should only be used to make management aware of the possible differences of approach or attitude that workers may display. Operational problems can be avoided if management realize that their style should be adapted depending on who they are addressing. For example, it may be necessary to monitor the use of jargon, colloquial expressions, directness, aggression, body language and humour (Goss-Turner 1992).

GAY AND LESBIAN WORKERS

There is a general perception that the hotel and catering industry contains a higher concentration of 'out' gay male workers than other industries. This may or may not be true, but what is likely is that the visibility of gay workers is more evident in hotel and catering occupations. It may therefore be true that hospitality companies offer a more protective work environment than most for gay and lesbian employees. This is not to say that problems will not arise.

There are no credible reasons why gay workers should feel unable to reveal their sexuality, yet to do so may create hostility among colleagues and/or management, which in turn can develop into discrimination. A survey carried out in 1993 by Stonewall, the gay lobbying organization, found that one in two lesbians and gay men had faced harassment at work, 48 per cent of whom were harassed specifically because of their sexuality. Forms of harassment ranged from jokes or teasing to more serious homophobic abuse and some even experienced physical violence (Collier 1995: 9) (see also Box 3.4).

Opinion formers in our society are generally agreed that forms of discrimination such as sexism and racism are unacceptable. However, the same cannot be said regarding homophobia. It is worth examining how the moral stance of the government and the explicit support of homophobia by sections of the media combine to legitimize discrimination against gay men and lesbians.

- Throughout the 1980s a central belief of the Thatcher government was that sexual permissiveness and other signs of supposed moral degeneration were a result of the break-up of the traditional family unit. The government was openly opposed to the 'promotion' of 'pretend' families.
- Homosexuality was viewed by many on the New Right as being immoral. As stated by Margaret Thatcher at the 1987 Tory Party Conference, 'Children who need to be taught to respect traditional moral values are being taught that they have an inalienable right to be gay' (Evans 1993: 126).
- Labour local authorities which adopted pro-gay policies were ridiculed by the Government. Some conservatives realized that there was political advantage to being viewed as the anti-gay party.
- In 1986 the Government placed control of sex education in the hands of school governors (parents). In September 1987 a Government

---

Box 3.4

Attitudes to gay people at work

In 1995, a survey for the Social and Community Planning and Research Group found that:

- 64 per cent of gay employees have hidden their sexuality from some or all of their work colleagues;
- 21 per cent of gay workers have been harassed at work;
- Eight per cent of gay employees believe they have been turned down for promotion because of their sexual orientation;
- Four per cent of gay workers allege they have lost their jobs on grounds of their sexuality.

Source:
Welch, J. (1996) The Invisible Minority. *People Management*, 26 September, 31.

directive stated that sex education should be based around informing pupils of the 'benefits of stable married and family life and the responsibilities of parenthood' (Weeks 1989: 295).

- Geoffrey Dickens MP, of the Conservative Family Campaign, summarized the attitude of many on the New Right regarding the 'promotion' of homosexuality when he said: '. . . not only with teaching and indoctrination in schools, but we've seen set up, gay and lesbian clubs all over the place . . . They entice and corrupt and bring others into their unnatural net' (Evans 1993: 127).
- Coverage of matters relating to homosexuality by the popular tabloid press has usually been harsh. Typical of the press attitudes were those expressed by Sun journalist, Gary Bushell, 'It must be true what they say about nobody being all bad . . . even Stalin banned poofs' (cited in Evans 1993: 123).
- The emergence of AIDS (acquired immune deficiency syndrome) and HIV (human immunodeficiency virus) and their close association with gay sexual activity undoubtedly strengthened homophobic attitudes.

Possibly spurred by the manoeuvres of government and the press and because of the emergence of AIDS, public feeling relating to homosexuality soured throughout the late 1980s. An opinion poll for London Weekend Television in 1988 displayed that support for legislation to legitimize homosexual relationships fell from 61 per cent in 1985 to 48 per cent in 1988, and over half of the respondents believed that homosexuality was 'unnatural'. It is easy to see that changing workers' attitudes and combating discrimination against gay men and lesbians in the workplace is no straightforward task.

The most worrying aspect of discrimination against gay employees is that they are offered no protection by law. Unless companies have an equal opportunities policy relating to gay and lesbian issues then workers have no means of appealing against discrimination in the workplace. Some commentators have argued the Sex Discrimination Act 1975 could be used as protection for gay workers because any discrimination which they receive is partly related to gender. However, this is stretching the scope of the Act and the reality is that UK law works against lesbians and homosexuals. For example, the Employment Protection (Consolidation) Act 1978 contains a clause which enables employers to dismiss someone for, 'some other substantial reason'. This clause has been used by employers on a number of occasions to dismiss employees purely on the grounds of their sexuality. Also, although not directly related to employment, Clause 28 of the Local Government Act 1988 which bans 'promotion of homosexuality' by local authorities, helps to perpetuate a culture in which equality for homosexuals is seen as a low priority.

Agitation for change in this area of equality in employment comes mainly from trade unions. However, most sectors of the hospitality industry have little or no union involvement. Unions do represent airline stewards and the British Airlines Stewards and Stewardesses Association and Cabin Crew 89 are known to lobby airline companies on gay employment rights issues. Examples of successful lobbying can be found. After pressure from both the above associations, British Airways have amended the term 'common law spouse' to 'partner' in their Staff Travel Regulations. Gay workers are now able to nominate their partners for BA's 90 per cent discount travel benefit. This prompted the *Sun* newspaper to suggest that gay stewards would be taking their partners to 'Botyswana' or Queensland. A gay BA steward, writing in the company magazine *Contact*, referred to problems of getting compassionate leave for bereavement, the wait for 'buddy rostering' so that couples can work on the same flights, the problems of changing pensions to accommodate same-sex partners and the fact that sexual orientation is not included in the BA Equal Opportunities Manual (Blundy 1995: 24).

Managers in the hospitality industry should not be influenced by the moral debate that surrounds this topic. It is not the privilege of managers or other members of staff to discriminate against gay men or lesbians on the basis of their beliefs on issues of morality. Any organization which makes claims to be an equal opportunities employer must have a policy relating to the employment of lesbians and homosexuals. Such a policy should afford the same rights to these employees as are enjoyed by their straight colleagues. It should also state that harassment will not be tolerated and outline the disciplinary measures that will ensue should this occur. The effective implementation of a policy of this nature is dependent upon commitment from all levels of management and clear communication by well-informed trainers.

AGE(ISM) AND YOUTH

The hotel and catering industry is heavily dependent on young workers. Figures supplied by Lucas (1995: 54) suggest that:

- some 42 per cent of all industry employers are aged less than 30 with some 40 per cent of these aged nineteen or less;
- a further 20.2 per cent of employers are in the 30–39 age category;
- only around 37 per cent of industry workers are aged 40 or more.

Thus, nearly two-thirds of all industry workers are aged 39 or less. It is unclear as to how reliable these figures are, derived as they are from 'official' sources (in this case a 1994 report of the Hotel and Catering Training Company). Impressionistically, they arguably appear to underestimate the number of young workers in the industry. Lucas and Jeffries (1991) examined the effects of declining numbers of organizations held to be problematic in the UK from the early 1990s onwards. In a postal questionnaire study of the managing directors of 300 hotel and catering organizations of which a response rate of 108 (36 per cent) is reported, the authors found that on respondents' own classifications, many firms relied heavily on young workers and women: 52 per cent had a higher proportion of women in the workforce; 15 per cent a higher proportion of men and 33 per cent had equal proportions of men and women. Most respondents were aware of the projected decline in the number of 16–19 year olds from 1990–94. Only 15 per cent of respondents stated that they had not introduced new recruitment and retention strategies in response to changing demography, though the authors note that such claims could reflect an exaggeration on the part of respondents. Some 84 per cent of respondents were enacting changes to try and reduce turnover though only 24 per cent had considered career breaks which might be considered important given the number of women in the industry.

Further evidence of employers' dependency on young workers comes from a variety of studies. Messenger and Makinson (1992: 253–5) offer a helpful insight into the age structure of a sizeable hotel company, De Vere Hotels. At the time of their writing the group comprised 25 three- to five-star properties employing some 3,958 staff, 61 per cent of whom were women, 62 per cent of whom were 30 or under (and of these 57 per cent were women) with 22 per cent under 20 years old. Lucas (1993) examined the employment practices of 38 restaurants in Greater Manchester and found that employment was predominantly young, despite difficulties with recruitment possibly associated with a relative shortage of youngsters. Some 57 per cent of units had the highest proportion of workers in the 16–25 age group with a further 31 per cent having the highest proportion in the 25–36 age group. Most employers were not actively pursuing alternative labour strategies and indeed, there was direct and indirect evidence of discrimination against older/mature workers. In a journalistic report on fast food employment, Williams (1994: 44) cited figures to the effect that, in Britain, Burger King then employed 3,000 workers of which 40 per cent were under 18 while McDonald's had some 60 per cent of its staff under the age of 21.

A later study by Lucas (1995: 241) which examined various survey data derived from her own research projects found that the majority of employers – some 51 per cent – employed the highest proportion of their work-force from among 16–25 year olds, while 37 per cent employed the highest proportion of their work-force from among the 26–35 year old age group with around 30 per cent of restaurants seemingly not employing anybody aged over 36. In some academic and other quarters, the hospitality industry's reliance on young workers has raised questions of 'ageism' (which of course applies as equally to the younger as well as older employee). This issue has had broader currency in employee relations concerns during the 1990s. In the context of the hospitality industry, an exclusive survey of age discrimination in the UK hospitality industry was reported in 1992 in the *Caterer and Hotelkeeper* (11 June: 44–46). The main findings of the survey were that three-quarters of people in the hospitality industry believe that age discrimination existed, though only one in five people admitted that their employer was guilty of ageism. According to the survey one in four people had experienced age discrimination, of these over a third were thought too old for the particular job. However, over a quarter of those responding reported that they had been turned away from a job because they were too young. Of the quarter of respondents who had experienced age discrimination, only one in twelve took action. This was most common in finding another job. Housekeeping staff were the least likely to believe that age discrimination existed within the hospitality industry. General managers were the most likely to believe that such discrimination existed.

The *Caterer and Hotelkeeper* survey was prompted by the magazine's regular discussions with employment consultants in the industry. The survey was based on the issue of 15,000 questionnaires randomly with the *Caterer and Hotelkeeper* edition of 23 April 1992. Some 12 per cent of questionnaires were returned, and 1,751 responses were analysed. An interesting finding of the survey was that 86 per cent of all respondents said that older people are more reliable, and 69 per cent agreed that they are better at customer care. Younger people were thought by 74 per cent of all respondents to be more adaptable, and by 70 per cent to be more career oriented. Almost two-thirds of all respondents were involved in some way in recruiting staff, and around three-quarters of these said that they preferred to employ experienced persons. However, younger people were regarded as easier to mould into a company's philosophies and styles of operation and a third of respondents involved in recruiting staff believed that younger people suited their image better. In an accompanying editorial, *Caterer and Hotelkeeper* (11 June 1992: 9) noted that age discrimination in the USA was illegal and deprecated negative attitudes to older workers in the hospitality industry. A selection of correspondence published in the *Caterer and Hotelkeeper* of 25 June (1992: 20) threw up a range of viewpoints, the most provocative of which were comments in a letter from Michael Gottlieb, proprietor of Smollensky's on the Strand, London. Gottlieb wrote:

> I fail to understand why employers ought not to be able to discriminate about potential employees on the basis of age, at least for those who are in contact with the public. We are in a business where image counts as much as content. Of course it is unfair to turn down older people with the required technical skills to do the job, but so what? It is not a perfect world.

Age discrimination in employment is not a problem of the hospitality industry alone. However, 'ageism' is one of those 'isms' that is growing in importance as an issue and, as with other areas of equal opportunities, it is important that employers are sensitive to the arguments attendant on debates about the relative merits of older employees *vis-à-vis* younger workers. Growing and vociferous comparisons against the 'cult of youth' promise to make this area one of continuing interest for employee relations.

DISABLED WORKERS

The employment of people with disabilities is a contentious issue. Whether due to lack of understanding, fear or ingrained prejudice, it is an area that generally receives little formal attention from managers in the hospitality industry.

Legislation has achieved little in terms of creating employment opportunities for those with disabilities. Under the Disabled Persons Acts of 1944 and 1958 companies with twenty or more staff were required to fill three per cent of positions with individuals who were registered as disabled. Furthermore, if employing a lift or car park attendant employers had to try to take on a disabled person. Under the Companies Act 1980 it became the duty of employers with more than 250 staff to publish a statement in their company's annual report detailing how the policy relating to disabled workers was operating. Unlike any other legislation concerned with discrimination, the Disabled Persons Acts introduced quotas and created criminal offences, but did not give individuals any rights of redress over discriminatory behaviour. These laws were unworkable and unenforceable.

It was not until 1994 that changes were made with the introduction of the Government's 'Access To Work' scheme, designed to help those with disabilities find and keep work. The Government established a fund from which employers can obtain financial assistance for specific projects such as making adaptations to premises, paying fares to work and providing specialized services. Decisions about grant allocations are made in response to individual requests, rather than on the basis of predetermined criteria. The sum of £21,000 is the limit that can be spent on one person over a five year period.

In 1995 Parliament passed the Disability Discrimination Act, to be effective from December 1996, which, for the first time, gave people with disabilities legal protection against discrimination in the workplace. The introduction of this Act is undoubtedly a turning point in the fight to ensure equality of opportunity for people with disabilities. The Act defines disability as a physical or mental impairment which has a substantial and long-term adverse effect on a person's ability to carry out normal day-to-day activities. The specific objectives of the legislation are to defeat discrimination not only in the job selection process but also in terms of the promotion and development prospects and dismissal procedures of those already in employment. Discrimination will have been deemed to occur if an employer treats a disabled person less favourably than others because of their disability, or if the employer refuses to make reasonable adjustments to terms and conditions of employment to allow disabled persons to work effectively. These 'reasonable adjustments' are governed by codes of practice that, whilst not legally binding, are likely to influence industrial tribunals' interpretation of the law. This is the second aspect of the new Act: disabled employees can seek redress for discrimination through the industrial tribunals system (see Chapter 11 for a discussion of this system). At the time of writing, three codes of practice have been issued, concerned with access to goods, facilities, services and premises; employment; and the definition of disability (for further information see Little 1996; Croner 1996).

Although the stated intentions of the Act are commendable it does have certain shortcomings. The legislation provided for the establishment of two advisory organizations. These are the National Disability Council (NDC) which advises the Government on matters relating to disability discrimination, and the National Advisory Council on the Employment of People with Disabilities (NACEPD) which advises the Department of Education and Employment. The NDC and NACEPD are purely advisory bodies and do not, unlike the Equal Opportunities Commission (EOC) and the Commission for Racial Equality (CRE), have a wider responsibility for campaigning against discrimination. Critics doubt whether the new legislation will act as a force for change if it is not supported by a single campaigning organization. Worries have also been expressed because the financial resources being allocated to disability are greatly overshadowed by the sums given to tackle other types of discrimination. The CRE has a budget of £15 million, the EOC receives £6 million, whereas the NDC receives only £250,000 (Preston and Scott-Parker 1995:19).

Even before this legislation was enacted the number of members of the Employers' Forum on Disability was increasing, indicating a rising interest amongst employers in matters relating to disability. The Forum works to improve the job prospects of those with disabilities by advising employers.

In 1993 the Institute of Manpower Studies published *Employers' Attitudes Towards People with Disabilities*, the results of a survey of 2,205 companies. In the industry sector entitled 'Distribution/Hotels', 52.8 per cent of respondents employed people with disabilities, which was below the industry-wide average of 56.7 per cent. Those companies which did employ disabled people stated that the benefits they experienced included having dedicated and motivated staff and an enhanced public image. Worryingly, nearly half of the respondents could identify no benefits in employing disabled people (see Box 3.5).

Box 3.5

Disability action in the hospitality industry

The introduction of the Disability Discrimination Act has forced hospitality organizations to address issues relating to the difficulties which are faced by disabled people. Few companies can yet have tackled the issues as effectively as the Greenbank project, a registered charity which aims to offer employment and training opportunities for people with disabilities.

The layout of the restaurant has been central to its success. Its

design, both front and back of house, related to the specific requirements of people with disabilities. The project dispels the widely held
view that the employment of disabled people in kitchens presents a
series of insurmountable problems.

There are other examples of hospitality organizations which began
to face this challenge before the introduction of the Disability Discrimination Act. With the assistance of Holiday Care Service, a
charity which co-ordinates travel and holidays for disabled people,
Mount Charlotte Thistle Hotels group undertook a nationwide review
of the facilities for the disabled in all its hotels. The results of this
review enabled the group to classify 39 of its hotels using criteria laid
down by the National Accessible Scheme. The scheme defines three
classifications:

- accessible to independent wheelchair users;
- accessible to wheelchair users travelling with assistance;
- accessible to those with limited mobility but able to walk a few
  paces and up to a maximum of three steps.

It is intended that such classifications will help disabled customers
assess which hotels best suit their requirements.

Mount Charlotte Thistle Hotels group have also begun to adapt
facilities in their hotels to suit guests who have disabilities. Some
£325,000 has been spent on the Mount Royal hotel in London to
improve facilities. Alterations have included providing lifts with
Braille on the buttons and a voice announcement system; electro-
nically operated doors; wooden-floored bedrooms; appropriate toilet
and shower facilities and reception desks that are a suitable height. In
addition to physical alterations staff at the Mount Royal have
received disability awareness training. The group's efforts in this
area have been recognized. In 1995 the company won the Holiday
Care Service award for the best hotel of 20 rooms and over.

Mount Charlotte Thistle Hotels, along with other groups including
De Vere Hotels, Hilton National and Inter-Continental Hotels, is a
member of The Hoteliers' Forum, an organization which aims to
increase the accessibility of hotels for disabled guests and staff.

This is an area of the hospitality industry about which management
have to be educated. As stated by Maundy Todd, Chief Executive of
the Hotel and Holiday Consortium, 'We need to give the industry the
information and tools to assist them in making things more accessible, they are not experts in accessibility.' Despite the initial capital
input that is required to make adaptations to premises and methods of
operation, hoteliers will hopefully realise that the result is worthwhile. As Maundy Todd adds, 'Companies should look on the act
positively – as there will be benefits – instead of looking for loop-
holes. It will open up opportunities.'

Source:
Caterer and Hotelkeeper, 22 February 1996, pp. 60–2.

As has been shown throughout this chapter discriminatory practices cannot be combated simply by fulfilling legal requirements. It is necessary to create a non-discriminatory environment by tackling the root cause of any prejudice or apprehension that may exist. In respect of disabled workers the now defunct Manpower Services Commission, at the Government's request, published a *Code of Good Practice on the Employment of Disabled People* in November 1984. Aspects of this code still offer sound advice on the integration of those with disabilities into the workforce. Covered in this code are the following topics.

1. The employment of disabled workers must be given considerations at the highest level within the organization.
2. A reference for potential employees making them aware of issues such as:
   (a) legal requirements and financial assistance;
   (b) the fact that the term 'disabled' encompasses many conditions;
   (c) health and safety concerns;
   (d) advice on increasing the number of employees with disabilities;
   (e) points relating to induction and training, etc;
   (f) options for those who become disabled while in employment;
   (g) stressing the need for communication to all employees about the realities, as opposed to the assumptions, of employing disabled workers; and
   (h) designating a single person to take responsibility for maintaining policy.

Consideration of all such points will help with the formation of strategies to successfully integrate disabled workers into any organization. Requiring special mention is point 2(b) above. It is a fair assumption that much of the apprehension that exists concerning the employment of those with disabilities stems from the fact that the term 'disabled' is so broad that it can be misleading. It is essential that managers examine potential workers' abilities in relation to the job, rather than dwelling on disabilities. Also of vital importance is the need to monitor the effectiveness of any policy so that weaknesses can be identified and adjustments made. In 1994 the fast food giant McDonald's undertook an audit on workers with disabilities in an attempt to identify shortcoming in its procedures and promote a positive attitude towards working with disabled people. This notion of encouraging a positive attitude to disability can also be formalized with the 'Positive About Disabled People' initiative. Organizations which support this initiative are identified by the 'Positive About Disabled People' tick symbol in job advertisements. The scheme which was introduced in 1990 and relaunched in June 1993, denotes that employers have demonstrated a number of commitments to disabled people. These commitments are (Torrington and Hall 1995: 369):

- guaranteed job interviews for all disabled applicants who meet the minimum criteria for the job;
- consultation with current disabled employees;
- retention of disabled workers;
- efforts to raise disability awareness, via things like disability equality training; and
- production of an annual review of the commitments and the achievements that have been made.

It is foolish to categorize all people who have some physical, sensory or mental impairment as automatically being unable to take up employment in the hospitality industry. Managers must approach this issue with an open mind, tackle each individual case independently and strive to create a non-discriminatory atmosphere in their workplace.

REVIEW AND DISCUSSION QUESTIONS

1. Differentiate between moral and pragmatic reasons for equal opportunities in employment.
2. What is sexual harassment?
3. Sketch a programme you might employ to train workers in your company about the unacceptability of racial discrimination and harassment.
4. Should gay and lesbian workers enjoy the same employment opportunities as all other workers?
5. Assess the proposition that there are no limits to the jobs that those with disabilities can perform in the hospitality industry.

4 Training and Development

The costs of recruiting and engaging a new member of staff are considerable – not only the direct costs like advertising, agency fees, paper-work, interview time, but many hidden or indirect costs. For example the expenses incurred in training and supervising new entrants, as well as those they are replacing, overtime that may be paid during staff shortages, an increase in wastage and losses while new staff settle in, customer irritation and low staff morale if staff turnover is high.

(Employee Relations for the Hotel and Catering Industry, 7th edn, Hotel and Catering Training Company 1990: 43 cited in Mullins 1992)

TRAINING

As the quotation above suggests, training is expensive – it is thus important to get it right in order to ensure cost-effective delivery of customer services (see Box 4.1).

Training starts before the employee walks through the door of the place of work for the first time. However, learning about the employer starts with the job advertisement and continues through the selection process. As a result 'training', in its widest sense could be deemed to have begun, albeit subliminally, several weeks, or even months, before a new employee is added to the payroll. It is important at this stage to make a clear delineation between training or development as a result of some initiative taken at work, and education that is undertaken before and is mutually exclusive to the work situation. Education at school, college or university may be undertaken as part of an individual's development programme, but for the purposes of this discussion, achievements in these areas outside and prior to employment will be regarded as qualifications required to gain employment, and thus not within the employer's control.

Formal training on starting work is usually associated with induction, the first rung for many on the ladder of human resource development. Formal, recorded, training of the employee should commence as the new recruit walks through the door of the premises on day one. Basic information will be in the new employee's possession as part of the

---

Box 4.1:

The costs of training in the hospitality industry

Hogarth, Siora, Briscoe and Hasluck (1996) in a report for the Department for Education and Employment compared the costs of training in several industries over a 3–4 year period. Of five industries listed, hotels and catering was the second most costly. The figures were as follows:

Construction	£41,002	(four years)
Hotels and catering	£37,465	(four years)
Electronics	£35,663	(four years)
Electrical engineering	£34,869	(four years)
Banking	£29,205	(three years)

Source:
Hogarth, T., Siora, G., Briscoe, G. and Hasluck, C. (1996) *The Net Costs of Training to Employers*, London: HMSO (source cited in *Skills and Enterprise Executive*, 3/96, August, p.3).

---

content of the formal offer of employment. However, the broadening, deepening and reinforcing of the company's activities and standards *vis-à-vis* the recruit is contained in the induction package.

Dangers associated with induction training include using the course as an indoctrination exercise rather than one of gentle assimilation. In addition to this the use of an inflexible, standard induction package will have the singular feature that it will suit no one! Obviously, certain elements will be common to all new starters, for example health and safety standards, fire and emergency procedures, and the availability and use of staff facilities. A staff handbook may also be issued. Thereafter individual needs are going to vary with the level of entry to the company, the area of operation and specialist roles.

Good induction is not a half-day course involving a human resource specialist and (if available) the new recruit's supervisor. Induction is carried out over a period of time, involves a variety of people, contains a follow up procedure and demonstrably benefits both the organization and the employee. Furthermore, induction should 'know its place', in that although the importance of the process must not be diminished, it must be recognized that induction training is an exercise in helping the employee to become as efficient as possible in as short a time as possible with the least disruption as possible to the department in which they are to be employed. Induction may take several weeks to complete. The sheer quantity of information to be transmitted makes it an impossibility to cover in-depth induction in a short period of time. Formal training sessions with reinforcing over a period of weeks is essential. A sample induction checklist should be constructed in order to convey the range and depth of information that is to be assimilated. In addition to the material covered in this list – which could be applicable to all new employees – induction germane solely to an individual's needs in terms of their specific duties and area of operation should be included. Recording induction training, ideally countersigned at appropriate junctures by new recruits and countersigned by trainers is incontrovertible evidence of having received and understood relevant information and is a vital, if cumbersome, check on the administrative efficiency of the induction process (see Box 4.2).

Keep 'handouts' to a minimum – they get lost. An easy-on-the-eye but apposite staff handbook containing basic information on the operation and expected standards of behaviour, as well as information on company policies covering aspects of employment, is issued as the norm in large companies with individual units supplying a supplement to cover aspects relating to their situation only – for example, social activities, staff accommodation house rules, use of hotel facilities, and

---

Box 4.2

Issues to be considered during induction

- Geography of the workplace, including location of equipment, staff and customer facilities, fire exits and fire alarms, together with location of fire-fighting equipment and evacuation procedures.
- Employee facilities, including locker space, rest rooms, car parking and telephones, including constraints on usage where appropriate.
- The department – where it fits in the organization; lines of authority; the new employee should be introduced to relevant departmental staff and others as appropriate.
- Personal quality standards, including personal hygiene and sanitation; individual obligations to ensure safety; dress codes and uniform policy.
- Communication standards including procedure for requesting time off; reporting in when sick; reporting accidents; informing supervisors/managers of changes in personal status (e.g. change of address); grievance and disciplinary procedures.
- Main duties, including responsibilities and expectation of the job; hours of work; issue job description where this has not already been done; relationships with others, including arrangements for team and group work where appropriate.
- Entitlements, including refreshment and meal breaks time off; holidays; pay and other remunerative entitlements; where or how to receive salary; rights and obligations under Equal Opportunities and related policies.
- Development issues, including training requirements and opportunities; equipment usage (and demonstrations of operation); procedure for performance appraisal.

so on (see Chapter 3). Smaller organizations have a more *ad hoc* approach, but formal delineation, publicly displayed and acknowledged by the employee (i.e. signed for) avoids any dispute as to ignorance in the event of a problem.

Induction systems should be used as a two-way street; on the one hand making the employee welcome and comfortable with new colleagues as quickly as possible and, on the other, giving the assurance that the system will consider personal potential for development and that the mechanism for this exists. Identification of the geography of the workplace and the key players therein avoids embarrassment. The use of a mentor system, i.e. an informal 'guide', usually at the same level and in the same department, to keep the new person 'right' has been popular in recent years in many organizations, and is not without its merits as long as the mentor is able to convey the right information in the right way. Skill is required in mentoring and those involved require specialist training to do the job well.

Traditionalists still refer to the notion of the 'induction crisis'. This arbitrary period, usually considered to be about the first six weeks of the new recruit's employment, is considered critical in influencing the person to stay by making a positive impression. Such romantic, even vaguely patronizing, ideas, in times of economic stringency and job shortages are regarded as passé. Nevertheless, the concept of easing the new employee into post quietly and providing formal and informal support as an incentive to achieve peak efficiency as quickly as possible is as valid today as ever it was.

THE TRAINING PROCESS

Training has been defined as 'A planned process to modify attitude, knowledge or skill behaviour through learning experience to achieve effective performance in an activity or range of activities. Its purpose, in the work situation, is to develop the abilities of the individual and to satisfy the current and future needs of the organization' (MSC 1981 cited in Beardwell and Holden 1994: 336). This is a wide-ranging remit, but the confusion with education which has a more abstract, formal and lengthier connotation must be established at the outset. At the risk of stating the obvious – something often sadly neglected – the benefits to be accrued from competent, apposite and regular training as part of the individual's career development include:

- reducing the learning time for new employees, allowing them to reach optimum efficiency as quickly as is possible;
- the corollary of the above – improving performance in the present job;
- by assuring competence, reducing the amount of time, energy and resources spent by managers correcting faults and errors;

- assisting transition of the organizational culture to employees in terms of standards of service and behaviour;
- helping to integrate the employee into the organization and thus perhaps assisting in reducing levels of staff turnover; and
- by influencing attitudes of employees to achieve support for company policies in areas including customer care, total quality management (TQM) and health and safety at work.

Training as an adjunct to solving operational problems must be recognized. For example, training of newly promoted supervisory staff in the skills of human resource management has its advantages in minimizing dissatisfaction and grievances among subordinates.

The benefits of training or retraining staff to satisfy current human resource needs has the advantage of not only motivating employees but also either eliminating the need for expensive recruitment or recruiting at a less skilled level of employment – recruits commanding lower salary scales. Furthermore, training 'raw' recruits when the labour market has a scarce supply can be advantageous. For example, training a pool of banqueting staff to the standard of the establishment using previously unskilled people has several advantages. Sadly, the drawback of the staff being promptly poached by competitors is a risk to be taken and a suitable strategy to combat this is required.

Training is often thrust upon employers as a result of changes in technology; changes in the law; changes in the make-up of the labour market, e.g. the increased sophistication of information technology (IT); changes in regulations regarding food hygiene; and changes in demography which restructure the labour market. Finally, and by no means least, the benefits to the individual of training are incalculable in terms of job enrichment, promotional potential, salary increment and job satisfaction.

IDENTIFYING TRAINING NEEDS

Finding out who needs training and why involves an analytical process. Contributions in assessing an individual's training requirements come from several sources, for example:

- personal requests for training;
- observation on the part of a supervisor identifying a remedial, upgrading or new training need; and
- a new job (via promotion or transfer) indicates that the person concerned requires training as indicated by the requirements of the job specification particular to the activity.

More broadly-based training needs are often identified as a result of organizational problems in production and/or service. Symptoms include:

- low productivity;
- high production costs;
- poor control;
- excessive waste;
- employee dissatisfaction;
- poor discipline;
- high labour turnover; and
- high absenteeism.

Finally, training needs arise from ongoing situations and from purposive organizational strategy. Anticipating training needs can help alleviate or eliminate the problems itemized above. Innovative programmes are the result of, *inter alia*:

- an expansion of the business;
- bringing new products and/or services on line;
- new technology;
- organizational changes; and
- human resource planning needs, e.g. promotion, transfer, recruitment and retirement.

As a result, training plans should be contrived to work at a corporate and individual level in order that true synergy of purpose can be achieved.

TYPES OF TRAINING

In this section we consider the main types of training strategy available to the organization.

Sitting by Nellie

The cliché 'sitting by Nellie' has been damned by many and accepted as perhaps one of the least efficient methods of training, not only on the grounds of its potential for passing on bad habits, but also for its lack of formalized structure and guarantee of content being adequately covered. Despite this, training *in situ* using operatives themselves skilled in training techniques has a vital role to play. Training of skilled and semi-skilled operatives lends itself to this method easily. Similarly, remedial and 'top up' training can be efficiently carried out. Short, formal recorded training sessions are amalgamated with the working routine with supervised application of new skills to the work situation. This is ideal for the likes of restaurant service, housekeeping, front of house, portering and some unskilled kitchen duties. Learning in the working environment encourages an easy transition to working practice, skills can be learned quickly and individuals or small groups can be accommodated. It has the added advantage of being a highly economical form of training delivery. On the down side, the temptation is to hurry the training, missing or inadequately covering important elements with the result that trainees are not completely confident before being 'let loose' on customers. This can have results that may be comic to the observer, but embarrassing and stressful to the trainee and infuriating to the customer. Furthermore, and more importantly, the potential loss of income arising from a failure of service standards should be considered.

Coaching

Coaching can take place 'on-site' in the work environment or it can involve divorcing the training situation from the operational circumstance which also has its advantages. However, making the training experience as 'real' as possible, while at the same time being able to use mistakes as observable points in the learning process for corrective action, highlights specifics without embarrassment. There are several variants on the simulation theme that are used depending on the content of the training operation.

Reducing the concept to its simplest for the demonstration, the 'show and do' situation affords the ease of the expert replicating the operation (e.g. a point of restaurant service, a room servicing operation, operating a computerized booking system) and takes the trainee through a series of controls and progressive tasks where they can be observed and corrected. The demonstration technique can also be employed when abstract concepts are being taught. For example, customer care skills, telephone skills and some communication skills, where a company style is employed, requires demonstration with replication on the part of the trainee (although role-playing exercises, q.v., will be used in tandem).

Formal training

Formal training covers a multitude of techniques and contexts and more often than not will involve off-site training, for periods of one or more days, often in the form of an assessment centre (see Chapter 2 and Box 4.3 below). Often lasting anything from a day or part thereof, to perhaps three days maximum, short workshops provide an ideal medium for small group work. Workshops suit the purpose when, for example, upgrading company policy, explaining new legislation, introducing new information technology systems and installing Total Quality Management procedures, in short a quick burst of information for immediate application! Where this training involves formal education for qualification, regular release to an educational institution for study is usual.

Much formal training focuses on some variation of the 'classroom' situation. The straightforward lecture is good for dealing with large numbers of people being given the same information over a relatively short period of time. In addition to this, presentation of material can be closely ordered. On the down side, because those attending tend to be passive listeners, it is difficult to tell without some kind of examination just how much has been absorbed. One-way communication in this

---

Box 4.3

Assessment centre training and development at Novotel

A reorientation of the company's strategy began in 1993 with revised management assessment centres for all Novotel managers commencing a year later. These one-day assessment centres were intensive and included an in-tray exercise; three half-hour role playing interviews with a demanding boss, an angry customer and an underperforming member of staff; and case studies. All the unit managers attending the assessment centre were scored on thirteen abilities grouped into four broad areas. Each 'ability' consisted of five observable key criteria on which managers' performance was rated. The four groups and thirteen abilities were:

CONCEPTUAL SKILLS
- perception
- judgement
- initiative

APPLICATION SKILLS
- decision-making
- decision implementation
- organization and planning

INSPIRING SKILLS
- leadership
- delegation
- follow-up and monitoring

RELATING SKILLS
- adaptability
- interaction with others
- written communication
- oral communication

As a result of the assessment centres, managers' strengths and weaknesses were identified with a view to completing up to thirteen three-day courses at the rate of about two a year on each of the 'abilities' assessed.

Source:
Littlefield, D. (1995) Menu for change at Novotel. *People Management*, 26 January, pp. 34–6

---

situation can be boring and difficult to follow for long periods. Those not used to a lecture situation can find that masses of information thrust at them in quick succession is difficult to follow. Nevertheless, as part of an educational whole in conjunction with complementary tutorials, essays, case studies, simulation exercises (e.g. the ubiquitous 'in-tray exercise') and group projects, the benefits are many. For smaller groups where more discreet exercises requiring individual contribution is a must the conference 'seminar' style of training is ideal. The benefit of strict organization coupled with oral participation by delegates under skilled instruction or direction is an efficient vehicle for learning. Clearly, numbers must be relatively small, and the process can be slow as a result of the encouraged discussion of topics to reinforce learning.

Case studies as a training technique have been used for many years. Groups are set a problem around a contrived situation. Unlike the methods discussed above, where some new knowledge is to be disseminated, the case study is a means of applying extant abilities with the view to their refinement and expansion by developing latent abilities. Extreme care must be taken in devising the 'case'. Off-the-shelf products can be bought in. Backup in the form of teaching notes and guidance for tutors is essential to maximize the effectiveness of the course. Tutors themselves must be fully briefed on their roles and how to control the activities of the group. Indeed, it is axiomatic that in all forms of training, trainers themselves are properly skilled and/or formally qualified to perform their tasks (see Box 4.4)

Out-placement – industrial release

This system of training, whereby employees are placed in another company or unit to immerse themselves in the philosophy and operational tactics of others has the advantage of allowing the trainees to have all the benefits of learning without the operational responsibilities. Eclecticism is vital in that the trainees are encouraged not to see the out placement locale as the ideal, but more of a reservoir from which to draw ideas for adapting and possible installation. All areas can be included here from basic mechanical activities (e.g. styles of service, computer procedures, security systems) to customer care activities, management communication methods, and hierarchical responsibility models.

Opinions vary as to the efficacy of this mode of training. The initial hurdle to vault is that of suspicion on the part of the receiving busi-

---

Box 4.4

Characteristics of a good trainer

PERSONAL ATTRIBUTES

- Genuine warmth of personality
- Sincere concern for others
- A degree of personal charisma

SOCIAL SKILLS

- Ability to convey enthusiasm
- Clarity in articulating ideas
- Patience
- An ability to put others at ease
- Good at responding to questions and giving answers

TECHNICAL SKILLS

- Sound knowledge
- An ability to be concise in communication
- Personally and professionally well-organized
- Good teaching and reinforcement skills

nesses as to exactly why the trainees are there. On a less paranoid note, observation, even limited participation, can be constructive. If the participants can observe and inwardly digest what is being experienced, taking the view that this is not an alternative to be copied, but a means of seeing how the other half lives and extracting anything that may be of use. There is also much to be said for recognizing that this is the wrong way for you. The trick is to analyse objectively and use the experience as a catalyst for improvement elsewhere. The difficulty is a lack of control of homogeneity, resulting in a limited application for out-placement as a vehicle for training. Finally, extended absence from work over consecutive weeks is expensive.

Out-placement – study for formal educational qualification

Day release facilities (normally to colleges or universities) are widely used not only for craft training but also for management courses, often over a period of years. Clear advantage can be drawn from the increased skill of the delegate via training with minimal infraction to day-to-day duties. Block release for study purposes, for example full-time degree study, is rare for obvious economic reasons although management staff in many organizations increasingly pursue Masters of Business Administration (MBA) courses.

New ground was broken with the installation of the National Vocational Qualification (NVQ – S(Scottish) VQ north of the border) scheme. Courses in many disciplines establish standards of competence. Five grades range from basic foundation courses (1) to senior management level (5). Installation of courses can be undertaken in colleges, schools, training centres and in workplaces at company level. As an alternative to traditional school qualifications' General National Vocational Qualifications were piloted in 1992, and were formally instituted the next year. Three levels of achievement were devised including a foundation Level (1), and Intermediate Level (2) and 'vocational 'A' Levels – the Advanced Level (3). They are designed for young people of 16 and 17 in the first instance.

The National Council for Vocational Qualifications sits in judgement over the system of competence (the ability to do a real live job according to laid down standards) training. Personified by the Hospitality Training Foundation, the remit of which is, *inter alia*, to validate qualifications in the NVQ system be they installed in schools, or colleges or training centres or *in situ* – on companies' premises. The awarding body physically issues the document to the student on completion of an NVQ module. Examples include City and Guilds, BTEC, SCOTVEC, RSA. External and internal verifiers are accountable to the awarding body for maintaining standards, the former being an expert in the area under examination, but who does not work for the organization, the latter, a senior manager in the company, co-ordinating the activities of the in-house assessors. A second line assessor could be required in place in large organizations with complex training networks. Approved centres, i.e. where the training takes place, are as discussed above. The starting point for this maze is the local TEC or Further Education College. Thereafter follow expert advice.

Government as the motivator for training

Incentives have been increasingly provided by Government and its agencies to channel individuals into training opportunities via the employers' auspices, or under their own steam at educational establishments or at work covering the full gamut of education.

In 1990 the Government initiative, Investors in People (IIP), actively encouraged employers to take cognizance of the asset that should be developed to its optimum, viz.: people. Cynics declaim that this is an exercise in stating the obvious. Nevertheless, formalizing and vocalizing universals in human resource management encourages greater awareness by systematizing aspects of the specialism, concentrating on key areas deemed to be appropriate. The main thrust of IIP involves: (see also Boxes 4.5, 4.6 and 4.7):

- a conscious evaluation of the place of training and the investment required therein as a yardstick against achievement and a guide for future efficiency;
- publicly declaring intent to develop employees' potential to the benefit of both the employee and the company;
- positively actioning training tailored to individual's needs;
- seeing training as an ongoing process to be regularly reviewed and revised where necessary; and
- chronologically the process is one of Commitment, Planning, Action and Evaluation.

Local Training and Enterprise Councils (TEC) (Local Enterprise Companies in Scotland), set up by Government initiative in conjunction with local employers to promote training according to local needs, far from being some kind of draconian network of coercive bodies intimidating firms into training for training's sake – and levying a hefty fee to boot – are designed to encourage employers to take seriously the concepts of Investors in People and help implement them. Help with appraisal of training needs from IIP experts is available. Assistance with the installation of National Vocational Qualifications is part of the TEC remit. Negotiate with the organization and talk money in terms of funding they provide as initiative for training. This will not be 100 per cent, but can be useful. Recognition by the local TEC as an Investor in People and receiving an award to that end indicates certain standards.

RESPONSIBILITY FOR TRAINING

Primarily responsibility for training rests with line managers who are in a position to evaluate and plan training strategies to suit not only the

Box 4.5

HCIMA brief on Investors in People

TECHNICAL BRIEF

No 29

Investors in People

1. **INTRODUCTION**

Investors in People is an award of public recognition achieved by companies who pursue business success through the continuous development of their management and staff.

It aims to help businesses improve their performance by realising the full potential of their staff. It is based on the experience of many successful UK companies. This amalgam of good practice has demonstrated that performance is improved by a planned approach to:–

setting and communicating business goals

and

developing people to meet these goals

so that

what people can do and are motivated to do, matches what the business needs them to do.

The basis of Investors in People is a National Standard which provides indicators to which an organisation can work and a benchmark against which progress can be measured.

Once organisations are assessed to have met this Standard, they can be publicly recognised as an Investor in People.

Whilst the achievement of the Award provides benefits in the eyes of potential recruits, current employees and not least customers, the real bottom line benefits are brought about by the journey to meet the indicators and the increasing involvement and contribution from the workforce at all levels.

A company's involvement will only be effective if the belief in achieving the aims of Investors in People comes from the very top of the organisation.

2. **GETTING STARTED**

The first step on the Investors journey is to find out how strong your business' commitment is to its people.

A survey of a cross section of management and staff with questions based on the Investors Standard and tailored to the level of employee will give you an indication as to how committed they feel your organisation is and what there may still be to do.

Having established what there is to be done, this is developed into an action plan showing clearly the action to be taken, by whom and when. The speed of the journey is determined by the business in the light of how much there is to do and the operational constraints of the business. The business benefits from the actions taken – the achievement of the Award is the recognition that the company has achieved the Standard.

There are 4 stages:

Commitment

Planning

Action

Evaluation

Commitment

An Investor in People makes a public commitment from the top to develop all employees. A letter of commitment is sent by the Chief Executive/Chairman/Proprietor/General Manager to the business's local Training and Enterprise Council.

An Investor in People will ensure that the business has a flexible plan which sets goals and targets as to how employees will contribute and how development needs will be met.

It develops communication of where the organisation is going to all employees and the contribution they will make to this.

Planning

An Investor in People reviews the training and development needs of all their employees and identifies these in the Business Plan, agreeing individual needs with each employee.

Action

An Investor in People takes action to train and develop individuals on recruitment and throughout their employment and encourages all employees to contribute to their own job related needs.

Evaluation

This is usually the most difficult stage for any organisation. A continuous assessment of the competence and commitment of all employees is made against business goals/targets and the effectiveness of training in meeting these established. Importantly as goals/targets change, the effectiveness of the workforce to meet these future needs is reviewed.

3. WHAT ARE THE BENEFITS?

Investing in People adds teeth to quality programmes.

Real benefits to an Investor in People organisation can be expected in:

  Improved performance

  Increased personnel motivation, commitment and loyalty

  Greater customer satisfaction

  Organisational reputation

4. THE ASSESSMENT

The Training and Enterprise Councils are the bodies who administer the assessment for the Investors in People Award, either through their own trained staff or through trained assessors from outside companies. Whilst a portfolio is asked for from companies being assessed demonstrating how they meet the various indicators through the evidence of practical working documents, much greater weight is attributed by the assessors to the interviews they conduct with a wide and balanced cross section of management and staff.

The aim is to establish how each individual business/organisation achieves the Standard, for there is no rigidly determined way of meeting the 24 indicators of good practice – eg while most organisations will have in place a formal appraisals system for their management and senior staff, in many businesses a recorded "job chat" may well meet the needs for junior and part time staff, and perfectly adequately suit a small organisation. The assessor will determine achievement of the Award from evidence from the workforce of what actually happens within the organisation. Assessments are made every 3 years and an organisation will have to have demonstrated how its achievement of the Standard has developed in that time.

In order to ensure conformity of the National Standard, the assessors are required to appear before a TEC panel, to demonstrate the thoroughness of their assessment.

5. TO LEARN MORE

Contact the Training and Enterprise Council which covers the county or borough in which your business is situated. The achievement of the Investors in People Standard by all organisations is an aim of all the 82 TECs (and LECs in Scotland).

Being individually administered by Chief Executives of local businesses the methods they adopt to assist organisations in the commitment and achievement of the Investors in People Award varies considerably.

All provide –   information

         practical assistance

         and various levels of funding if consultancy help is required

6. THE COSTS

The real costs are in management time.

Each organisation will have to pay the cost of the assessment. This will be determined by the size of the workforce but will probably take between 1-5 days and is normally charged at £500 per day.

For those companies seeking consultancy help for the Diagnostic Assessment and Action Plan or in the implementation of the plan there is usually TEC funding available to help with the cost.

7. AN INVESTOR IN PEOPLE COMPANY...

An increasing number of companies and organisations of all types and sizes are choosing to become Investors in People. Whilst they will be seen as high quality organisations the real benefit experienced is in their operational performance.

"We can only reach our maximum potential as a business by helping each individual reach his/her full potential".

Further reading:

Each of the 82 TECs (LECs in Scotland) have a wide range of booklets, these are usually available free of charge

Booklets particularly recommended are:

Ref No. IIP 37 (rev.)	The Benefits of Being an Investor in People
Ref No. IIP 28	Revised Investing in People
Ref No. IIP 29	The National Standard – Links to Assessment Indicators
Ref No. IIP 46	How Do We Measure Up

This technical brief has been prepared with the assistance of Mr Steve Samuel FHCIMA, Gayton Consultancy.

HCIMA 191 Trinity Road, London, SW17 7HN Tel 0181 672 4251 Fax 0181 682 1707

February 1995. This document has no copyright restrictions. Registered Charity No: 326180.

Printed on environment-friendly paper.

Box 4.6

Investors in People: impacts on the industry in England and Wales

- Some 79 per cent of employers recognized as Investors in People believe that IIP has improved the quality of their work-force and two-thirds believe IIP has made a positive contribution to business performance.
- Recognized employers are almost twice as likely to have a formal training budget as those not involved in IIP.
- Employers involved in IIP are also likely to be involved in other training-related initiatives – 70 per cent of those involved in IIP are also involved with NVQs.
- At September 1995, some 2,476 employers were recognized as Investors in People with a further 17,290 committed to reaching the standard.
- DeVere Hotels is one of the notable hospitality industry companies to be awarded IIP and the Managing Director is reported as saying that labour turnover has fallen by 30 per cent in a year and adverse comments about staff by customers by 31.8 per cent in six months. Improved business performance is also attributed to IIP – Sales at DeVere in the six months to March 1994 were up 10.3 per cent and operating profits 15.3 per cent.

Sources:
Skills and Enterprise Network (1995) Investors in People makes an impact. *Skills and Enterprise Executive*, 5 November, p. 1.
Williams, M. (1994) 'DeVere proves 'Investors' pays', *Caterer and Hotelkeeper*, 26 May, p. 13.

needs of individuals, but also the long-term goals of the department in their charge. Efficient appraisal, as discussed in Chapter 8, is the foundation on which much planning for training is built and when the formal identification of training needs is instigated. In addition to this generation of information, the line management function includes an institution of new training directives from external sources as the situation arises. Examples include training in new technologies, new procedures, and new health and safety legislation. So far the discussion has ranged from methods of training to avenues of training. Applying the principles, various areas and levels of training can be identified.

Skills training

Within itself, levels of skill as a progression to higher and broader things, for example with chefs, is easy to identify. However, the

> **Box 4.7**
>
> *Investors in People and the Hospitality Industry*
>
> - The number of organizations in the hospitality sector involved in Investors in People doubled in the year to August 1996 but this was still below the national average for participation.
> - Only 19.5 per cent of hospitality industry employees work for an Investors in People employer compared to 25 per cent of employees across all industries.
> - The New Inn at Tresco on the Isles of Scilly saw sales revenue increase by 12 per cent, repeat business by 18 per cent, year on year as a result of achieving Investors in People: in addition, a reduction in staff turnover meant a saving of £20,000.
> - Rockley Park in Poole, Dorset, saw a 20 per cent increase in bottom-line profitability and repeat business: the Park caters for over 100,000 guests every year and employs 250 staff in high season.
> - The De Vere hotel group employs around 2,700 people. In the two years it worked towards achieving the Investors in People standard, average room occupancy rose by 12.6 per cent and sales by 15.6 per cent, despite a recession.
> - Investors in People UK and the HCIMA (Hotel and Catering International Management Association) produced in 1996 a self-help pack entitled *Shaping your team for success* aimed at encouraging small and medium-sized businesses in the hospitality, tourism and leisure industries.
>
> *Source*:
> Chapman, M. (1996) An opportunity that's too good to be missed. *Caterer and Hotelkeeper*, 1 August, p. 22.

acquisition of skill could be a 'one-off', e.g. fire and safety training cannot be assumed as complete after the half-day course. Periodic upgrading and refresher courses are essential.

Supervisor training

When entering the more esoteric fields of human resource development the straightforward 'show and do' is not enough. Participative techniques are commonly used as a means of developing inherent skills in addition to more structured theory which forms the foundation. Areas of instruction can include: interpersonal skills, customer care and safety oriented courses. An obvious overlap with skills training can be identified in terms of content, however delegation and instructional skills are a component to be highlighted. Control of staff in the work situation should be made distinct from the more draconian sounding disciplinary procedure. Often the distinction is blurred since many supervisory posts are held by skilled workers and there is an automatic amalgamation.

Management training and development

Management training and development, while using all the principles and methods discussed elsewhere in this chapter, concentrates on developing skills geared toward the executive decision-making process rather than the hands-on craft element or the supervision and organization of operational activities. Individuals' experience and ability is applied to requirements and the two are matched.

Training – a continuous process

Training is never completed. As well as the constant process of training new employees and retraining and diversifying the training of established personnel, training programmes themselves become obsolete, or elements of the content of programmes cease to be apposite due to the march of technology or a change in legislation or company direction. As a result, a rolling plan of revision, renewal and amendment is vital if a valid training function is to continue (see Box 4.8). Establishing a communication system of opinion on the quality and relevance of training from the trainees goes part of the way to satisfy this need. Newby (1992: 100) suggests that the flippantly named 'Happy Sheet' submitted by the departing delegate as not much more than a gut reaction to the course has several limitations including the observation that it can veer towards the judgmental rather than the appreciative. Furthermore, there is no way of telling from the document just how much information will survive and be applied in the workplace, ergo, assessment of the effectiveness of training takes place at the point of usage, i.e. the workplace. Techniques are various but are based on observation of performance of the trainee and/or testing the new knowledge or skill via a written or practical test against a benchmark of acceptability. The result of this exercise will determine whether any follow-up training is required. Consequently, as part of the individual review procedure, training recommendations become an indigenous part of appraisal, identifying training needs (see Chapter 8).

Evaluation and upgrading training: the training cycle

Drawing together the complexities of the types and availability of training, implementation of training requires a straightforward sequencing. If carefully constructed, with the proviso that it is not sacrosanct, a good training plan can be seen as a living, maturing, changing, complement to a business rather than a necessary evil to be tolerated at best and

Box 4.8

Team hospitality at Whitbreads

A pilot scheme involving 92 pubs in the Whitbread group in 1995 indicated that Team Hospitality training resulted in improved customer service, increased sales and reduced staff turnover.

The scheme built on an earlier programme aimed at raising standards of service which, although little more than an induction, made employees aware of and confident in, *inter alia*, points of law, food hygiene and products available. For passing a simple test a 'silver' award was given. Further training raised participants to a 'gold' and 'diamond' level. Hourly rates of pay reflected the level of qualification. Coupled with this, managers were encouraged to develop staff discussion groups as part of the communication system.

Reform came about as management at board level observed competitors fine-tuning new customer care skills, leaving the Whitbread policy at a comparative disadvantage. A new approach was seen as a priority. The result was an encouragement 'from the top' of managers to concentrate on team building as the fulcrum needed to improve customer service. Sceptical managers had to be convinced that this fundamental cultural change could indeed lead to increased sales and profits.

Staff working parties were set up to produce a set of standards of good practice in units identified as being in one of the three discrete sectors identified, i.e. food-led pubs; those serving a local community; and those offering special attractions, for example music, that would appeal to customers from further afield.

To avoid stereotyped 'have a nice day' styles of service, the instruction was to develop the personal confidence of employees and thus display individual personalities via a pleasant manner and confidence in an ability to do the job.

Having completed a two day group training skills course, each house manager and one other member of staff involved in the pilot scheme undertook a six-week period of structured training in their respective outlets. The experiment proved highly successful and all 1,650 pubs were thereafter included. A target of 30,000 trained staff by the end of August 1996 was set, the cost to be £1.5 million.

The old silver badge scheme was retained but amended by increasing the pass level on the test, and instituting a Team Hospitality Award to pubs with over 80 per cent of staff at the 'silver' level. The 'Award' status must satisfy set standards of training, team meetings, operating standards and customer satisfaction. Quarterly audits are carried out to verify continuity when team meeting minutes and action plans are examined. 'Mystery' customers adjudicate the customer satisfaction remit. Apart from a plaque and visit from a senior executive, winners of the Team Hospitality Award can decide on a party in celebration, or a points system to be redeemed against catalogue goods in a 'Share Inn Success' promotion. After each six month reassessment, an 80 per cent score on all four measures results in further points being awarded.

The results of the pilot were striking. When compared against a control group of 'untrained pubs', sales were found to be significantly higher and staff turnover down in the pilot group. Increased staff morale and personal confidence were evident with both part- and full-time employees. Furthermore, the involvement of staff in the design and implementation of change was seen as a vital component in this achievement. Whitbread were confident of further success over time with the system.

Source:

Arkin, A. (1996) Pulling ahead of the pub crawlers. *People Management*, 18 April, pp. 36–7.

resented as a time-wasting intruder at worst. Seven easy stages can be identified as follows.

1. Closely examine the potential trainees (that means everyone) and the job(s) they do. This sounds daunting, but if accurate job descriptions exist, much of the spadework is removed.
2. Compare the job descriptions with the realities of the individual and find the gaps and/or lack of experience, or areas requiring remedial work.
3. Establish and clarify training objectives for individuals and the company/unit/organization. Strategies should be established for all levels of training.
4. Decide on the courses required, where and how they take place, and their content.
5. Establish the best format for each course.
6. Run the course!
7. Evaluate the training and take action as required.

A diagrammatic illustration of a systematic approach to training is shown in Figure 4.1.

Training is a constant, training is an essential, training is an ethos, but most of all training is a means to an end, the improved performance of the company via the improved performance of the individual. Use training to serve the organization, not to disrupt its real work!

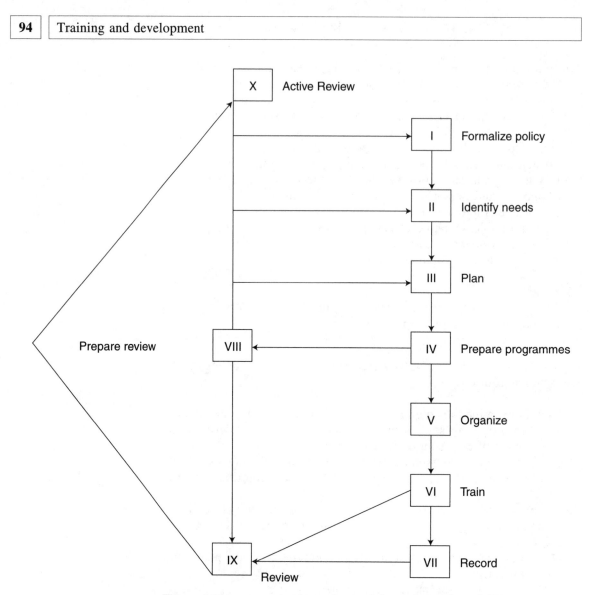

Figure 4.1 A systematic approach to training (adapted from HCITB)

REVIEW AND DISCUSSION QUESTIONS

1. Examine the case study shown in Box 4.9 below. Identify the benefits to the Harry Ramsden's organization of undertaking this type of training strategy.
2. Identify the likely training needs of staff in an independently owned three-star hotel with 50 rooms, located in a rural location and dependent on coach business to a large degree.
3. Outline advantages and disadvantages of Investors in People for hospitality organizations.
4. Does training make a difference to quality?
5. What sort of training do hospitality managers require?

Box 4.9

Training at Harry Ramsden's

Harry Ramsden's won a 1995 National Training Award for its role in getting long-term unemployed people back to work. Together with local Training and Enterprise Councils, groups of 50 people are put through a pre-training course in areas such as food hygiene and customer care. These people are all long-term unemployed (out of work for more than six months) and are directed towards vacancies at the restaurant chain. However, local recruiters are not told who has completed the pre-training course so as to prevent bias in selection. Instead, Ramsden's objective is that 20 per cent of new employees should be those who have been unemployed for six months or more. All new staff attend in addition a two week training programme so they can practise running the Ramsden restaurant.

Source:
Merrick, N. (1996) Sole not dole. *People Management*, 7 March, p. 7.

5 Staff health and welfare

A belief that staff health and welfare have direct implications for the success of organizations has encouraged a number of companies to introduce policies aimed at creating and maintaining a healthy workforce, policies which often have implications extending beyond the workplace into employees' non-work life. At face value this appears to be a positive trend. However, there are important ideological questions involved relating to the extent to which employers should have control over their employees' activities outside the workplace. There is also a certain irony in the fact that supposedly inclusive welfarist policies may in fact help to marginalize workers who do not conform to desired norms, such as those who are overweight or who smoke or drink heavily, even if such factors do not have a bearing on occupational abilities. This is potentially more relevant in the hotel and catering industry than in many other sectors, as those who are perceived to be non-conformist may not be considered suitable for contact with the public. It is therefore essential that the introduction of welfare policies should be in an attempt to fulfil business objectives and these should be formulated so as to avoid imposing a moral code on employees.

What follows is an examination of the main areas in which well-constructed and sensitively implemented policies relating to employee welfare can benefit both staff and organizations. Topics covered in each sub-section of this chapter could form individual policies within a broad staff welfare strategy.

ABSENTEEISM

Employee absence is one of Britain's greatest industrial relations problems. Britain has, persistently, the highest rate of absenteeism in Europe (Williams 1993). In 1987 the CBI estimated that the cost of non-attendance and sickness in Britain was £5 billion, a figure which had risen to £11 billion by 1993 (Lucas 1995: 245). Despite the scale of this problem employee absence remains an industrial relations problem which is rarely tackled in strategic terms. The fact that there is confusion about how best to tackle absenteeism is understandable. It is difficult to address a problem for which the causes are so varied and complex, encompassing genuine illness, stress due to personal circumstances, stress due to the workplace environment and idleness.

It is probable that absenteeism exists to a greater extent in the hospitality industry than in many other sectors. Factors such as the casual nature of employment contracts, employees' lifestyles, the stressful nature of workplace environments and low wage rates combine to encourage high levels of worker absenteeism. In certain workplaces there is a shared acceptance amongst staff of the legitimacy of absence from work. This is what commentators have termed an 'absence culture'. Simplistic punitive measures imposed by management are unlikely to reduce the levels of illegitimate or stress related absence. Worker absence cannot be eradicated, but in workplaces in which relationships between management and staff are strong and all employees feel valued the levels of absence are likely to be lower than the norm.

Achieving acceptable levels of staff attendance has to be viewed as a strategic issue if hospitality organizations are to overcome the problem to any degree. There are a number of means by which this aim can be incorporated into strategic plans, some of which have been suggested by the Audit Commission (1990: 4–7). These are as follows.

- Commitment of top management. Senior management should display the seriousness by which it views absenteeism by issuing staff attendance levels that line managers must try to achieve and by writing a personal letter to every member of staff explaining the company position on absence from work.
- Examination of work environment. It may be helpful to examine the workplace environment to identify any problems that may be encouraging absenteeism, then following this up with appropriate action.
- Suitable training for managers. Poor management will lead to high rates of staff absence. It is pointless setting attendance targets and appearing committed to solving the problem if management is not suitably trained.
- Recruitment. Information about employees' attendance records in previous occupations should be obtained from referees.
- Employee Assistance Programmes (EAPs) (see pp 107–9 below). It may be that referral to an EAP counselling session or an appropriate external counselling service could help an employee to overcome whatever personal problem is the cause of their absence from work. Monitoring of the topics that are discussed at EAP sessions may show that absenteeism is due to a particular workplace problem of which management are unaware.

In addition to these measures there are a number of administrative procedures that may help to control staff absence.

- Employees must inform management in advance if they are going to be absent from work. Failure to do so should be considered misconduct.
- Medical certificates should be passed to management to confirm rea-

sons for absence. Some organizations only require medical certificates for absences of a certain time period, usually over three days.

- Absence leave forms should be completed by employees who have been granted time off. This should help to prevent disputes about whether absence has been approved.
- Attendance records are essential to satisfy the requirements of Statutory Sick Pay legislation (see pp. 109–11 below).
- Attendance records also enable management to track patterns of absence. These may occur in particular departments within a workplace or on particular days of the week. It is often easier to identify a cause of absence from work if a trend can be identified.

According to Williams (1993) a CBI survey found absence levels to be 16 per cent higher in companies that kept minimal records of absenteeism rather than a more precise centralized computer system. In this and a later report, Williams (1994) identified Swallow Hotels as ready to install a monitoring system; De Vere had run such a system for two years (with, according to the group personnel director, a positive – i.e. downward – effect on absenteeism); contract caterers Gardner Merchant also had a computer monitoring system; and Stakis' computerized system allowed the company to observe that absenteeism was higher in its Scottish units than those in England.

Whatever tactics are adopted there will always be employees who suffer from what one commentator refers to as 'non-digitus extractus' (failure to extract the finger) (Janner 1982: 6). Management must reserve the right to take disciplinary action against staff for whom it can be proved that their absence from work has no legitimate basis. A standard disciplinary procedure should be followed, as described in Chapter 11. In conclusion therefore, it can be seen that the causes of staff absence are complex and varied. To overcome the problem successfully management must adopt a strategic approach to achieve acceptable levels of attendance.

AIDS AND HIV

Despite the topics of HIV infection and AIDS arousing much controversy, the employment implications of HIV/AIDS have not figured too highly in associated debates. This is probably, as Kapila and Williams (1990) suggests, because HIV and AIDS are as yet unlikely to have had a significant impact upon the lives of most working people in the UK. However, this situation may change if pessimistic forecasts of the growth in levels of infection become reality. The UK experience contrasts greatly with that of the USA where HIV infection is far more widespread. Estimates suggest that employers in the USA rank HIV/AIDS as one of their top three concerns, with one in five employers having at least one worker who is infected with HIV or who is suffering from AIDS (Bunker 1990: 8) (see Box 5.1).

Box 5.1

HIV/AIDS in the UK: Some Facts

- As of June 1995 24,502 people were reported to have contracted HIV (0.04 per cent of the population). Of those 11,501 had developed AIDS (0.019 per cent of the population) and 7,571 had died (0.013 per cent of the population).
- In the year July 1994–June 1995 there were some 2,590 new reports of HIV (compared to 2,461 for the previous year).
- Globally, AIDS affects the most economically active age group. The Institute of Actuaries calculates that by the year 2000, death from AIDS could account for $\frac{1}{10}$ of all working years lost in the UK due to death before retirement.

Sources:
Labour Research (1995) World Aids Day. December, p. 22.
The Economist (1995) *Pocket Britain in Figures*, London: Hamish Hamilton.

There are a number of reasons why HIV/AIDS has particular relevance to the hotel and catering industry.

- **Age composition and accommodation arrangements**. Many organizations within the industry rely to a great extent on young workers. This is the group perceived to be most at risk of infection through high risk behaviour, whether that be intravenous drug abuse or unprotected sexual intercourse. It is possible that there is a greater concentration of high risk behaviour when many young workers are living together in shared accommodation.
- **The perceived high concentration of 'out' homosexual males working in the industry**. Despite research showing that homosexual males have now changed their sexual practices to a significant degree, there may be a number who became infected before the risks were apparent.
- **Employers' reaction to the fears of the public**. Despite medical assurances to the contrary, the public may feel that there is a significant risk of HIV being transmitted through food. In their attempts to avoid the emergence of such fears employers may not take on those who are perceived as belonging to high risk groups.

Accepting medical advice about the means of transmission we can see that the risk of becoming infected while engaging in normal workplace activities in the hospitality industry is minimal. This being the case, management almost has a duty to provide guidance and training aimed at preventing discrimination against those who are perceived to belong to high risk groups or who are known to be HIV positive.

Adam-Smith and Goss (1993) have identified a variety of ways in which individuals may respond to the perceived risk of infection in the workplace.

- **Rational response**. Here it is assumed that individuals fully understand the risks that are involved in an occupational setting and that their opinions on the subject are based on sound reason. However, when dealing with an area that is shrouded in so much fear, responses are not often so rational.
- **Bounded rationality response**. Here it is assumed that people's perceptions of risk are exaggerated because they have been formed on the basis of flawed information. In such cases it is likely that individuals will believe that certain circumstances present risk of infection, when in fact no risk exists.
- **Subjective response**. Here, as the phrase suggests, it is subjective beliefs, often on moral issues, that determine individuals' perceptions of the risks of infection in the occupational environment. In such cases workers are likely to completely disregard medical advice concerning risks and create their own set of beliefs.

Such insight into the possible reactions of workers is of great assistance in the formation of training programmes designed to change attitudes and behaviour. It is vital that employers create effective equal opportunities policies relating to HIV and AIDS before their implementation is required, so as to avoid any human resource crisis which may occur in the future. As stated by Patrick Nicholls MP, then Under Secretary of State at the Department of Employment, at a national seminar in 1990 entitled 'HIV/AIDS in Employment' (cited in Kapila and Williams 1990: 114):

> Employers should now be drawing up sensible, humane guidelines to cope with the likely upsurge in the next few years of HIV infection and AIDS among their staff. AIDS is a problem that will not just go away.

A number of organizations have provided information for companies wishing to establish an equal opportunities policy relating to HIV/ AIDS. Comprehensive guidelines come from the support charity The National AIDS Trust, and other organizations have issued their own guidelines specifically aimed at employers including, for the hospitality industry, the Hotel and Catering International Management Association (HCIMA, see Box 5.2). The National Aids Trust guidelines for workplace AIDS policies are as follows (Arkin 1994).

1. The policy must address both HIV and AIDS separately and the company's response to each should acknowledge that they are separate conditions. HIV and AIDS can be integrated into existing policies such as those relating to sickness leave.
2. In an integrated policy, mention must be made of HIV and AIDS to ensure that staff can obtain the information they need on company practice without having to ask specific questions.
3. Any policy must state that discrimination, in any respect of company

Box 5.2

HCIMA brief on Precautions against AIDS

TECHNICAL BRIEF

Precautions Against AIDS

No 2

1. **INTRODUCTION**

    1.1   AIDS (Acquired Immune Deficiency Syndrome) is a serious public health hazard. The essential approach is to observe normal practices of good hygiene. Certain specific precautions are also recommended.

    1.2   The HCIMA Technical Advisory Group has issued the following notes for guidance after consultation with the Health and Safety Executive. The notes are not claimed to be exhaustive but, if followed carefully, will reduce any risk of infection by the AIDS virus.

2. **THE MEDICAL FACTS**

    2.1   AIDS is caused by infection with a virus known as HIV. This virus breaks down the body's resistance to other infections. At present there is no cure for AIDS.

    2.2   In the majority of known cases AIDS has been passed from one person to another through sexual intercourse. Other common causes include using contaminated products or needles and syringes for drug injections and blood & plasma transfusions.

    2.3   Although the virus has been found in a number of body fluids infection has been known to have been transmitted only by semen, blood and possibly breast milk.

    2.4   There is no medical evidence to suggest that the virus is transmitted in food or drink, or through the air by coughing or sneezing. Nor is it passed on by shaking hands, sharing a meal or by using the same toilet facilities as an infected person.

    2.5   Outside of the body, the virus is easily killed by heat (*temperatures of 77°C/171°F and above*) and by household bleach and a number of other chemicals.

3. **HOUSEKEEPING**

    3.1   Take special care with used razors, razor blades, and hypodermic needles. Dispose of them in impenetrable (*e.g. metal or hard plastic*) containers. beware of such sharp objects when emptying waste bins from toilet areas or bathrooms.

    3.2   Do not provide guests with electric shavers unless with a disposable or freshly-sterilised head.

    3.3   Employ a safe disposal system for sanitary towels, nappies (*diapers*) etc.

    3.4   Ensure high-quality laundering and safe handling of soiled linen.

    3.5   Ensure that towels are not used by more than one person. In public toilets this will normally require either warm-air dryers, disposable towels (*with lidded waste receptacles*), or automatic roller towel dispensers.

4. **CATERING & BAR SERVICE**

    4.1   Strictly observe Codes of Practice on food handling.

    4.2   Strictly observe hand wash procedures.

5. SPECIAL FACILITIES

5.1   Swimming pools, spa baths and whirlpools: ensure that the water treatment plant is operating correctly, that strainers etc are clean, and that chlorine and pH readings are within manufacturer's recommended limits at all times.

5.2   Hairdressing, manicure and pedicure: enforce relevant Codes of Practice including sterilisation of instruments before each use.

6. MOPPING-UP

6.1   Always wear disposable waterproof gloves when mopping-up spillages of blood, semen, vomit or excreta. Ensure that the gloves have no holes or splits in them.

6.2   Mopping-up materials must be disposed of safely. They should be placed in a sealed bag and incinerated. Where incineration is not possible the contents of the bag should be disinfected with household bleach or other approved disinfectant.

6.3   Sterilise surfaces with household bleach (*one part in ten of water*) or other approved disinfectant.

6.4   Normal machine-washing will disinfect contaminated clothing.

7. FIRST AID

7.1   First aiders should always wash their hands before and after applying dressings.

7.2   First aiders should always, before treating any casualty, cover any exposed cuts or abrasions on their skin with a waterproof dressing. When treating a wound, any person who is suffering from skin disease, chapping or an open or unhealed wound of the hand which cannot sensibly be covered with waterproof dressings should wear disposable gloves. After use, these gloves should then be washed again with soap and water.

7.3   No case of infection has been reported from any part of the world as a result of giving mouth-to-mouth resuscitation. Therefore first aiders should not withhold such treatment if they judge it necessary.

8. TRAINING

8.1   Display hygiene and cleaning procedures prominently.

8.2   Train and periodically re-train staff in these procedures.

8.3   Instructions and training in more than one language may be necessary.

9. AIDS AND EMPLOYMENT

9.1   Refer to appropriate company policies or to public bodies such as the Department of Employment and the Health and Safety Executive.

9.2   For personal advice and information contact one of the agencies listed below and/or refer to a company doctor or general practitioner.

FURTHER ADVICE

Department of Health AIDS Information Service, telephone help line 0800-555777
Health & Safety Executive and Employment Medical Advisory Service; listed in telephone directories under Health & Safety Executive.
Terence Higgins Trust telephone help line on 0171-833 2971.

FURTHER READING

AIDS – What Everybody Needs to Know – Health Education Council, Dept A, PO Box 100, Milton Keynes, MK1 1TY
AIDS and Employment – by the Department of Employment and the Health and Safety Executive; available from the Mailing House, Leeland Road, London W13 9HL
AIDS & First Aid – Confederation of British Industry; CBI, Centre Point, 103 New Oxford Street, London, WC1A 1DU
Clean Catering: A Handbook on Hygiene in Catering Establishments – HMSO London
Hepatitis B and AIDS; Association of Domestic Management, 1988

HCIMA 191 Trinity Road, London, SW17 7HN Tel 0181 672 4251 Fax 0181 682 1707

December 1995. This document has no copyright restrictions. Registered Charity No: 326180.
Printed on environment-friendly paper.

activity, against anyone who is HIV positive or who has AIDS will not be tolerated.

4. The policy must contain a clear statement on confidentiality, explaining the way in which confidential information will be treated.

5. The policy should state clearly that AIDS will be treated in the same manner as any other progressive or debilitating illness.

6. The policy must make clear, by outlining or referring to discipline and grievance procedures, what action will be taken if staff breach the terms laid down.

7. The best model policy will cover areas such as opportunities for redeployment, retraining, flexible working, compassionate leave and so on. Where possible these should apply not only to those infected with HIV but also to carers.

Obviously the successful implementation of such a policy would be ideal. However, when dealing with such a controversial topic difficulties are bound to arise. It is therefore essential that those chosen to communicate the policy can do so in a credible fashion. It may be advisable to involve an expert, possibly with a medical background, who could add weight to the messages contained in the policy. Interactive training sessions provide a means of monitoring the attitudes of employees and are therefore useful in the development of future sessions. These should be followed with the distribution of written material so as to reinforce the importance of the topic. No policy will meet with success unless all levels of management are seen to be committed. As with every area of an integrated equal opportunities policy, failure to implement each element should be regarded as avoidance of management's responsibilities. Consideration must also be given to the legal aspects of HIV/AIDS in the workplace and the possible consequences of discrimination. The controversial issue of screening employees can arise in the hospitality industry due to the perceived risk of having workers in direct contact with the public. The taking of blood samples without first securing valid consent from employees constitutes a criminal assault. Also, consent from employees to take blood samples does not give permission to employers to conduct HIV testing.

Regarding discrimination against persons with HIV or AIDS, this is mainly covered by both the Sex Discrimination Act 1975 and the Race Relations Act 1976. As noted by Gaymer (1990: 15), a refusal to employ males or blacks because at present more homosexuals and Africans are registered as having AIDS would amount to unlawful direct discrimination. As an example, Dan Air was found to be in breach of the Sex Discrimination Act 1975 because it attempted to exclude males from its cabin crews. Dan Air unsuccessfully argued that it did not wish to employ homosexuals because of the concentration of AIDS sufferers in this group and that the only way to fulfil this aim was to exclude male applicants. Claims of unfair dismissal or constructive dismissal may be brought against employers under the Employment Rights Act 1996 and the Industrial Tribunals Act 1996 if workers are sacked or forced to resign under pressure due to their HIV status, or the perceived risk which they present.

Forecasts suggest that the problem of HIV and AIDS is a growing one and that in years to come it will greatly affect groups other than those which have already suffered most severely. This being the case employers must now develop policies which may avert future difficulties. It is essential to attempt to create a work culture in which discrimination will not be tolerated if the effective management of human resources is to be maintained.

ALCOHOL MISUSE

Alcohol misuse is undoubtedly the single largest cause of workplace disruption in the UK. The consequences of heavy drinking amongst employees becomes apparent in a variety of ways including absenteeism, impaired efficiency, poor judgement and irritability, all of which are likely to have an adverse effect on productivity. The detection of alcohol-related problems can be difficult as all the aforementioned symptoms can be attributable to a number of other factors such as genuine sickness or stress. Difficulties are compounded when workers cover up for the over-indulgence of their colleagues, either through loyalty or because they, too, enjoy drinking heavily. The problem of alcohol abuse would appear to be greater throughout the hospitality sector than in most other occupations. Research highlighted by the Institute of Personnel Management (Dickenson 1988: 17) gives details of liver cirrhosis mortality amongst British males in a variety of occupations. In first position on this list are publicans and they are closely followed by a number of other hospitality sector occupations. This research presents a grim picture of the extent of alcoholism amongst hotel and catering workers. It is possible to offer some informed speculation as to why alcohol abuse should be worse in this sector:

- the fact that much activity centres around the service of alcohol, thus ensuring a culture in which alcohol consumption is seen as socially acceptable;
- because hotel and catering outlets are often very sociable environments in which to work, employees may become involved in excessive drinking through social pressures;
- the levels of stress often experienced by hotel and catering employees as a result of the frenetic nature of many workplace activities: this can lead to abuse of alcohol because drink is viewed as offering a short-term release from stress; and
- shiftworking, which enables employees to drink before coming to work, or to drink excessively the previous day if an early start is not required.

It is often the case that management turns a blind eye to problem drinking amongst staff, either because this may be seen as infringing workers' personal liberty, or because to tackle the problem would mean that management may have to transform its own behaviour. The formation of an alcohol-related policy can help to stem the problem. Before considering the most appropriate contents of such a policy, management must be clear about what it is that it hopes to achieve. Objectives are likely to include the maintenance of a healthy workforce, the creation of more stable workplace relationships, the communication of the inherent dangers of being drunk while at work and less altruistic factors such as the need for high productivity. As with all aspects of welfare policy, the desire to present the company as being innovative in matters of staff welfare should not in itself be a policy objective, although this may result from the effective implementation of the policy.

Fulfilment of the aforementioned objectives requires a policy that guarantees assistance for employees with a problem. Consideration should be given to the following areas:

- a statement of commitment from senior management;
- a guarantee that the policy applies to all employees, irrespective of position in the organizational hierarchy;
- information on how to gain advice from either an internal employee assistance programme where these exist (see below pp. 107–9) or external specialist agencies;
- a guarantee that time off work will be granted as for other conditions of ill-health provided appropriate medical advice is sought and acted upon;
- responsibility for the maintenance of the policy should be given to one member of staff;
- details of training that each member of staff must undergo to be told of the company's attitude towards heavy drinking; and
- an assurance that problem drinkers who refuse help will be disciplined.

The implementation of an alcohol policy is a sensitive issue as it involves challenging people's attitudes. If the policy is introduced in a confused manner, without the assigning of appropriate responsibilities and the involvement of all employees then it may appear as a paternalistic intrusion into the private affairs of workers. Lack of management commitment may lead to the policy being marginalized and being seen as for 'addicts' only. It is essential for managers and supervisors to understand the expected benefits of such a policy and secure their involvement by training them to recognize the symptoms of heavy drinking amongst employees. Monitoring such a policy is also vital to its success. By comparing levels of absenteeism, lateness, and accidents at work before and after the implementation of the policy it should be possible to gain an indication of its effectiveness. It is also necessary to keep records on individuals to assess their personal improvement and how this relates to the alcohol policy. If the policy appears to be successful then this should strengthen the company's commitment to staff welfare issues.

COUNSELLING

Employees' problems and anxieties, whether caused directly by work or of a more personal nature undoubtedly affect their ability to undertake their responsibilities in an appropriate manner. As a first step towards further help, management should be able to perform a counselling role. It is realistic to assume that informal counselling can be the most effective means of improving a member of staff's performance, given that their poor performance is due to a specific difficulty rather than general incapability.

In many cases counselling will be instigated by members of staff approaching management with their problems. However, management must be aware of behavioural characteristics that can signify that counselling of a member of staff may be necessary. Those displaying sudden changes in performance standards, irritability, regular absenteeism, obsessive practices or some other form of unusual behaviour, may be experiencing personal difficulties that counselling could solve, or at least provide a starting point for further assistance. Certain individuals are undoubtedly better predisposed than others to provide counselling. The qualities that define an effective counsellor are largely dependent on personality and attitude and include the ability to listen, to be non-judgmental, to have genuine regard for others, to be trustworthy and discreet, to have self-knowledge and of course to be able to give objective advice. Managers can be trained to become better listeners and can be reminded of the need for discretion, but to develop regard for others and to gain self-knowledge requires a fundamental change in attitude. The provision of counselling by management should not, therefore, become a formal and structured part of organizational activities. To do this would force the involvement of those managers who could never offer effective counselling. Poor counselling can be dangerous. If a manager gives inappropriate advice then this can exaggerate and perpetuate workers' problems. The hope is that if hotel and catering organizations move towards a more welfarist approach to human resource management they will recruit and develop those who have impressive interactive skills and should therefore be more likely to provide counselling on an intuitive basis.

One of the most beneficial outcomes of staff counselling is the positive effect that it can have on a workplace atmosphere. In hotel and catering establishments this can often be tense due to the frantic nature of workplace activities and having management which continually criticizes workers will surely worsen the atmosphere. However, management which appears tolerant, open and willing to help staff overcome their difficulties is more likely to be rewarded with motivated staff operating in a positive workplace atmosphere.

Bereavement

There are innumerable reasons why workers may be under stress that could be helped by some form of counselling. It is, however, worth making specific mention of bereavement, possibly the most powerful source of stress and anxiety, and one of the events most likely to be encountered by all employees at some stage of their working lives.

Every person responds differently when they experience the death of a relative or close friend. Ability to cope depends on a number of factors, one of which is the nature of the social networks in which the bereaved person is involved. In the hospitality industry, relationships between work colleagues are often intense and will be tested should a member of staff become bereaved. It is also the case that workers who are living in staff accommodation will not have the continuous support of relatives and non-work friends after they return to work. Management must attempt to create an open and supportive environment in which workers feel able to express their emotions. Management should not follow the common cultural characteristic of being unable to approach the subject of death.

Embarrassment and awkwardness often lead people to avoid discussing a person's loss, thus denying them the opportunity to express how they feel. As in other areas management need not attempt to adopt the role of professional counsellor. What it can do is have the confidence to listen. Staff must also be reassured of their job security should they wish to take time off work after the death of a friend or relative. Management must also be prepared to deal with the death of a member of staff. It is important to remember that every worker will deal with this situation in a different way. A poor response from management could have a devastating effect on the work environment.

EMPLOYEE ASSISTANCE PROGRAMMES

Employee assistance programmes (EAPs) are professional counselling schemes established by employers in an attempt to limit the negative impact that employees' personal problems will have on their productivity. EAPs are a relatively new phenomenon, appearing first in the US during the 1970s and being introduced by some UK companies in the mid 1980s. Their introduction widened the scope of existing schemes that were designed to combat specific problems such as excessive drinking.

It is unlikely in the hospitality industry, a sector not known for its progressive human resource management practices, that EAPs will become a standard element of personnel practice in the next few years (but see Box 5.3). At face value they may appear expensive to operate, while providing intangible benefits. However, it is possible to argue that EAPs are particularly applicable to hospitality organizations. For example, consideration should be given to the nature of the hospitality

Box 5.3

Employee assistance programmes at Whitbread

It may seem surprising to find a hospitality organization leading the way in employee welfare, despite management's repeated assertion that staff are the sector's most valuable resource. However, Whitbread plc, one of the UK's largest hospitality organizations, has done precisely that by establishing an employee assistance programme.

The programme began as a pilot scheme in 1988 in Whitbread's Sheffield brewery and in Gloucester and Cheltenham. The apparent success of the scheme led to its swift adoption by all of the company's operating divisions.

The programme is called 'Person to Person' and is controlled by Focus, an organization which employs professional counsellors and specialist support staff such as financial advisors and solicitors. Whitbread employees contact Focus by telephone and can, if necessary, arrange face-to-face interviews.

Whitbread's acceptance of an employee assistance programme is based on the assumption that employees' motivation is closely linked to their personal well-being. Those members of staff who are experiencing problems, whether these are of a personal or work related nature, are unlikely to perform to their full capacity unless their problems can be resolved.

Whitbread highlight other benefits which can be gained through the introduction of an employee assistance programme.

- A high level of staff morale amongst employees is likely to be reflected in their attitude towards customers and colleagues.
- Rates of staff turnover are reduced if employees are content at work.

Based on the nature of employees' contacts with counsellors, Ian Anderson, Whitbread's EAP manager stated, '. . . I wouldn't say this industry is more problem prone or stressful than others.' However, when this statement was made the EAP was only available to Whitbread's management and supervisory staff. The results may be different now that the company has extended the service to include those operative staff at the bottom of the pay hierarchy.

Source:
Hardcastle, S. (1994) Lifeline. *Caterer and Hotelkeeper*, 6 October, pp. 64–5.

industry work-force. As discussed elsewhere in this chapter, excessive drinking amongst employees seems to be commonplace. This can cause a number of problems, some of which will impair employees' abilities to work effectively. Also, the industry contains a high proportion of young people, the group most usually associated with the UK's spiralling problem of drug abuse. The potential damage that this can inflict on individuals is huge and the consequences for the workplace cannot be ignored. EAPs have a role to play in this respect. Furthermore, by helping to create a stable work environment EAPs can encourage company loyalty and reduce staff turnover, absenteeism and lateness. They can also provide advice for employees who find themselves in financial difficulties, a common problem considering normal wage rates.

EAPs can be operated either 'in-house', using appropriately qualified company employees, or by an external agency. Consortia can provide EAPs for independent hospitality organizations. It may be true that in-house systems can be more tightly controlled and tailored to the specific requirements of individual companies. However, there is more potential for breaches of confidentiality, lack of trust amongst staff and subsequent lack of credibility. Programmes that are operated by external agencies can more easily guarantee confidentiality. If choosing such a system it is essential to check that counselling staff have appropriate qualifications and that they have an understanding of the nature of the hospitality industry and of the typical problems faced by workers.

It is likely that the majority of enquiries to EAP staff will come directly from employees. However, management and supervisory staff must be trained to identify human characteristics that can signify that referral to an EAP counsellor may be required. Attendance at EAPs must not be viewed by employees as an opt-out from improving their performance. If they fail to seek assistance, or deliberately avoid following the advice that they are given then disciplinary procedures should ensue. As with all human resource initiatives it is essential to monitor the success of EAPs. As well as looking at rates of usage and the feedback from clients it is helpful to keep precise records of staff turnover, absenteeism, lateness and accidents, so that trends can be identified.

SICK LEAVE

The necessity for tight controls on employee absenteeism need not run counter to the adoption of a humane approach to absenteeism that is the result of genuine illness or injury. Managers who are automatically suspicious of employees who do not attend work are unlikely to secure desirable levels of staff loyalty.

Statutory Sick Pay, which is in some cases paid in full by employers and in others employers can claim rebates, will be discussed later. This should not be confused with Occupational Sick Pay (OSP), which is not compulsory and the details of which are entirely at the discretion of employers.

Accepting that few hospitality companies are renowned for their forward thinking approach to staff welfare and given the lack of trade union involvement in the industry and the transient nature of the workforce it is not hard to imagine why OSP arrangements are rarely applied to workers in the industry. However, for companies that are adopting a welfarist approach to securing employee loyalty and motivation the formation of OSP arrangements can be an effective tool. Staff are more likely to respond in a positive manner to employers who display genuine concern and provide some financial security for sick or injured employees. The rates of OSP that are provided will obviously vary between employees and will be dependent on a number of factors such as wage rates, seniority, length of service and duration of absence.

The original legislation relating to Statutory Sick Pay (SSP) was the Social Security and Housing Benefit Act 1982. This has been refined since then, most notably through the introduction of the Statutory Sick Pay Act 1994. The legislation is fairly complex and this is not the text in which to deliver a detailed explanation, yet it is essential to have an understanding of its most significant aspects which are as follows.

- Employees are entitled to SSP if their period of incapacity for work is four or more consecutive days.
- The period of entitlement lasts for the duration of the employee's incapacity to work, although responsibility for payment may shift to the State after an allotted time, or until the individual is no longer employed.
- Until the introduction of the 1994 legislation SSP that was properly paid was fully recoverable from the Government. However, because absenteeism has been such a problem in the UK the Government chose to shift more of the burden for the payment of SSP on to employers. This, it is hoped, will encourage employers to introduce more effective absenteeism control measures. The system of rebates has been retained for small employers (e.g. those with National Insurance Contributions of £20,000 or less in 1993–4 would have been eligible for 100 per cent reimbursement of the payment that they made for staff absences of over four weeks).
- Women are now entitled to SSP on the same basis as men. They receive payments for any periods of illness starting before the age of 65.

It should therefore be clear that in order to administer SSP procedures in the required manner it is essential to keep accurate records, especially of absence dates, dates on which staff are entitled to SSP, the sums to which employees are entitled, dates on which staff are not entitled to SSP and the completion of the statutory forms, all of which are available from the Department of Social Security. It is likely that this newest legislation will greatly increase the financial burden on employers, not only through the higher levels of SSP that they will have to pay, but also due to greater administration costs. The best hope for employers is to minimize this burden through the introduction of effective absenteeism control measures.

In certain cases there may be no alternative to the termination of a member of staff's employment due to recurring or continuous illness. In such cases recognized dismissal procedures must be followed, as described in Chapter 11. A decision to dismiss a member of staff on grounds of illness is an extremely sensitive issue that could have unpleasant repercussions. Such a decision must be taken only after a period of detailed consultation with the member of staff involved and possibly with medical representatives and other members of staff. Janner (1982: 41) offers a useful list of points that should be considered before terminating employment due to illness. These include:

- length of service – more flexibility would be expected for an employee who has many years of service;
- duration of absence – if absence is for an extensive period then dismissal may be more justified;
- the effect of absence on work and on the work-force – if the absence of an employee is disturbing workplace practices to a great extent then dismissal may be justified;
- frequency and length of previous absences – if an employee suffers periods of absence with much regularity then dismissal may be a viable option; and
- the prognosis – consideration must be given to the likely return date of an employee and his or her likely capacity for work on their return.

It is also worth considering whether alternative, less demanding work could be found for an employee who is troubled with illness, rather than resorting to dismissal.

SMOKING

In the UK the climate of opinion concerning smoking has changed markedly since the early 1980s. Not only has there been a significant decline in the number of UK citizens who smoke cigarettes, but less people are now willing to accept smoky conditions at work, probably due to increased awareness of the alleged dangers of passive smoking. This trend is reflected in the number of employers who have now adopted smoking related policies. As noted by Goss-Turner (1992), the Institute of Personnel Management reported that in 1982 only six per cent of UK companies had smoking related policies, compared with 20 per cent in 1989.

Fears about the possibly harmful effects of passive smoking led the World Health Organization in 1986 to encourage member governments to introduce legislation that would: 'ensure that non-smokers receive effective protection, to which they are entitled, from involuntary exposure to tobacco smoking in enclosed public spaces, restaurants, transport and places of work and entertainment' (Jenkins *et al.*, 1989: 4). As yet no legislation relating to smoking in enclosed public spaces has been introduced in the UK. Any organizations that introduce smoking related policies do so on their own initiative.

The majority of companies in the commercial sector of the hospitality industry are unlikely to have followed the trend and taken action on smoking. Before entering hotel and catering occupations staff presumably realize that much of their time is likely to be spent in a smoky atmosphere. It is therefore doubtful that a large proportion of staff will campaign for smoke-free zones as are provided for workers in other occupations. It is more often the case that any smoking restrictions are related to hygiene and fire prevention measures.

However, this should not mean that the rights of non-smokers who work in the hotel and catering industry should be disregarded. Employers who have adopted a progressive welfarist attitude towards their staff should regard it as their duty to provide workers with areas which are smoke-free. It is unlikely that relying on the courtesy of smokers would be effective. A formal policy is usually required which, if written in response to the views of smokers and non-smokers, should meet with little resistance. The process should begin by surveying staff opinion, probably by means of a confidential questionnaire. In organizations with many units the logistics of holding staff surveys can be complex. One person in each unit should be responsible for administering the survey and ensuring returns from a representative sample. In most cases a smoking related policy will cover the following areas:

- an assurance to non-smokers that there will be designated no-smoking areas (in hotel and catering operations this may be a staff common room that is used during official breaks from work);
- designation of areas in which smoking is permitted during official breaks from work;
- a statement that smoking is only permitted during official breaks and never in view of customers;
- mention of regulations that are in fulfilment of the Health and Safety at Work Act 1974;
- appointment of one person to oversee the policy and to whom any complaints should be addressed; and
- an assurance that failure to comply with the policy may lead to disciplinary action being taken.

The benefits of such a policy are numerous and include:

- lower rates of absenteeism;
- reduced fire risks;
- lower cleaning costs;
- increased productivity (staff taking numerous smoking breaks is disruptive); and
- improved inter-staff relations.

Obviously the implementation of a smoking related policy should be carried out in a sensitive manner, especially in organizations that have no history of involvement in staff welfare. It is helpful to warn staff well in advance of the policy actually taking effect to allow a period of readjustment. Emphasis should be placed on the health issues involved, but care must be taken not to sound like a crusader for the anti-smoking lobby. A successfully implemented policy can be presented as further testament to a company's commitment to the welfare of its staff.

STRESS

In very broad terms stress can be defined as the experience of being under pressure to an extent that affects normal behaviour. There is now a general realization that stress and stress related illness are major causes of absenteeism and sub-standard performance at work.

There is a degree of truth in the assumption that the levels of stress experienced by workers are directly related to the importance they place on their occupations relative to other aspects of life. The fact that many workers in the hotel and catering industry work part-time, on a casual basis or in relatively unskilled jobs may imply that workers place relatively little importance on their occupations and that stress is therefore less prevalent than in other industries. There are, however, a variety of reasons why the nature of workplace activity that is particular to the hospitality industry can place workers under a great deal of stress. These include the following.

- **Physical characteristics of the workplace**. Staff often have to operate in difficult conditions such as cramped restaurants or over-heated kitchens.
- **Physically demanding activities**. Many occupations involve activities that are tiring and require a great deal of stamina.
- **Manic nature of workplace activities**. Hotel and catering units can become extremely busy. Staff often have to perform tasks at great speed, without many breaks and for long periods of time.
- **Interaction with customers**. Interaction with difficult customers is an undoubted source of stress. This can become exaggerated when factors such as under-staffing or lack of training result in slower service and therefore more disgruntled customers.
- **Employees' lifestyles**. As noted elsewhere in this chapter many workers in the hotel and catering industry have routine access to alcohol. Drinking may relieve stress on a very short-term basis, but problems are likely to arise while trying to perform at work during the aftermath of a drinking session.
- **Relationships with colleagues**. Hotel and catering units are often very sociable work environments. Stressful situations can arise through soured relationships.
- **Low wages**. Many workers in the hotel and catering industry are receiving poor wages and may be facing financial difficulties.

In addition there are work-based causes of stress (stressors) that are not particular to the hotel and catering industry, such as disliking managers or supervisors, being set unrealistic targets, feeling insecure about future job security and being denied promotional opportunities. Sources of stress from outside the work environment can have an effect on employees' ability to work to their full potential. Included in this category could be problems with family, friends or partners, health concerns or bereavement.

It is essential to view stress limitation as a natural component of a strategy designed at increasing staff productivity. Rather than labelling certain employees as those who simply cannot cope under pressure, it is advisable to examine ways in which stressors in the work environment can be reduced and in which staff who are experiencing some personal stress can be helped. Employee stress reduction policies should be based on the premise that stress results from a lack of control. When staff are under pressure it is those who can maintain control who avoid a build up of stress. There are a number of measures that management can implement to make employees feel that they are in control while involved in workplace activities, each of which reflects sound human resource management. These include the following.

- **Staffing arrangements**. Avoid understaffing during busy periods, provide adequate supervision and allow breaks from work for a reasonable length of time.
- **Stress management training for managers**. Those in charge of workplace activities must be taught to anticipate the arrival of tension and be able to implement appropriate stress limitation measures.
- **Staff induction**. New staff must undergo welcoming and informative induction training that will set them at ease from day one.
- **Staff training**. Staff must be trained to perform every aspect of their job. Inability to complete tasks can be a powerful source of stress.
- **Setting clear objectives**. Staff must be aware exactly what is expected of them and completion of tasks should be recognized.
- **Staff meetings**. Staff meetings should not simply be sessions during which management passes on information and sets demands for staff. Staff should be provided with the opportunity to give suggestions to management and express any sources of dissatisfaction.
- **Personal stress reduction techniques**. It may be helpful to provide staff with information regarding techniques for stress reduction such as meditation, muscle relaxation and breathing exercises.
- **Employee Assistance Programmes**. The structure and operation of EAPs are discussed elsewhere in this chapter. However, it is worth mentioning their specific application to stress reduction. Staff who are experiencing personal difficulties that are affecting their workplace performance may find that referral to an EAP could provide solutions to their problems. EAPs also have a role to play in assisting management with the identification of sources of stress in the work environment. These can then be tackled by management.

Accepting that stress is now a major cause of workplace disruption, it is essential that management addresses the problem. The adoption of a staff welfare approach using the aforementioned guidelines is likely to limit employee stress and help maintain acceptable levels of productivity.

STAFF HANDBOOK

A staff handbook can be a useful means of communicating statutory and company specific policies and procedures to employees, especially those relating to health and welfare. By clearly distinguishing between contractual and non-contractual conditions of employment a staff handbook can help prevent the occurrence of disputes between management and staff. It should, however, be remembered that a staff handbook can actually precipitate disputes if it contains promises that are not fulfilled. Such a publication can also be of assistance to the induction of new employees by making them feel welcome, by explaining the company's ethos and by detailing what is expected of staff. Most importantly, a staff handbook allows management to outline unambiguously the extent of welfare-related policies in operation.

It is helpful to produce staff handbooks in a loose-leaf format so that additions can easily be made. The contents vary depending on the nature and size of each organization. However, in order to offer comprehensive information the following areas should be included.

1. Introduction
   (a) welcome to the company by senior management;
   (b) information regarding the nature of company interests and activities.
2. Contractual conditions
   (a) hours of work;
   (b) wages, incentives and benefits;
   (c) health and safety requirements;
   (d) dress code.
3. Non-contractual conditions
   (a) equal opportunities policies;
   (b) training, development and promotional opportunities;
   (c) staff welfare policies;
   (d) employee representation;
   (e) performance appraisal;
   (f) disciplinary and grievance procedures.

REVIEW AND DISCUSSION QUESTIONS

1. Why is staff health and welfare more than a matter of simply 'caring' by the employer/manager?
2. The manager of a restaurant is approached by the senior sous chef who alleges that the head chef is HIV positive. This 'information' was garnered as a result of overhearing a telephone conversation in

which the head chef appeared to be talking to a medical adviser. The sous chef and his colleagues are threatening to walk out unless the head chef is removed. Advise the manager on his options.

3. Is the best form of work-counselling that which leaves people to resolve their own problems?

4. How do you encourage employees to give up smoking in the workplace?

5. With a group of friends, identify occasions when you have experienced stress and examine the symptoms and remedies you have employed.

Health and safety in the workplace   6

The kitchen was like nothing I had ever seen or imagined – a stifling, low-ceilinged inferno of a cellar, red-lit from the fires, and deafening with oaths and the clanging of pots and pans. It was so hot that all the metal-work except the stoves had to be covered with cloth. In the middle were furnaces, where twelve cooks slipped to and fro, their faces dripping sweat in spite of the white caps.

(Orwell 1995: 8)

Promotion of safety and health at work is an essential function of good management. We are not talking about legal responsibilities. The job of a director or senior manager is to manage. The boardroom has the influence, power and resources to take initiatives and to set the pattern.

(Robens Committee Report, cited in Armstrong 1993: 772)

Despite the view of the Robens Committee (whose report provided the cornerstone for the Health and Safety at Work Act (HASAWA) 1974) that health and safety represented a key managerial issue, traditionally it has often been perceived by organizations and managers as relatively unimportant within an overall human resource management approach. In these terms it may be seen by organizations as something that is bureaucratic and rule-bound and simply a case of meeting certain statutory duties, in articulating a policy that meets bare minimum requirements (Goss 1994; Goss-Turner 1992). Indeed, within a wider public policy sense, safety at work may only be perceived as important when a major disaster occurs, leading Nichols to note that 'aside from newsworthy events . . . safety is rarely an important public issue' (Nichols 1975: 217). When such events occur however, official inquiries into disasters such as Zeebrugge, Clapham Junction and Kings Cross demonstrate a failure of managers to provide adequate training and supervision and a lack of awareness of unsafe systems of work (James 1990).

Whilst only 'high profile' disasters may make the news this should not hide the daily cost of poor health and safety management in the workplace. The Health and Safety Executive (HSE) (1993) notes that every working day in Great Britain two people are killed, and over 6,000 are injured, leading to the loss of 31 million working days – this being more than 30 times that lost through strike action. As well as pain and discomfort for the victim there is add on cost for business as a result of poor health and safety management.

Clearly then it is important for organizations and managers to be aware of their obligations and duties in not only meeting the expectations of the law, but perhaps more importantly in seeing the role of health and safety as a key human resource management issue. In this way organizations can be thought of as having both a legal and ethical responsibility to ensure safety in the workplace. These are the key themes of this chapter: to outline and discuss the legal obligations and policy in practice, and to locate both within a context that emphasizes the centrality of health and safety to human resource management policy.

One further point by way of introduction relates to the particular context of the hospitality industry. Within the industry all workplaces are covered by health and safety legislation. In many respects the dangers inherent in the workplace are magnified in these settings (Aston 1995; see also Lucas 1995: 237–8 who offers an excellent criticial discussion of health and safety in the hospitality industry from an employee relations point of view). This may be a reflection of features like the labour intensive nature of the industry; the high level of manual labour activities such as lifting, pushing and pulling of awkward loads; the need to meet deadlines in serving customers speedily; and the dangers apparent in a hot and humid kitchen (e.g. wet and slippery floors, potentially dangerous tools and equipment, etc.). Consequently the HSE (1993) characterizes hospitality as a high risk industry, with a higher rate of accidents compared to other parts of the service sector. Thus, the food industry is rated third in the league table of accidents, ahead of construction and metal manufacturing (*Health and Safety at Work*, 1994). In 1992/3 there were 2,635 reported injuries to people working in hotels and catering, three of which were fatalities (Drummond 1994). More recently *Hospitality* (August/September 1996) reported on the accident reports submitted by employers in the hospitality industry to suggest that the number of major injuries had risen between 1986/7 to 1994/5. The report also noted that in 1995 employers reported 472 major injuries (equivalent to an amputation or worse) and 2,408 over-three-days injuries, often fractures. From these figures it was estimated that a serious injury occurs in the hotel and catering industry about once every three hours. Therefore, this gives a greater resonance to the need for hospitality managers to be fully cognisant of health and safety legislation, including recent initiatives emanating from the European Union (EU); and also to appreciate the role good health and safety management may provide in not only reducing working days lost to accidents, but in enhancing organizational effectiveness, improving efficiency, industrial relations and productivity.

THE LEGAL FRAMEWORK

As we have already noted there is a need for organizations and managers to have a well thought-out and comprehensive health and safety policy to ensure a safe and efficient workplace. Such a policy though should not just rest solely on an adherence to statutory minimum requirements. Notwithstanding that, health and safety is now the most regulated area of employment in organizations today (Institute of Personnel and Development 1994), with several major initiatives stemming from the EU's attempts to harmonize health and safety across European work places. These regulations, which will be discussed in some detail later, have sought to clarify and make explicit duties that were already legal requirements under the Health and Safety at Work Act (HASAWA) 1974.

To understand the role that HASAWA plays in regulating workplace safety it is important to begin with its rationale and intent, and then go on to discuss its scope and effectiveness in ensuring the health and safety of all employees and customers. Torrington and Hall (1995: 508) note that HASAWA is 'an attempt to provide a comprehensive system of law, covering the health and safety of people at work'. In this sense HASAWA imposes a duty on employers to ensure, so far as is reasonably practicable, the health, safety and welfare of all their employees. The key provisions of the Act are (Armstrong 1993: 800; Torrington and Hall 1995: 508–13):

- to install a safe working system;
- to provide safe premises, a safe working environment and safe equipment;
- to employ trained and competent personnel;
- to give adequate instruction and supervision necessary for the job;
- creation of new bodies and reinforcement of existing authorities with responsibility for enforcing HASAWA, i.e. the Health and Safety Commission, the Health and Safety Executive, the Health and Safety Inspectorate (covering agriculture, mines and quarries, nuclear installations and factories) (it should be noted that the commercial sector of the hospitality industry is covered by local authority inspectors and HSE inspectors cover the institutional sector) and the Employment Medical Advisory Service;
- creation of non-legally binding Codes of Practices, which may still be used to assess employers' efforts in a given health and safety area if a legal case arises (time off for the training of health and safety representatives, for example); and
- a statutory duty on all employers to consult employees about measures taken to maintain and improve standards of health and safety. This was later modified in the Safety Representatives and Safety Committees (SRSC) Regulations 1977 to give trade unions an exclusive right to appoint safety representatives who in turn could request safety committees. Although non-unionized workplaces may

conceivably have had a safety committee consisting of employees and managers, in reality Lucas (1995: 239) notes how 'joint committees for health and safety alone are almost entirely absent from hotels and catering'. However this situation now seems set to change with the implementation of the EU inspired Health and Safety (Consultation with Employees) Regulation 1996 (HSCE) which came into force on 1 October 1996. The HSCE regulations now mean that where no trade union recognition exists or the work-force is non-unionized, the employer is now required to consult either directly with employees, or with a new group created by the regulations – representatives of employee safety (ROES).

There is also a duty on the employee to observe health and safety rules and instructions and act with due care and attention in the workplace. Failure to do so may lead to dismissal. Clearly, though, the main accountability is on organizations and managers who carry the prime responsibility for implementation of the HASAWA. Failure to do this may lead to criminal proceedings against the individual manager responsible and the employing organization. James (1990: 55) makes the point that accidents are rarely due to carelessness or incompetence on the part of employees, but are more frequently the outcome of wider organizational and managerial failings. He cites an HSE analysis of 1,000 fatal accidents, which found the vast majority could have been avoided, and that management failure was the primary cause in 60 per cent of accidents and employees were at fault for only 12 per cent of the accidents.

In addition, employers also have a common law duty to provide a safe place to work, safe systems of work and competent fellow employees (Goss-Turner 1992: 157). This point may be particularly important in the sense that employers are often 'hypnotized by minimum legal requirements', and fail to remember or act upon 'their common law duties of care and good faith to employees'. This last point is important in illustrating the fact that some organizations and managers may view health and safety legislation as nothing more than a requirement to conform to certain statutory minimums. This may be seen, for example, in the written statement on health and safety that all organizations employing five or more persons must prepare under the HASAWA. Companies with less than four employees, which may cover a number of hospitality organizations, are not required to write a policy statement, but good organizational practice would suggest that this should be done. Armstrong feels that such a statement should be a basis for organization, action and control, and thus:

> The general policy statement should be a declaration of the intention of the employer to safeguard the health and safety of his employees. It should emphasize four fundamental points: first, that the safety of employees and the public is of paramount importance; second, that safety will take precedence over expediency; third, that every effort will be made to involve all managers, supervisors and employees in

the development and implementation of health and safety procedures; and fourth, that health and safety legislation will be complied with in the spirit as well as the letter of the law.

(Armstrong 1993: 753–4)

Although such statements are intended to illustrate top management's commitment to health and safety, a number of writers suggest that in many organizations these statements remain at the level of rhetoric, rather than denoting a true commitment (Torrington and Hall 1995). Such a view may reflect the vagueness of the Act (Howells and Barrett 1982); the conflict between the need for increased efficiency, output and production and health and safety (Bratton and Gold 1994); the decline in union organization (James 1992); and the relative lack of success in punishing errant employers for health and safety breaches, due in part as James (1992: 104) notes, to the lack of funding for bodies like the HSE and Factories Inspectorate. He writes that 'Standards of occupational health and safety have deteriorated significantly since the end of the 1970s' and advocates a stronger legal framework to improve health and safety in the workplace. This has ostensibly been achieved with the implementation of a number of new EU Directives on health and safety (Aston 1995). Before any discussion of these though it is necessary to briefly mention the Control of Substances Hazardous to Health Regulations (COSHH) 1988.

COSHH 1988

The COSHH regulations, which are part of the HASAWA, actually came into force on 1 October 1989 and apply to all workplaces. The regulations again place certain requirements on the employer to protect employees working with substances hazardous to their health, by 'regarding the way and extent that such substances are handled, used and controlled' (Torrington and Hall 1995: 513). These include obligations to:

- assess the risks to health caused by workplace exposure to hazardous substances, taking into account the particular circumstances of the workplace, and decide what precautions are necessary (in all but the simplest cases, the assessment should be recorded and where circumstances change, the assessment should be reviewed);
- prevent such exposures or, where this is not reasonably practicable, implement control measures;
- ensure that control measures are used and that equipment is properly maintained and procedures observed;
- where necessary, monitor atmospheric contaminants and keep records of the measurements obtained (where records refer to individual exposures, they should be kept for 30 years, or in any other case for five years);
- carry out, and record, health surveillance in certain areas; and

- inform, instruct and train employees about risks and the precautions to be taken.

A thorough understanding of the scope and intent of the COSHH regulations may be particularly important for hospitality managers due to the high level of accidents in the catering industry involving contact with hot surfaces and harmful substances (e.g. oven cleaners) (HSE 1993; McDermid 1993).

To date then we have considered statutory legislation that has emerged and developed in the United Kingdom, we now need to go on and describe the new legislation emanating from the EU and discuss its effect on hospitality workplaces.

THE EUROPEAN FRAMEWORK

A key element of closer European integration is perceived to be the need for a 'Social Dimension', which has sought to extend regulation in a number of areas in the workplace. To date, the UK Government has vigorously opposed such moves in its belief in a deregulated labour market (Goss 1994). It is not within the remit of this chapter to discuss the wider implications of this debate, other than to note that in one area at least the Government has not been able to veto attempts to increase regulation in the workplace. This is the area of health and safety, where directives emerging from the EU are governed by Qualified Majority Voting (QMV), which means that no one state alone can block measures with which they disagree.

Consequently, the adoption of a number of binding EU Directives, as from 1 January 1993, has introduced the most fundamental change in health and safety legislation since HASAWA (Torrington and Hall 1995). Indeed the Confederation of British Industry (CBI) (1994) feels that it presents European governments and employers with the greatest challenge they have faced in the field of health and safety legislation. However Drummond (1994: 38) views the new regulations in a more relaxed manner, asserting that 'The new regulations were no great shake up for the catering industry'. Despite Drummond's view, Peters (1993: 13) believes the new regulations are useful for hospitality organizations in making 'management duties more explicit in areas where the Health and Safety at Work Act left managers with little or no guidance about how to organise and structure good health and safety management'. In order to assess this we will examine the new regulations in more detail.

The regulations – dubbed the 'six pack' by the Confederation of British Industry (CBI) (1994) – effectively enlarge upon the obligations imposed on employers by the HASAWA by requiring specific risk assessment, review and monitoring arrangements, health surveillance, training, protective and preventive measures and emergency procedures. Further to this the HSE (1993: 2) has suggested that the new regulations 'introduce a number of requirements which deal specifically with the hazards responsible for most deaths, injuries and ill health in the catering industry'.

Thus the new regulations concentrate on areas which have the highest level of risk in the industry. The HSE (1993) sees the main causes of accidents and ill health in the catering industry as:

1. slips, trips and falls;
2. contact with hot surfaces and harmful substances (these two categories are said to account for more than 70 per cent of major accidents in the catering industry, Drummond 1994);
3. lifting and manual handling;
4. the dangers of falling objects – generally equipment falling off shelves;
5. dermatitis; and
6. work-related upper limb disorders.

It is noteworthy that most of these categories fit into the Factories Inspectorate's so-called 'big four' causation group – 'handling and lifting', 'machinery', 'persons falling' and 'falling objects' (Nichols 1975) – which again demonstrates the need for a well thought-out safety policy in the hospitality work setting. We will now explore the so-called 'six pack' to understand its potential impact on hospitality organizations in improving safety within the workplace.

The Management of Health and Safety at Work Regulations 1992 as amended by the Management of Health and Safety at Work (Amendment) Regulations 1994

This is the most important directive in the way it provides an over-arching framework, with the other directives which cover more specific areas being characterized as 'daughter directives'. As its name implies, this directive seeks to avoid accidents at work by good safety management techniques. Consequently, the directive is an attempt to encourage organizations and managers to adopt a wide-ranging and systematic approach to identifying risks, and in response to that to provide preventative and protective measures (Boella 1994). This is most obviously manifested in the key concept of risk assessment or 'hazard spotting' (McDermid 1993), which is common to all the sets of regulations. In undertaking risk assessments, employers have firstly to identify all the hazards in the premises, which in the catering industry include mincers, slicers, use of chemicals, slippery floors and so on (HSE 1993), then assess the associated risk and the likelihood of harm coming to employees (for a useful summary of how to undertake a risk assessment exercise see Drummond 1994). Having identified such risks, employers then have to think of ways of eliminating or reducing the risk as far as it is practicably possible. Employers with five or more employees must also record any significant findings from the risk assessment.

The notion of risk assessment has proven somewhat problematic for hospitality organizations and the British Hospitality Association (BHA) has described the procedure as 'time consuming and bureaucratic' (cited in Drummond 1994: 38) and a logistical nightmare for smaller organizations. There have also been disagreements about the practical consequences of risk assessment. For example, Drummond (1994) cites an Environmental Health Officer who suggests that slippery kitchen floors will remain a virtually insurmountable problem, whilst McDermid (1993: 14) quotes an HSE inspector who suggests that 'The idea that this is a problem area we can do nothing about is a myth'. Given the high level of slips, trips and falls on floors made treacherous by water, fat and vegetables, a more proactive approach would seem appropriate within the new legal framework. Such a proactive approach is outlined by the HSE (1996) which describes a range of practical 'good practice' measures to substantially lessen the risk of slips and trips. These measures encompass a range of environmental, organizational and individual factors that can be addressed in relation to a number of causative factors. For example, individually employees can lessen risk by cleaning as they go, reporting contamination of the floor surface, maintaining suitable footwear and walking appropriately to the circumstances (HSE 1996: 2).

The Workplace (Health, Safety and Welfare) Regulations 1992

These workplace regulations suggest that catering organizations should place a good deal of emphasis on the conditions of their floors in ensuring a safe working environment. The regulations also expect organizations to maintain healthy surroundings in relation to ventilation, lighting and so forth. The final component of the Workplace Regulations is concerned with employees' welfare and the sufficient provision of washing facilities, sanitary conveniences and similar services.

Provision and Use of Work Equipment Regulations 1992

As the names suggest these regulations place a duty on employers to make sure that employees have suitable and properly maintained work equipment, are fully aware of any risks in using such equipment and appropriately trained to use such equipment.

Manual Handling Operations Regulations 1992

These regulations attempt to ensure organizations properly assess any risks to employees in lifting and carrying loads. In this way any significant risks should be identified to minimize the possible risk of injury. Boella (1993) suggests that in catering, for example, many loads should be moved on wheels rather than carried manually.

Personal Protective Equipment at Work Regulations 1992

These regulations are important in requiring employers not only to provide protective equipment, but also to have regard to health and safety factors in the use of such equipment and finally train staff to ensure such equipment is used in a suitable manner.

Health and Safety (Display Screen Equipment) Regulations 1992

Boella (1993) suggests that approximately seven million people are now working with visual display units (VDUs) including an increasing number in the hospitality industry. Perhaps because of this Peters (1993: 13) opines that these regulations have 'created the most comment and interest because they are new and quite radical'. In this sense they seek to ensure that staff have properly designed and ergonomically sound workstations and take regular breaks. These regulations then have sought to specify obligations which employers have in creating and maintaining a safe workplace and both organizations and managers should be clear that failure to meet the regulations will lead to criminal prosecutions.

The above constitute the so-called 'six pack'. There are two further directives which may have some impact on hospitality organizations.

Construction Design and Management Regulations 1994

These regulations apply to health and safety in circumstances where new premises are being constructed and old areas refurbished (see Box 6.1).

Working Time Directive 1993

The possible introduction of this directive caused much controversy in the UK in 1996 (see Box 6.2).

This chapter has endeavoured to address the macro issues of the role of health and safety in a wider human resource management policy, and also the micro issues via a discussion of the minutiae of health and safety legislation and its effect on the workplace. The intent has been to demonstrate the centrality of health and safety to good management. In that sense James (1990: 58) sees poor health and safety as a microcosm for bad management more generally within the organization and suggests that 'Weakness in safety management will often signify broader failures in management within organizations'. When we realize that around 80 per cent of accidents are preventable in the catering industry (Drummond 1994), this message (and its implications) would seem to be slow getting through to hospitality managers. A related point is Lucas' (1995) view that authoritarian management and a lack of workplace involvement are contributing factors to poor health and safety practices in the hospitality industry.

Box 6.1

HCIMA brief on CDM relations

TECHNICAL BRIEF

Health & Safety for New or Refurbished Catering Premisies   *No 32*

CDM Regulations

---

1.   INTRODUCTION

Health & Safety issues in the catering industry have become a major part of the caterer's life, as new legislation begins to bite.

The accident rate in the catering world is very high and the risk to all users, staff and visitors alike, of catering premises can lead to serious legal and personal consequences for owner/occupiers.

Unfortunately, not a great deal of publicity is given to this area and consequently, this brief is intended to be a layman's guide of what to do and where to obtain information, when planning to build or refurbish a catering facility.

2.   LEGISLATION

In 1994, changes to the Health & Safety at Work Act places the onus fairly and squarely on the developer, occupier or owner of catering premises to protect all people involved from risk of accident when using their facility.

However, when refurbishing, or building a catering facility, all sorts to trades can be employed on the site, making Health & Safety regulations difficult to implement and control. Prior to 1994 the legal responsibility for Health & Safety management during the design and construction of premises was unclear.

This area of weakness in Health & Safety legislation was addressed by the introduction of 'CDM' regulations (Construction Design & Management) in 1994. The objective of these regulations is to minimise potential Health & Safety risks and hazards, both during the construction of and subsequently the operation of, all developments, including catering.

The CDM regulations apply to any site where five or more people will be work at the same time or any design or demolition work.

Therefore, all involved in refurbishing or rebuilding a catering facility are required to comply with these new regulations.

3.   HOW WILL THE REGULATIONS AFFECT YOU?

The CDM regulations place new duties on clients, planning supervisors, designers and contractors to plan, co-ordinate and manage Health & Safety through all stages of work.

ANYONE WHO APPOINTS A DESIGNER OR CONTRACTOR HAS TO ENSURE THAT THEY ARE COMPETENT AND WILL ALLOCATE ENOUGH RESOURCES TO COMPLY WITH HEALTH & SAFETY LEGISLATION

The Client: Should take ultimate responsibility for the appointment of a competent designer/contractor.

The Designer: Should ensure that all possible measures are taken to provide Health & Safety guidance.

The Planning Supervisor: Should have overall responsibility for developing the Health & Safety plan.

The Contractor/s: Should have responsibility for implementing the Health & Safety plan.

4.   IN PRACTICE

Wherever a new build or refurbishment facility is worked upon the CDM regulations apply and unfortunately design costs will increase to cover the additional cost of planning supervision, responsible for Health & Safety, throughout construction.

Particular care needs to be taken when a unit continues to operate, while building is taking place.

All interested parties in the Design and Construction chain must take an active part in developing and managing the CDM regulations and work as a team to ensure implementation.

A successfully completed CDM programme should ensure that Health & Safety issues are addressed during construction and not left to operators or employees to find out the problems afterwards.

5.   ONCE OPERATIONAL!

The development of a Health & Safety policy with guidelines and training for employees is essential. Training can be given commensurate with the employees tasks but all employees should have sight of the Health & Safety policy document with a brief synopsis giving basic instruction on how to avoid risks, what they are likely to be and the reporting procedure in case of accident.

The regulations to protect employees and the public are now numerous and anyone involved in the catering industry, whether already working in a catering operation or intending to build or refurbish, should take steps to know the law and its implications.

If in doubt, **SEEK PROFESSIONAL ADVICE.**

Suggested Reading:-

a)   "Managing Construction for Health & Safety" Construction (Design & Management) Regulations 1994
            Price: £7.95

b)   "A Guide to Managing Health & Safety in Construction"
            Price: £8.50

c)   CDM Regulations: How the Regulations affect you.
            HSE Books, PO Box 1999, Sudbury, Suffolk, CO10 6FS

            Phone 01787 881165   Fax: 01787 313995   Price: Free

This brief has been prepared with the assistance of Rodger Flanagan AHCIMA.

HCIMA 191 Trinity Road, London, SW17 7HN Tel 0181 672 4251 Fax 0181 682 1707

July 1996. This document has no copyright restrictions. Registered Charity No: 326180.
Printed on environment-friendly paper.

Box 6.2

The 48 Hour Working Time Directive

As has been noted elsewhere the ability of the UK government to resist implementation of EU legislation is contingent on whether any issue requires unanimity or can be passed by qualified majority voting (QMV) by member countries. Directives passed under QMV have to be implemented in member states in the EU. Council Directive 93/104/EC was one such directive, as it was introduced as a health and safety measure. Despite this, the Government of John Major sought to challenge the legality of this directive via the European Court of Justice (ECJ), but eventually lost the case in November 1996, as the ECJ ruled that working hours were a health and safety issue as opposed to a more general social issue. This means that companies have to introduce the measures contained within the directive.

The directives' main provisions are:

1. the directive limits the maximum working week to 48 hours a week, but only as averaged over a four-month (or longer) period;
2. workers are entitled to 11 hours' rest in 24 hours;
3. night workers are limited to an average of eight hours' work in 24;
4. employees are now entitled to three weeks' paid holiday, rising to four weeks by 1999;
5. where the working day is longer than six hours, workers will be entitled to a rest break;
6. in each seven-day period, workers will be entitled to one day's rest, in addition to the above 11–hour period set out above; and
7. free health assessments must be made available to night workers.

Prima facie the directive looks to have a radical intent and wide-ranging practical implications for organizations. In particular, the extension of paid annual leave to the UK, the only EU country not to previously have a legal right to paid holidays, will effect around 2.5 million workers, mostly part-timers and women. Moreover just over 4 million workers have less than three weeks' leave and 6 million have less than four weeks' leave (Milne 1996). Also though, in making it illegal for employers to force staff to work more than 48 hours a week, a significant step was taken as it removed the element of coercion forcing employees to comply with such requests. This is particularly important when we recognize that the UK has the highest percentage, within the EU of workers working over 48 hours a week. Current estimates suggest that around 22 per cent of UK full-time employees currently work more than 48 hours a week, the next country is Ireland with nine per cent and the majority of EU countries have seven per cent or less (Wintour and McSmith 1996).

However, in reality many commentators point to the symbolism of the directive as opposed to its actual practical impact and in that sense there are a number of exemptions to the directive:

1. Workers having to work more than 48 hours from time to time, e.g. a large order.
2. Workers in seasonal jobs (including tourism) – with the period of seasonality being classified as up to 12 months, so as an example a waiter in a seaside hotel could be required to work 70 hours a week for half the year, if during the off-season their hours were reduced to 26 or fewer.
3. Workers in industries where long hours are inherent.
4. People who work extra hours to earn overtime.
5. Transport and fishing workers and junior doctors are also exempted from the holiday allowance.

Nonetheless, on balance the measure does seem set to incur extra costs to organizations, particularly hospitality organizations. Estimates of the overall cost to all industry go as high as £1.7 to £2 billion, with the British Hospitality Association (BHA) predicting that the cost to the hospitality industry will be between £75 to £100 million (*Caterer and Hotelkeeper*, 31 October 1996). Based on a sample of 700 of the BHA's members, who employed 53,000 people, the BHA suggested that around two-thirds of the businesses surveyed have staff who work more than 48 hours a week, and that a third of employers surveyed had staff who did not receive four weeks leave. On that basis the BHA deputy chief executive Martin Couchman, suggested that the industry should 'be prepared for a real shock'. Equally though there were more sanguine reactions from business generally due to the scope for flexibility within the directive, and also within the hospitality industry. Moreover, for larger organizations, it may pose less of a problem as more developed personnel/human resource policies would seek to address such issues already. For example, Janet Grey, Head of Human Resources at Jarvis Hotels, suggested that the directive was unlikely to have much impact on larger companies, such as Jarvis, which already operates a 39–hour week and offers more than four weeks holiday (*Caterer and Hotelkeeper*, 31 October 1996).

Sources:
Caterer and Hotelkeeper (1996) Hospitality faces £100m bill for EU directive. 31 October, p. 8.
Milne, S. (1996) Four million get extra holiday rights. *Guardian*, 12 November, p. 10.
Wintour, P. and McSmith, A. (1996) A time bomb at work. *Observer*, 10 November, p. 10.

Consequently it is important for senior management to foster the right culture within the organization, although the development of a safety culture has to be supported by adequate resources and training, and not just exist at the level of rhetoric. Within the hospitality industry Aston (1995: 28) believes that 'most larger companies have taken their responsibility seriously with properly trained and appointed safety officers', however he does question whether medium and smaller companies are doing enough in encouraging and actively supporting a safer workplace. Once again it appears there may be a dichotomy emerging between large and small organizations within the hospitality industry. In many respects this should not surprise us as it mirrors the findings of other research suggesting a growing gap in the extent to which large and medium/small companies are pursuing what could be seen as relatively sophisticated and progressive human resource management policies (Lucas 1995; Price 1994; Wood 1994). Notwithstanding this, it would seem to be vital for all organizations operating in the hospitality industry to realize the consequences of an under investment in health and safety is still too great in the pain and misery caused by unhealthy and unsafe working conditions, and that organizations have a moral and ethical responsibility to ensure the welfare of their employees, which should transcend any short-term bottom line considerations.

REVIEW AND DISCUSSION QUESTIONS

1. For what reasons should health and safety be seen as a key human resource management issue?
2. Why might hospitality workplaces be considered particularly dangerous?
3. In what ways can a thorough training programme minimize the risk to individual employees in the hospitality industry?
4. What is meant by the notion of risk assessment and why is it important?
5. Suggest why it might be important to have a safety representative, even if there is no trade union representation within the workplace.

Employee involvement $\boxed{7}$

The notion of some kind of employee influence in organizational decision-making is one that seems to attract much support amongst government, employers and employees, thus reflecting Bean's (1994: 160) view that 'It is generally conceded in the liberal democratic world that working people should have a right to participate in the making of decisions which critically affect their working lives'. Though the quote suggests a consensus and convergence on the need for employee influence in decision-making, in reality there are likely to be sharply differing views on the scope, level and intent of participation. Blyton and Turnbull (1994), for example, suggest a continuum from no involvement through to workers' control, although in reality most organizations are likely to fit somewhere in between in the categories of receiving information, joint consultation and joint decision-making, which in a generic sense are likely to be characterized as being either employee 'involvement', 'participation' or 'industrial democracy' – although these terms are not totally agreed upon and the discussion will acknowledge the debate over terminology and interpretation of what they represent (Hyman and Mason 1995; Marchington 1992, 1995; Salamon 1992). A key element to this discussion is the increasing influence at the supra-national level via legally binding directives emanating from the European Union (EU) reflecting Hyman and Mason's (1995: 134) assertion that 'There is little doubt that the UK's future approach to employee participation will be influenced either directly or indirectly by European initiatives'. Indeed, the British trade union movement is looking increasingly to Europe for answers to the problems of falling membership, recognition and bargaining coverage and sees potential success in the remodelling of employee representation along European lines (EIRR 1994b).

Such considerations may have a particular resonance in the hospitality industry and mirror Lucas' (1995: 264–66) view that a more corporatist dimension, partially embodied in the European approach to participation and industrial relations, may signal the way forward to reform the 'poor' industrial relations which characterize hotels and catering. An understanding of the concept of industrial relations is crucial to any discussion of employee participation and this forms the central analytical framework for this chapter. In this way the chapter will firstly develop an understanding of industrial relations (or increasingly employee relations, recognizing Bratton and Gold's (1994: 283) view amongst others that industrial relations is an 'anachronism' in the 1990s) and the role played by the key 'actors'; the government, employers (and their organizations) and employees (and their representative arm, the trade unions). Such an analysis will recognize the differing perspectives to managing the employment relationship, which in turn will affect participatory approaches. We will then be in a position to go on and assess in greater detail the differing views of participation and speculate on future development, particularly via the EU.

EMPLOYEE OR INDUSTRIAL RELATIONS?

In her recent work, Lucas (1995: 4), chose to talk of employee relations in the hotel and catering industry, rather than industrial relations. Such a view, in part, denoted an attempt to conceptualize the management of the employment relationship in hotels and catering as being qualitatively different from traditional 'mainstream' industrial relations, not least because employee relations in the hotel and catering industry 'exemplify one extreme of British industrial relations'. Such an extreme represents 'unbridled individualism' (Lucas 1994: 3), which finds its expression in organizational terms by a lack of formal industrial relations arrangements. Thus as Price (1994) suggests, employment practices in the hospitality industry remain informal and unregulated and nowhere near Storey's (1992) ideal-type personnel and industrial relations, which implies the existence of clearly written policies and procedures, well defined payment structures, recognition of trade unions and strong personnel/industrial relations practitioners. In this respect the hospitality industry has largely represented the antithesis of the organized manual work-force in manufacturing, which could be thought of as characterising 'industrial relations' (Salamon 1992).

This dichotomy is challenged by Gospel and Palmer (1993: 3) in their suggestion that industrial relations are 'certainly not restricted just to the study of blue-collar manual workers and "industrial" does not just mean manufacturing industry. The subject covers all areas of paid employment and all forms of work organization'. However, Lucas (1994: 2) cogently argues that notwithstanding such a view, hotels and catering and the service sector generally have been consciously neglected in 'mainstream' industrial relations research, in favour of research on the organized manufacturing sector. This is despite the fact that recourse to the industry could provide us with some insight into 'what is industrial relations in contemporary Britain?'. In this way the hospitality industry does provide an extreme, arguably, increasingly, such an extreme provides a template for other sectors of the British economy in the management of people in the organization (Riley 1993; Thomas 1996).

So although Lucas recognizes that the terms industrial and employee relations are broadly similar, some awareness of how they may be conceptualized as different is also equally important. For the purposes of this chapter industrial relations is thought of as denoting formal arrangements and the presence of trade unions and collective bargaining in managing the employment relationship (a collectivist/pluralist perspective), whilst employee relations is conceptualized as unitarist and individualist, and in hotels and catering, at least, contributing to 'poor' industrial relations, exemplified by more dismissals, high labour turnover and more accidents and injuries (Lucas 1994). Nonetheless it should be made clear that employee relations is not necessarily synonymous with 'poor' industrial relations and in more general terms it could equally be argued that employee relations denotes an approach to managing the work-force which is closely connected to a progressive and sophisticated HRM approach.

To begin to understand these considerations we should examine the differing perspectives on the employment relationship as these essentially provide the point of departure for understanding the historical development of participation and industrial relations and the way in which the employment relationship has increasingly been reconfigured in contemporary Britain. Gospel and Palmer (1993: 11–34) and Salamon (1992: 29–39) provide a detailed description and analysis of these differing perspectives from which several key points can be extrapolated.

Marchington (1992: 213) utilizes the metaphor of a football team to illustrate the unitarist perspective to suggest that 'Unitarists are keen to view organizations as football teams, in which all participants are aiming for the same goal, have similar objectives and are not in conflict with one another'. Thus the unitary perspective sees the organization as a cohesive and integrated team, where everybody shares common values, interests and objectives to achieve the goal of the efficient functioning of the enterprise. Within this 'unitary utopia' the key element is the recognition of the managerial prerogative and the corollary of the unrestrained 'right to manage', where managers act in a benign and rational manner for everyone's benefit. As a result of this a unitary view of the employment relationship would be framed and constrained by the idea that conflict and dissidence are unnecessary, undesirable, irrational and deviant behaviour. So any conflict that arises is rationalized as being a reflection of frictional rather than structural problems within the organization. Consequently, trade unions are viewed as being an unimportant and unnecessary intrusion into the organization. One final point about the unitary perspective is the need to recognize that there may be differing styles of management ranging from authoritarian to paternalistic, and the latter in particular may underpin a more sophisticated unitarism which finds organizational expression in talk of human resource management (Goss 1994). Unsurprisingly, the unitary view of the employment relationship is held by management because of its legitimation and reinforcement of their position, and the authoritarian form of unitarism can be said to be particularly prominent in the hospitality industry (Wood 1992). The 'them and us' attitude which unitarism eschews is something that is accepted as being integral to the various pluralist perspectives on the employment relationship. In this way conflict is accepted as being inevitable and rational because of the plurality of interests in the organizational setting, though the resolution of such conflict is given very different forms in the variations of the pluralist perspective. Gospel and Palmer (1993) delineate three such variations.

First is liberal collectivism and collective bargaining, characterized as liberal due to the limited role of government and collective because of its support for collective organizations, who further employees' rights and interests by undertaking collective bargaining. This effectively institutionalizes conflict in the bargaining process undertaken by employers and trade unions. A key element of this process is the recognition that these arrangements allow for conflict to be resolved through compromise and negotiation, although collective bargaining may in reality be concerned with power bargaining or possibly 'winner takes all' type bargaining. In such a process the relative economic strength of employers and trade unions can determine the eventual resolution of any such dispute. Liberal collectivism, and the formalized procedures it represents, was largely accepted as 'good practice' in the post-war period and in many respects represents the archetypal notion of 'industrial relations' which was discussed earlier (Sisson and Storey 1993).

A second variant on the pluralist perspective starts from the point that corporatism and the active state envisages a tripartite arrangement between government, employers' and employees' organizations, who coalesce for the purposes of joint regulation. Corporatism as a concept may in reality not be so clear cut, with a number of writers disagreeing on what form it may take. For example, in the British context, Crouch (1977) has talked of bargained corporatism, which arguably reached its height with the Social Contract between the Labour Government and the trade union movement in the 1970s, where as a quid pro quo for wage restraint from the trade unions, the government enacted several favourable pieces of legislation that encouraged trade unionism and collective bargaining. Various forms of corporatism are also apparent throughout Europe, although they can be considered qualitatively different from the traditional British approach, premised as they are on notions of social partnership and social dialogue. As has already been noted it is this model to which British trade unions are increasingly looking to improve their position, and conceivably this could be achieved via a greater number of EU level directives, despite the British Government's rejection of the social dimensions of European integration.

The final variant of the pluralist perspective is that of liberal individualism and neo *laissez-faire*. This perspective also views conflict as inevitable in the relationship between employers and employees, but rejects the idea that such conflict can be pursued within a collective framework. It is axiomatic then that such a view is antipathetic to collective bargaining and trade unions, which are seen as being impediments to the smooth working of the free market. Consequently, the employment relationship is based on employment contracts freely negotiated between employers and employees and determined by market forces and common law. Conflict arises in this negotiation stage as employees seek the highest level of reward, best conditions and least exacting work, whilst employers seek the lowest level of payment, least costly conditions and most efficacious and flexible use of labour. Thereafter it is assumed that the relationship will be conflict free and in this sense there is a clear overlap with the unitary perspective. Once again it is characterized as liberal because of a lack of state involvement and individual due to the rejection of any influence from combinations. It is generally accepted that the Conservative administrations of Margaret Thatcher and John Major have vigorously pursued policies which have attempted (and largely succeeded) to create a liberal individualistic framework and conditions in which employers clearly 'call the tune' in the workplace. One clear example of such policies is the wide-ranging legislation which has radically changed the basis of the employment relationship, and is characterized as denoting a shift in support of collectivism to a more explicit individualist ideology. In simple terms this again represents the shift from industrial relations to employee relations (see McIlroy 1991 for a comprehensive review of the key statutes of the 1980s).

A further related point of the shift to this individualistic view of the employment relationship is the extent to which this approach represents 'an outdated hangover from the nineteenth century' (Gospel and Palmer 1993: 24). Certainly as we have already noted Riley (1993: 8) suggests that industrial relations in the hotel and catering industry have always been characterized as reflective of a 'nineteenth-century backwoodsman mentality', but in relation to the wider contemporary industrial/ employee relations landscape, Riley warns apocalyptically that 'If that looks like the past, it also looks like the future'. Similarly, Lucas notes somewhat resignedly that while the liberal individualist and neo *laissez-faire* approach is associated with the 1980s, 'this approach, or at least a close relation to it, has underpinned managerial thinking in the hotel and catering industry since the 1960s' (Lucas 1995: 86).

In addition to unitarism and pluralism, a final major perspective is the Radical/Marxist perspective which views the employment relationship not so much in organizational terms, but in a much wider social, political and economic framework. In this way capital and labour are conceptualized as being engaged in an unceasing 'power struggle'. Such a struggle though is not even, and is waged very much on capital's terms. Within this perspective Marxists or neo-Marxists argue that trade union power is illusory and unequal to that of capital and this helps to maintain the illusion of a balance of power. In its purest form the Marxist perspective suggests that only by the working class gaining workers' control will real equality be established. Increasingly such a dogmatic view is untenable in contemporary market-driven economies though this does not reduce the legitimacy of the radical perspective in providing the theoretical framework for more critical views of the employment relationship.

TRADE UNIONS

From the foregoing, clearly the hotel and catering industry can be seen as unitarist and individualistic. Trade unions, collective bargaining and industrial disputes in hospitality services are largely absent. Given the suggested effects of unbridled individualism such as inefficiency, poor quality of working life and low productivity it is perhaps surprising that there is virtually no trade union presence in the industry. In order to assess why this is the case we need to briefly define what a trade union is, examine the objectives of trade unions, and show how they have been severely emasculated in recent years, before examining why they have been so clearly excluded in the hospitality industry.

Salamon (1992: 78) defines trade unions as 'any organization, whose membership consists of employees which seeks to organize and represents their interests both in the workplace and society and, in particular, seeks to regulate their employment relationship through the direct process of collective bargaining with management'. In this way unions can be thought of as representing the sectional needs and interests of their members, something that entails them fulfilling a number of functions as follows.

- **Power**. Trade unions seek to protect and support the individual via a collective voice, by acting as a countervailing force to employers and as pressure groups in the wider society.
- **Economic regulation**. Unions seek to maximize the wages and conditions of their members within the framework of the contract of employment.
- **Job regulation**. The establishment of joint rule to protect members from unilateral management actions and provide a voice in decision-making within the organization (economic and job regulation are the key processes in collective bargaining) is a major function of trade unions.
- **Social change**. Unions seek to develop a society which reflects the aspirations and political ideology of their members.
- **Member services**. Trade unions provide a range of benefits and services to members.
- **Self-fulfilment**. Unions allow individuals to develop outside the immediate confines of their jobs and participate in wider decision-making.

A wide range of factors has contributed to a decline in trade union membership such that some commentators talk in the most apocalyptic terms for the future of the trade union movement. For example, Guest (1995: 137) suggests that 'Approaching the twenty-first century, trade unions appear to have been a phenomenon of the twentieth century to which we prepare to say good-bye [although] their departure from any serious and significant role would be a tragedy', particularly with rising job insecurity, the growth of inequality and arbitrary treatment in the workplace. Legislation which has severely emasculated the trade union movement and collective bargaining, and mass unemployment and structural changes in the economy with the shift from manufacturing to services have seen trade union membership decline from 13,289 million in 1979, a density of 54.2 per cent, to approximately 8.5 million in 1993, a density of 35 per cent. Indeed it is now suggested there are more shareholders in the United Kingdom (9.26 million) than there are trade unionists (Hendry 1995). Nonetheless, despite Guest's pessimism he is concerned to suggest how trade unions could reconfigure their role into the twenty-first century to avoid extinction and a key to this is a shift away from their traditional adversarial collective bargaining role to one premised much more on notions of 'social partnership' as seen in the rest of Europe. Furthermore within that scenario clearly any future for the trade union movement is, to a large degree, contingent upon their ability to organize in the service sector, although their efforts to date in the commercial hospitality industry suggest that certain parts of the service sector remain extremely difficult to organize. Lucas (1995) demonstrates this point by extrapolating figures from the third Workplace Industrial Relations Survey (WIRS 3), which was carried out in 1990. These figures demonstrate that trade union density (at around three per cent) in hotels and catering is substantially lower than other private sector services, despite similarities in workplace size, status of establishments, level of specialist personnel expertise and experience and proportion of female employees. Why is this so?

Given the acknowledgement of poor employment practices in the hotel and catering industry it is unsurprising to find Lucas (1995: 96) asking two key questions; 'Why have the vast majority of workers in the hotel and catering industry not joined trade unions?' and 'Why have trade unions failed to organize workers in the hotel and catering industry to any significant extent?'. Aslan and Wood (1993) and Macaulay and Wood (1992) offer some answers in two small-scale studies of managerial and employee attitudes. In this way their discussion is contextualized by recognizing the conventional reasons forwarded for low levels of trade union density. These include the following.

- **The ethos of hotel and catering**. For example the suggested conservatism and individualism of the work-force and reliance on informal rewards create a 'dog eat dog' culture which is antipathetic to trade unions.
- **The structure of the work-force**. The work-force has a high number of part-timers, women, casual and seasonal workers, plus the added problem of high labour turnover. Even in a situation where statutory recognition rights existed in Germany, Royle (1995) found that trade union membership in McDonald's was still only around five per cent, with the NGG trade union seeing low levels of union membership as

being due to high numbers of part-timers, shift working and high levels of labour turnover.

- **Employer and management attitudes**. As we have already noted the industry is characterized by a unitary view of the employment relationship that sees no role for trade unions. Consequently employers and managers are hostile towards trade unions and pursue an actively non-union policy. This is nicely illustrated by Lord Forte's assertion that 'I am not anti-union . . . [but] . . . I will not allow the unions to bully our management or staff'. Consequently, he writes later, 'we have a very straightforward relationship with the unions . . . We, the company, believe that we have sole responsibility for the people who work for us and that is our duty to look after them' (Forte 1987: 119 and 160). Reiter (1991) and Royle (1995) also outline how Burger King and McDonald's have pursued a vigorous anti-union stance.

- **The role of trade unions**. Although trade unions would appear to face difficult circumstances in attempting to organize in the hotel and catering industry, it is also suggested that there has been a lack of an effective strategy, a situation arguably exacerbated by a lack of shop steward organization. Such a situation has not been improved with the historical conflict between the Transport and General Workers Union (TGWU) and the General, Municipal and Boilermakers' Union (GMB) over who should organize in the industry and the loss of several high profile recognition disputes. Recent evidence suggests that this situation has not changed and, if anything, has got worse from the trade union point of view (Royle 1995; 1995a; Thomas 1996).

Within that context it is nevertheless interesting to examine the findings of the two studies by Macaulay and Wood (1992) and Aslan and Wood (1993). In respect of the former, the results of an employee sample showed support for trade unions in three broad areas – general (e.g. stopping exploitation and supporting peoples' rights) pay (e.g. ensuring proper pay) and conditions (e.g. protection against unfair dismissal, pursuing grievances or responding to sexual harassment) but this is tempered by a sense of fatalism in terms of the likely success of trade unions organizing hotels and catering, although such fatalism should not preclude a more proactive approach by the trade unions because as Macaulay and Wood (1992: 27) opine 'The research reported here suggests that there is indeed a latent positive disposition towards unions which could be capitalized on by unions themselves . . . [and] indifference to trade unions [was] more as a function of the neglect of workers by unions than as some pervasive reactionary helplessness'.

Similarly Aslan and Wood (1993: 64) found some equally interesting attitudes amongst managers. First, they noted how 'In an abstract sense, there was a general if uneasy consensus among all respondents that unions had a role to play in the hospitality industry'. The key point here though is the recognition that acceptance of trade unions was in the abstract and managers generally were much happier with non-union hotels. This reflected the notion that managers enjoyed the freedom from restriction of trade union regulation, as trade unions were perceived as being likely to interfere with the managerial prerogative, slow down decision-making processes and create dual sources of authority within their organizations. Managers rationalized their views via an 'interior dialogue' where they acknowledged trade unions might have a role to play in the industry, 'followed by a rejection of any need for unions in their own unit/organization and finally to outrigthly contradicting the initial premise' (ibid.: 67). In sum, although there is no one reason for low trade union density, the more important point is that it remains difficult to see any great change in the future.

The lack of success for trade unions illustrates in many ways the type of participatory arrangements likely to be found in hospitality industry workplaces. For example, under the traditional liberal collectivist model of industrial relations, collective bargaining was often seen by trade unions and others as the most important manifestation of workers' participation in organizational decision-making (Bean 1994). This is exemplified by the much quoted passage from the Donovan Report of 1968 (1968: 54, cited in Blyton and Turnbull 1994: 206):

> properly conducted, collective bargaining is the most effective means of giving workers the right to representation in decisions affecting their working lives, a right which is or should be the prerogative of every worker in a democratic society.

Consequently, in many workplaces for much of the post-war period, notions of involvement and participation were confined to the representative democracy of collective bargaining. Changes have been apparent since the 1960s and 1970s with initiatives seeking to extend employee influence beyond collective bargaining with other representative mechanisms such as worker directors. These initiatives can clearly be seen as reflecting the prevailing collectivist ethos apparent prior to 1979. The 1980s though saw the rise of involvement mechanisms which have sought to encourage a more direct relationship with individuals as organizations attempt to create greater commitment from employees. To begin to understand these trends we should firstly be clear of the difference between the various terms connected with debates on participation and involvement in the workplace.

As we have already noted there is a definitional and terminological debate about the meanings of terms such as 'employee involvement', 'employee participation' and 'industrial democracy' (Blyton and Turnbull 1994; Marchington 1995). Hyman and Mason (1995) in an overview of developments on the question of involvement and participation, suggest that increasingly talk of industrial democracy – which denotes a fundamental change in the balance of power in society generally and the workplace specifically, such as the establishment of employee self-management – has little currency in contemporary market-driven economies. Consequently we are left with the notions of 'employee involvement' and 'employee participation', which represent the 'two principal and in many respects contradictory approaches to defining and operationalising employee influence' (Hyman and Mason 1995: 1; and see Box 7.1)

EMPLOYEE INVOLVEMENT

Salamon (1992: 341) defines employee involvement as 'measures introduced by management intended to optimize the utilization of labour and

---

Box 7.1

Employee involvement and participation compared

Employee Involvement	Employee Participation
Management inspired and controlled	Government or workforce inspired; some control delegated to workforce
Geared to stimulating individual employee contributions under strong market conditions	Aims to harness collective employee inputs through market regulation
Directed to responsibilities of individual employees	Collective representation
Management structures flatter, but hierarchies undisturbed	Management hierarchy chain broken
Employees often passive recipients	Employee representatives actively involved
Tends to be task based	Decision-making at higher organizational levels
Assumes common interests between employer and employees	Plurality of interests recognized and machinery for their resolution provided
Aims to concentrate strategic influence among management	Aims to distribute strategic influence beyond management

Source:
Reprinted from Hyman, J. and Mason, B. (1995) *Managing Employee Involvement and Particpation*, p. 25, by permission of Sage Publications Ltd.

at the same time secure the employee's identification with the aims and needs of the organization'. Employee involvement is seen as being very much a phenomenon of the 1980s and closely linked with human resource management, with its emphasis on unitarism and its organizational expression in initiatives such as empowerment, teamworking, autonomy and communication. Employee involvement is managerially initiated and characterized as direct, 'descending participation', which is task-centred as it attempts to involve all individuals in the workplace. In this way it seeks to provide employees with opportunities to influence and take part in organizational decision-making, specifically within the context of their own work group or task. Therefore it is intended to motivate individual employees, increase job satisfaction and enhance the sense of identification with the aims, objectives and decisions of the organization. Hyman and Mason (1995) outline three different approaches within employee involvement.

Downward communication flows to individuals and groups of employees

This form of employee involvement is amongst the most popular in Britain in the 1990s and encompasses a wide range of techniques. Communication dissemination to the individual can be via formal written media such as employee reports, house journals or company newspapers, there are also video presentations and lastly, the chairman's forum. Essentially, though, these forms of involvement are passive and Hyman and Mason (1995) suggest they are superficial and question the extent to which they denote meaningful involvement.

In a group sense, the most prominent method of downward communication is the use of team briefings. Team briefing is a system which allows for information from executive management to be cascaded down the line to the 'shop floor', with the intent that all employees know and understand what they and others in the company are doing. Such information is likely to encompass high level or strategic decisions, general information on company goals and performance and, finally, explain the reasons for change decisions. Marchington (1992) cites the Industrial Society booklet *Team Briefing* (Grummitt 1983) to outline the general objectives of improving efficiency and satisfaction and also some of the perceived specific benefits of team briefing which are that they:

1. reinforce the role of line managers and supervisors as leaders of their teams;
2. increase work-force and supervisory commitment to the primary task and also to the organization as a whole;
3. reduce misunderstandings if information is communicated to employees and prevent a considerable amount of wasted time and rumours over potential decisions;

4. help people to accept change via understanding of reasons for such change;
5. help to control the grapevine, not by preventing it, but by ensuring the employees receive the 'official' version of any decision from their manager; and
6. improve upward communication as people have the facts which allows them to fully contribute to organizational life.

In order to ensure the smooth and efficient running of a team briefing system, several key principles are suggested, namely:

- teams should comprise between 4 and 15 people;
- meetings should be on a regular prearranged basis and at least monthly;
- meetings should not last more than 30 minutes;
- general discussion should be encouraged;
- feedback and questions should be encouraged;
- the leader should be the manager or supervisor of the section concerned; and
- leaders should be trained in the principles and skills of team briefing;

This last point may be particularly important as Marchington (1992) notes how problems may arise if the skills of the team leader, who is doing the briefing, are not sufficiently well developed. Consequently there is a need for a thorough and rigorous training programme to ensure the person carrying out the briefing has the necessary skills. A further problem that may have particular resonance for the hospitality industry is the difficulty that arises where atypical working patterns exist. In this way extensive shift-working or a large number of part-timers may mean the provision of information via briefings is logistically complicated and costly. Lastly, Marchington sees the need to encourage a change in attitudes and management style to avoid the 'flash in a pan' syndrome. Therefore information must be relevant, comprehensive, meaningful and up to-date to avoid team briefings simply degenerating into a moaning session.

Upward communication flow employee involvement

Once again these are aimed at both the individual and the workgroup. Two main techniques can be identified. The first is paid suggestion schemes – one of the oldest forms of employee involvement and one reasonably common in the hospitality industry. A number of benefits are perceived to be attached to such schemes. First, they are believed to be a method of improving the self-motivation and commitment of workers, as they see their voluntary activity as being integral to company success. Second, there is supposedly a more instrumental and tangible benefit both to the individual, whereby employees are paid for ideas, and the organization, which may accrue cost savings from suggestions emanating from employees. For example, Goss (1994) cites the United Kingdom Association of Suggestion Schemes (UKASS) which claims savings of over £1bn could be made if all companies in the UK operated suggestion schemes.

The second area here is the attitude survey. These are likely to take one of two forms. First, there is a general survey to assess the 'state of the nation' within the organization, where employees can be encouraged to talk candidly about company activities and policies. Second, there are attitude surveys which allow employees to appraise their managers' performance. The suggested benefits are that such schemes make for better management, although this is contingent upon management accepting and acting upon the results of surveys, and improvements in the financial performance of the company (Bratton and Gold 1994: 183–4).

In a group sense initiatives seeking to encourage employees' involvement in upward communication are likely to be premised on the notion of improving quality within the organization and towards the customer. This is likely to find expression in quality circles (QCs) and total quality management (TQM). QCs originated in and have been adapted from Japanese organizations and began to appear in the UK in the 1980s. They have been defined by the Department of Trade and Industry as:

> a group of 4–12 people coming together from the same work area, performing similar work, who voluntarily meet on a regular basis to identify, investigate, analyse and solve their own work related problems. The circle presents solutions to management and is usually involved in implementing and later monitoring them.
>
> (Hyman and Mason 1995: 89)

The effectiveness of QCs is dependent on voluntary membership, a focus on problem solving and the need for systematic training. Some of the suggested benefits of QCs outlined by Ramsay (1991, cited in Goss 1994: 117) include:

- improved quality in products and services;
- suggestions leading to cost savings;
- increase employees' interest and commitment in jobs;
- encourages awareness and flexibility in responding to problems; and
- enhancement of supervisory authority and leadership skills.

Generally QCs seem to be less popular than they were in the 1980s (Goss 1994; Beardwell and Holden 1994) and this may be a reflection of three underlying problems highlighted by Hyman and Mason (1995: 91). First, QCs may not always be successfully transplanted into UK organizations and may remain culture bound reflecting the fact that 'their underlying "quality ethos" is not a concept readily accepted in Western organizations'. Second, QCs involve a fundamental reappraisal of relationships within organizations from the more traditional adversarial 'them and us' approach to one based on consensual relationships: such a shift may be particularly difficult in unionized workplaces. Third and relatedly, management may feel that QCs undermine their authority as they are expected to adopt a more participative style, which may involve them feeling as though they are losing control over traditional areas of jurisdiction.

A more all-embracing approach to quality is via the notion of total quality management (TQM) which is more concerned to promulgate an integrated view of quality via company wide improvements in quality both towards the internal customer (the employee) and the external customer. Baldacchino (1995) reports a case study of a luxury hotel where the implementation of a TQM philosophy was beset by a number of problems including employee suspicion of the rhetoric of TQM, empowerment and involvement when faced with the realities of redundancy, industrial conflict and the more prosaic problem of a 'them and us' attitude emerging over the car-parking situation for managers and employees at the hotel. Others claim several benefits for TQM, including improved organizational efficiency, greater employee involvement, consistently 'delighting the customer' by exceeding their expectations, and reduced labour turnover (Becker 1996; Hubrecht and Teare 1994; McDermid 1994 and Tse 1996).

An integral part of a TQM framework is the role of empowerment, which may be seen by some as being synonymous with greater employee involvement. In reality the concept of empowerment defies a universal definition of its meanings and motives, although in a participative sense it may be seen to involve greater involvement via mechanisms such as quality circles, suggestion schemes, team briefings, delayering, and autonomous or semi-autonomous workgroups (see Lashley 1994, 1995; Lashley and McGoldrick 1994 for an overview of this debate in the context of the hospitality industry). The result is that 'each of these initiatives is likely to represent different intentions by managers and produce different feelings amongst employees who are so empowered' (Lashley 1994a: 19), particularly in the extent to which they feel genuinely involved in organizational decision-making, as opposed to seeing empowerment as merely a euphemism for work intensification (Hyman and Mason 1995).

Nevertheless, the messianic qualities which have quickly been ascribed to the notion of empowerment demonstrate the speed at which this new buzz-word has entered the managerial and organizational lexicon as a byword for increased commitment, motivation and bottom-line organizational performance. The emergence of empowerment in the late 1980s and early 1990s as a key to future organizational success is one which can be seen to have a particular resonance for the hospitality industry, with its insistence on what Lockwood and Ghillyer (1996: 213) have termed 'dynamic quality' (where customers' expectations are not only met but exceeded). Empowerment is increasingly sold as being the key to achieving such quality but also as a means to enhance the commitment and job satisfaction of employees. To assess this view we should briefly look at empowerment as a means of devolving decision-making to employees; the ways in which empowered employees are likely to require substantial training and development; the changes required in the prevailing organizational culture; some of the benefits which are suggested to accrue from empowerment; some potential problems; and then conclude this section with a description of the implementation of an empowerment strategy in the Marriott organization.

As noted elsewhere, empowerment may actually encompass a variety of employee involvement techniques, though for clarity we will talk here of empowerment as being predominately about encouraging front-line staff to solve customers problems on the spot, without constant recourse to managerial approval. The decentralization of decision-making that this denotes is premised on the notion that employees will be allowed to exercise greater authority, discretion and autonomy in their dealings with guests. In reality the level of discretion allowed is likely to be contingent on the extent to which organizations utilize either structured or flexible empowerment (Brymer 1991). The former will set clear and rigid boundaries and parameters around what exactly the employee response should be to any given problem, the latter allows for greater latitude whilst still delineating expected responses, for example, Ritz Carlton allow employees to rectify a guest's problem and spend up to $2,500 in doing so. In this sense, the rhetoric of empowerment is about attempting to move decisively from a control-oriented organization to a commitment-oriented organization. Riley (1996: 171) pragmatically recognizes that whilst 'empowerment is giving the employees the right to "break the rules" to serve the customer' it is also nonetheless important to recognize that 'rules are always necessary for an organization. It is a balance between organizational rules and discretion which must be available quickly'.

Regardless of which strategy is pursued there is likely to be a need for substantial training and development of employees to ensure they have the requisite skills to operationalize empowerment strategies. This will require training in areas like: social skills, communication skills, decision-making skills, problem-solving skills, planning skills and team-working (Cunningham *et al.* 1996; Wood 1994). Relatedly there will also be a need to reorient managerial thinking towards a more facilitative and coaching style, which should also attempt to impart a greater sense of trust and confidence in the ability of the front line staff to make suitable decisions (Baum 1995). This does not mean that management's role is completely emasculated or abrogated but merely refined, although this may be particularly difficult for managers to accept (Riley 1996; Wood 1994). Equally it is important to create a 'no blame' culture wherein 'well-intentioned errors' are discussed in a supportive way in order that lessons can be learned from any mistakes in decision taking by employees (Cunningham *et al.* 1996: 146). Thus the intent is to sustain a continuous learning environment which attempts to encourage constant improvement.

This latter point can be seen as one of the obvious benefits of empowerment but there are others, including (Baum 1995; Cunningham *et al.* 1996; Lockwood 1996; Wood 1994):

- a reduction in social distance between customers and employees, so service is not seen as servility – for example, Ritz Carlton talk about 'Ladies and Gentlemen serving Ladies and Gentlemen';
- improved quality and guest satisfaction, due to a more responsive service delivery system;
- enhanced motivation and job satisfaction for employees, leading to greater commitment and reduced labour turnover;
- more time for managers to engage in strategic planning and customer responsiveness;
- cost savings and improvements from ideas generated by employees; and
- word of mouth advertising.

It is perhaps easy to get carried away with the idea that empowerment represents a panacea for all organizational ills. However, the same writers noted above also identify a number of potential problems. Chief among these is the notion of empowerment simply increasing risk and responsibility without any commensurate extra reward for the additional skills and discretion employees are expected to demonstrate. A second point is that of job security, as empowerment may be used to justify delayering, which in turn leads to a drastic reduction in the number employed by the organization. Clearly there are no easy answers to some of the conundrums suggested by these issues and consequently the implementation of an empowerment strategy needs to be carefully thought out by organizations.

The implementation of empowerment in the Marriott organization

Clutterbuck and Kernaghan (1994: 237–42) describe how during the late 1980s Marriott sought to improve their market position. In particular, the intense competition in the global hotel market and the oversupply of hotel rooms in the US, meant that Marriott had to develop new strategies to sustain their competitive advantage. The company saw little mileage in reducing prices or changing the physical product and instead sought to compete on the basis of offering superior service. This was to be based on a shift from a rule-bound and procedural customer service approach to a more proactive 'whatever it takes' total quality approach. Marriott saw a key role being played within this process by front-line staff, who would be given greater responsibility in order to meet the guest's needs. To facilitate such a change Marriott sought to create enthusiasm among the staff to achieve clearly defined goals; develop employees' problem-solving skills; and develop a company culture which supported continuous improvement. This involved comprehensive and prolonged training, with the extensive use of role plays and exercises. The creation of a supportive environment also allowed for coaching to address any problems, thus ensuring that employees would still not be afraid to use their initiative. One such example was the member of staff who lent a guest his track suit and brand new running shoes in order that the guest could go out jogging the following morning with President Clinton! In summary, Marriott's approach is considered exemplary by Clutterbuck and Kernaghan (1994: 241) who suggest that 'Marriott's empowerment process has resulted in a more energized, creative, and forthcoming work-force. Ideas are flowing from staff in all functions and at all levels. It has also had the effect on managers' roles, making them more people-oriented'. Whether such success can be universally diffused and repeated in other hospitality organizations remains to be demonstrated as does the extent to which empowerment represents the brave new organizational world for the 1990s and beyond.

Job restructuring

To some extent involvement, as outlined in the previous two categories, may be contingent upon some form of job restructuring, for example empowerment may be seen as job enrichment. This could be considered a more recent manifestation of job restructuring, whilst job rotation and enlargement may be considered as more traditional examples of job redesign to improve the quality of working life (Salamon 1992).

There is much debate as to the efficacy – in relation to issues like improving employee morale and raising productivity – and democratic intent of employee involvement, and particularly the extent to which the various initiatives represent 'pseudo-participation' in their lack of a challenge to the managerial prerogative. To begin to further understand this debate we can now go on and look at employee participation.

EMPLOYEE PARTICIPATION

Hyman and Mason (1995: 21) define participation as 'state [or supra-state] initiatives which promote the collective rights of employees to be represented in organizational decision-making, or to the consequence of the efforts of employees themselves to establish collective representation in corporate decisions, possibly in the face of employer resistance'. As has already been noted this may encompass collective bargaining, which was traditionally seen as the main channel for employee representation. For the purposes of this discussion, however, we will concentrate on joint consultation, works councils and worker directors as they denote attempts by employees and their representatives to become involved in areas of organizational decision-making beyond those normally covered by collective bargaining. Thus Salamon (1992) characterizes participation as being pluralist, power-centred, indirect, representative and 'ascending' in its focus on the managerial prerogative and attempts to extend employees' collective interest into a variety of areas and decisions at higher levels of the organization. The expression of employee interests over company decisions will, as we have already noted, be via joint consultation, works councils and worker directors.

Joint consultation

We should begin our discussion of joint consultation by recognizing that in many respects it is the perfect example of terminological and definitional debates about involvement and participation. In this way joint consultation tends to be characterized as having a borderline status between involvement and participation, not least because of its hybrid nature (Hyman and Mason 1995). To some extent much of this debate is about the role of joint consultation in unionized workplaces, and the extent to which joint consultative committees (JCCs) seek to compete with or work alongside traditional collective bargaining channels (Marchington 1992). At its simplest, joint consultation is a process whereby management seeks the views and opinions of employees, via elected representatives, before decisions are taken. A more measured analysis though would recognize Marchington's (1988) 'four faces of employee consultation', as follows.

1. **The non-union model**. Here the principle activity of the JCC is to educate and inform employee representatives, in order that they will accede to management thinking and feel less inclined to seek union representation. The range of information will be both of a 'hard' (business oriented) and 'soft' (welfare, social and personalities) content. Marchington suggests that as employee representatives are provided with a considerable amount of information they are more likely to accept management's interpretation of events and the managerial prerogative. Essentially, though, this type of JCC remains at the level of simply communicating information up and down the line and has minimal employee influence on actual decisions.
2. **The competitive model**. The intent of the competitive model is to essentially constrain militant expressions of trade unionism and render collective bargaining less meaningful by ensuring a more knowledgeable work-force, one aware of management plans and future prospects. This is achieved by the provision of high-level information to ensure a greater understanding of problems confronting the company and its management.
3. **The adjunct model**. This is suggested as being the most sophisticated form of JCC in its blurring of the distinction between negotiation (collective bargaining) and consultation (JCCs). Although the worker representatives are invariably trade unionists, management creates a more conducive climate for successful problem solving and negotiations by the provision of high-level and strategic information on areas such as trade prospects, business plans, orders, quality and customer relations.
4. **The marginal model**. These tend to be largely symbolic and

irrelevant to the main needs of the business, characterized as they are by the 'three Ts' – tea, toilets and trivia.

From a review of fairly limited sources, Lucas (1995) reports that consultative arrangements found in the hospitality industry tend to conform with Marchington's non-union model and seek to reassert and not relinquish managerial control.

Works councils

Hyman and Mason (1995: 32) suggest works councils are 'a representative body composed of employees (and possibly containing employer representatives as well) which enjoy certain rights from the employer'. Although prima facie JCCs appear similar to works councils in terms of structure, levels and coverage of issues, in reality, they can be conceptualized as different in their symbolic and practical intent. Thus in Europe they are likely to have statutory backing and operate within the corporatist arrangements outlined earlier, whereby trade unions/ employees and employers/managers meet in the works councils as 'social partners' to engage in 'social dialogue'. Therefore employees have two principal rights, first, the right to receive information on key aspects of company activity, such as production issues, personnel issues and health and safety, and second, the right to consultation on such issues prior to their implementation by management. Although works councils are a relatively rare phenomenon in the UK, this may change in the future with the EU's European Works Councils (EWCs) Directive. It is widely acknowledged that the works councils initiative is based on one of the two elements, the other being worker directors, of the 'best practice' model of co-determination found in (West) Germany (Hyman and Mason 1995). Fuerstenberg (1993) and Streeck (1984) provide comprehensive reviews of the development of the German model of participation, and in particular the underlying ethos of 'social partnership' and 'co-operation' in the enterprise. It is this *mutual incorporation of capital and labour* by which labour internalizes the interests of capital just as capital internalizes those of labour' (Streeck 1984: 416, emphasis in original), which seemingly the EU is seeking to create across Europe with EWCs Directive.

The Directive on the establishment of EWCs was adopted in September 1994, and according to the EIRR (1994a: 14) 'It represents the first successful attempt by the Community to create a transnational industrial relations/employee participation structure or procedure, and is thus a major milestone in the 37 year history of EC social policy'. The success of this measure has not been without a real struggle (see Cressey 1993) and in theory the Directive does not apply to the UK due to the Conservative government's opt-out from the Social Charter, and the Social Chapter of the Maastricht Treaty. In reality though, UK multinational companies will be affected and will have to comply and the UK work-force of European multinationals are likely to find the arrangements extended to include them (EIRR 1994a and b). This is a result of the Directive applying to undertakings with more than 1,000 employees in the EU, and a minimum of 150 employees in at least two member states of the EU, such a criteria is said to affect around 100 British multinationals (EIRR 1994a). Gold and Hall (1994: 177–78) describe EWCs as 'a transnational, pan-European forum of employee representatives within multinational corporate groups for the purposes of information disclosure and consultation with group-level management'. The EIRR (1994a) summarizes the practical implications of this in terms of issues such as:

- Scope – will the EWC encompass only EU countries or all European countries?
- Composition – how are seats to be distributed amongst employees in differing countries? And which employees will be eligible for selection?
- Organization – how many meetings per year? One meeting of the full EWC would be the norm, with sub-committees meeting on a more regular basis. Agendas will be usually set by management with input from employee representatives.
- Costs and time off – it is envisaged that all costs, such as travel, accommodation and subsistence, will be covered by employers.
- Content – the Directive sees consultation as being about 'the exchange of views and establishment of dialogue' cited in EIRR (1994a: 17). In the first European-wide information and consultation arrangements established by a British firm, United Biscuits agreed upon a forum for 'the exchange and information of views between management and employees with the aim of establishing a transnational dialogue' (EIRR 1994b: 20). Similarly agreements in other European organizations talk about 'trustful co-operation', 'promotion of social contracts', 'reflection and dialogue'. One company, Norsk Data, is much more specific in the range of issues to be discussed, such as structure, economic and financial situation of the company, development of the business, production, sales, employment, safety, environment, training policy and working methods (EIRR 1994a).

As far as the hospitality industry is concerned a number of companies are identified as being affected by the Directive, including Bass, Compass, Forte/Granada, Ladbrokes, Queens Moat House and Scottish and Newcastle. Another company operating in the UK, Accor, has already established works councils with workers from a number of European countries including France, Germany, Italy, Spain and the UK (Sangster, 1994). Seemingly any involvement in EWCs and the threat of any other European legislation is something which employers in the British hospitality industry actively oppose, as evidenced by the view of the British Hospitality Association that 'We support the opt-out from the Social Chapter because we're concerned about the international competitiveness of tourism' (cited in Sangster 1994: 10). Royle (1995; 1995a; 1996) also reports on how McDonald's has used a variety of means to avoid conforming to German legislation supporting the setting up of works councils in the company. Regardless of such opposition we have already acknowledged the fact that some UK multinationals, including the above named hospitality organizations, will have to comply with the Directive, which came into effect in September 1996, although organizations have up to three years to comply. Evidence would suggest that a number of European multinationals have already responded though, with the EIRR (1994a; 1995a) identifying a number of voluntary agreements, such that the figure had risen from eight in 1990, to 40 in 1994, and 54 by May 1995.

Worker directors

Although Pendleton *et al.* (1993: 1) have noted that 'The notion of worker directors has an inescapably "seventies" feel about it' recent pronouncements from the Labour Party suggest that worker directors may be back on the political agenda (Hosking 1994). If this were the case it would revive the type of debate that was apparent in the late 1970s when the then Labour Government sought to extend worker influence to the boardroom via the Bullock Committee of Inquiry on Industrial Democracy (see Marchington 1992 for an extended discussion of the Bullock Report and its implications). Ostensibly, worker directors would seem to represent a radical source of employee power in allowing for representation and influence over strategic decision-making processes in the organization. In reality, experiments with worker directors in the 1970s had a limited impact on those organizations (usually public sector organizations) which encouraged such arrangements (Chell 1983). Nonetheless Pendleton *et al.* (1993) provide an interesting account of the more successful role played by worker directors in two privatized bus companies. Significantly in both companies there were high levels of employee ownership and trade union membership which allowed for significant involvement and influence in strategic financial and commercial decisions.

This chapter has ranged over a number of issues current in the contemporary industrial/employee relations scene in the UK and in the hospitality sector in particular. In many respects the discussion is characterized by polarization on a number of issues. For example, industrial relations versus employee relations, unitarism versus pluralism, participation versus involvement, collectivism versus individualism. In very simple terms this can also be seen as a dichotomy between employers and the government on one side and the trade union movement on the other. The extreme dualism that these various positions represent can perhaps be reconciled by looking to Europe and the more consensual relationship between the 'social partners', and the economic success enjoyed by Germany, for example, in much of the post-war period. The recognition of a plurality of interests is determined within a consensual and co-operative framework which is often supported by state intervention to facilitate, as much as possible, the smooth running of relationships between employers and employees. The social partner-ship that this exemplifies can be compared to the differing tradition of 'them and us' which is characteristic of the UK. Whether such approaches can be reconciled within a framework of greater European integration remains extremely debatable, though Hyman and Mason (1995) certainly offer conditional optimism that UK industrial/ employee relations can take on a more European feel, via the accep-tance of the various EU initiatives on social policy. If there were to be greater convergence within Europe, employees in the UK may find a collective voice in decision-making which allows for the legitimate expression of views on a wide range of important and significant topics in the organization. Moreover this does not have to be at the expense of more direct involvement mechanisms, which as we have already noted seek to improve commitment and motivation on the part of the employ-ees. To conclude we should recognize Salamon's (1992) view that the most effective structure of employee influence in decision-making involves both direct (involvement) and indirect (participation) mechan-isms, a point endorsed by the EIRR (1995a: 26, emphasis in original) in their recognition that 'each form fulfils a different function within the organization, each of which helps to improve the quality of decision-making. They are complementary and best seen "not as *either/or*, but as *both/and*"'.

REVIEW AND DISCUSSION QUESTIONS

1. How can the differing perspectives on the employment relationship further our understanding of employment issues in the hospitality industry?
2. How might trade unions begin to address the issue of low union membership in the hospitality industry?
3. 'Participation schemes offer more "real" influence on organiza-tional decision-making than involvement initiatives?' Outline some arguments for and against this proposition.
4. Suggest how employee involvement schemes can improve relations in the workplace between managers and employees.
5. What is the likely impact of European Works Councils on hospitality organizations in the United Kingdom?

Performance appraisal

Appraisal is now a widespread feature of working life in private and public organizations alike. From being a technique once directed primarily at managerial workers, it has now been extended to many more levels of the employment hierarchy. Broadly speaking, appraisal as a human resource phenomenon comes in two distinct packages, what might be called reward-oriented appraisal and development-oriented appraisal. The essential difference between these two is that the first is, as its name suggests, oriented towards the judgement of performance and is reward-linked – i.e. it is linked to remuneration. In contrast, development-oriented appraisal is rarely or only tentatively linked to remunerative reward, instead being concerned primarily with the quantitative and qualitative enhancement of employee performance without there being obvious links to reward.

OBJECTIVES OF APPRAISAL

A convenient (if not wholly accurate) way of distinguishing between reward- and development-oriented appraisal is to regard the latter as an incomplete model of the former. This view leads to the observation that irrespective of the specific type of appraisal, appraisal as a process has certain generic features or objectives. These can be summarized as being to:

- ensure that each job in the organization is being performed according to specification and to identify for the benefit of individual job holders and the wider organization any sources of drift and the reasons for such drift;
- encourage better job performance by job holders through a mixture of self-generated standards for improvement (i.e. solicited from the job holders themselves) and external standards based on organizational imperatives;
- develop a perceptual model of performance based on individual job holders views of their own performance compared to those of the organization's management;
- derive for the whole organization an audit of skills, and some understanding of the relative performance of employees;
- identify skill and performance gaps within the organization; and

- identify both short and long-term promotable employees in the context of career and succession planning strategies within the organization.

These strategies of the appraisal process are crucial irrespective of whether the primary goal of the process is to reward or to develop. To talk of a 'process' however is to beg the question as to what form this process takes. This is modelled in Figure 8.1 from which it can be seen that appraisal is an ongoing and cyclical process – a crucial point to bear in mind as, in many organizations, the appraisal process is seen as being confined to the pre-interview and interview stages of the cycle

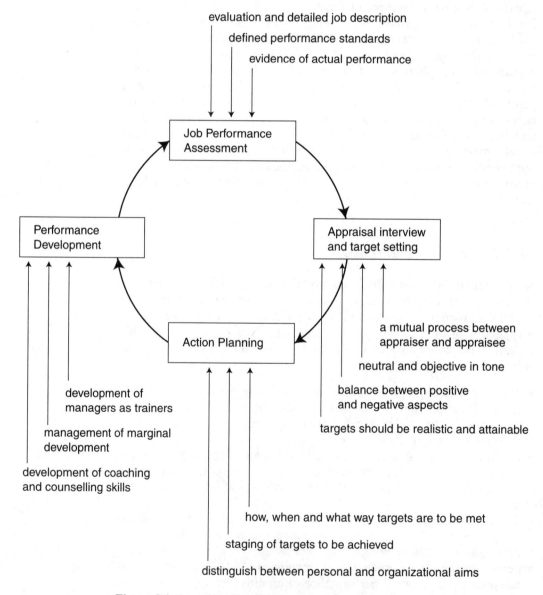

Figure 8.1 A model of appraisal

with the result that organizational resources are concentrated here, with little or no framework for sustaining the outcome of appraisal interviews through the subsequent period until the next round of such interviews.

REWARD-ORIENTED APPRAISAL

In reward-oriented appraisal systems, some effort is made to establish a link between job and job-holder performance, and pay and other rewards. As one might expect, the nature of such linkages are often contentious and controversial. Controversy can be further fuelled by the sheer momentousness of appraisal – ideally a long-term and continuous process which, however, normally peaks at the appraisal interview, the linkages of pay and performance in such a manner raises questions about how any system can function equitably and effectively to decide, in a single interview (or small number of interviews) the extent of an employee's reward(s). The reward-oriented appraisal can be further confounded by appraisal 'drift' where the developmental aspects of the process are sidelined and appraisal merely becomes a pay review.

A survey of seven case studies by the independent research organization Income Data Services (IDS) (1989) produced the following 'performance' factors which are often appraised.

- Job knowledge and abilities – being able to perform in all aspects of a job to a reasonable standard.
- Quality of outputs – including attention to detail and consistency in quality of output.
- Productivity – individual work rates and outputs.
- Attitude to work in terms of commitment, enthusiasm and apparent motivation.
- General demeanour and conduct – in terms of absences and reasons for absences and overall punctuality.
- Supervisory qualities – whether there is an ability to work independently and a capacity to offer leadership to others.
- Perceptual and anticipatory qualities – including an ability to interpret and anticipate job requirements and demonstrate originality in problem-solving.
- Co-operativeness and collaboration – with other workers in a team-oriented environment.
- Resource utilization – an ability to set personal priorities and plan and organize work schedules.
- Performance against targets – the most obvious measure, involving the level of attainment of the employee.

From the foregoing list a sense of the problems of reward-oriented appraisal can be readily gleaned. The central issue, precisely, is how any or all of the above performance criteria can be accurately and fairly measured. Some of the measures are, one might argue, fairly easy to measure in 'objective' terms, for example the level of absenteeism of a worker or their punctuality. Many of these performance criteria – probably most – rely heavily on a subjective assessment of the appraisee by the appraiser, even where these subjective judgements are lent some semblance of objective respectability by being converted to a score on some predefined scale. As Goss (1994: 52) notes, however, such scales are not uncommon in appraisal schemes giving rise to questions about their reliability and the overall fairness of reward-oriented appraisal systems. Set against this is the effort by several commentators to suggest that it is possible to find both favourable and less favourable arguments for the operation of reward-oriented appraisal schemes. Notable among these is Anderson (1992; see also Anderson and Evenden, 1992). In the view of Anderson, arguments in favour of reward-oriented appraisal include:

- appraisal linked to reward means that all parties to the process take appraisal more seriously;
- many people approve in principle of what they perceive to be the fairness of a relationship that rewards performance.

By way of contrast, the negative aspects of reward-oriented appraisal include:

- the possibility that the link between pay and performance will tend to obscure all aspects of the appraisal process unrelated to pay;
- the possibility that there is a downward pressure on performance standards within the organization as employees seek to influence appraisers to set and accept more limited performance targets;
- the fact that employers may focus disproportionately on those employees who are perceived as achieving a high level of performance, thus failing to address adequately the question of overall employee performance including those whose performance is weaker.

DEVELOPMENT-ORIENTED APPRAISAL

Earlier in this chapter, we considered 'the' objectives of appraisal. Review these objectives now (see above pp. 153–5). It should be clear that in the main, these objectives have a strong managerial bias – they are the objectives of appraisal which are most likely to be beneficial to the organization and managerial personnel within the organization. In both reward- and development-oriented appraisal, other objectives of appraisal, notably those which yield benefits to employees, should be considered important but, as we have seen, one of the potential dangers of reward-oriented appraisal systems is that they focus disproportionately on organizational objectives, especially the effort-reward relationship. In development-oriented appraisal, objectives 'friendly' to employees should be paramount and may include (Anderson and Evenden 1992: 220–1):

- to give employees the opportunity to obtain feedback from their supervisors and managers on how their contribution is viewed in the organization;
- allowing employees within a formal but friendly context to express their own views and feelings about their job, decide possible career development, and identify areas where performance might be improved and training and development might be appropriate to the attainment of career development and improved performance; and
- extending to employees an understanding of management and organizational expectation of their performance and their contribution in the overall scheme of things.

In an ideal world, these objectives, like those outlined earlier in the chapter, would, as we have suggested, be common to all forms of appraisal. In once again emphasizing this point, the intention is to highlight the view that any genuine appraisal system places duties and obligations on the employer to ensure that organizational expectations of employees are matched with a real commitment to providing the means necessary to employees to have a reasonable chance of meeting these expectations. An effective appraisal process then has resource implications beyond a simple reward dimension. Resources are required to ensure that training and development opportunities can be provided in pursuit of the objectives of appraisal.

In many development-oriented appraisal systems, reward is, of course, not a key issue. Such systems are, by definition, tailored to meeting an organization's essentially humanistic concerns and responsibilities for human resource development. Development-oriented appraisal is essentially diagnostic in nature, and many of the 'stick' elements of reward-oriented systems are absent. Instead, developmental approaches tend to rely more on 'carrots', if they rely on anything at all, to encourage more effective performance by employees. Such carrots include the possibility that the outcomes of development-oriented appraisal systems may (if positive) be used to support pay reviews; secure extra resources for individuals to undertake additional training; and prevent a diminution in status or responsibility (where appraisals tend to the negative). Of course, it can be argued that developmental-appraisal is a relatively pointless form of the art since it is denied any real impact. Several advantages of developmental approaches have been suggested, however, and these include (Holdsworth 1991, cited in Goss 1994: 55):

- greater emphasis on the assessment of both person **and** performance rather than the latter alone, leading to a much more effective and 'honest' system of developing objective self-awareness on the part of both appraisees and appraisers;
- greater openness in documentary procedures and hence greater potential for joint negotiation of the content of appraisal and subsequent action to build on appraisal; and
- greater stress on the appraiser-appraisee relationship with a conco-

mitant documentation in the use of 'big brother' in the form of the personnel manager/personnel department.

THE APPRAISAL CYCLE

We earlier noted that according to Anderson and Evenden (1992) the appraisal process could be conceived of as being cyclical in nature with four key stages. All too often, 'appraisal' is simply equated with just one of these stages – the 'appraisal interview'. Indeed, it is difficult to talk extensively about the appraisal process in general because so much hangs on that core event of the process – the interview. A careful reading of the preceding two sections of this chapter reveals that the authors of this book are not wholly innocent in this respect! Nevertheless, appraisal **is** a process that is more than just an interview and in this section we consider the four key stages as discussed earlier.

Job performance assessment

Core considerations in job performance assessments as are actually used by some organizations were examined in the earlier discussion of reward-oriented appraisal. As a matter of basic principle, however, job performance assessment must embrace the following:

- a properly evaluated and detailed job description;
- defined performance standards: wherever possible these should be unambiguous and refer to material and objective measures; and
- evidence of actual performance of the job by the job holder: this may be obtained in a variety of ways, for example by (a) observing actual performance and assessing against established criteria; (b) checking a job holder's record to establish whether there are any notable events recorded (positive or negative); and (c) checking with line managers and work colleagues.

In the hotel and catering context the second and third points above (and the latter's subdivisions) can be realized in a variety of ways. Performance standards may be rooms cleaned per shift; meals served per sitting and so on (see the later discussion on productivity). Peer review may be a useful integral part of appraisal where each member of a work group is asked to assess the others in that group on a range of criteria: clearly such a process must guarantee confidentiality and be designed in the first place with the aid of professional advice: local universities and colleges, the HCIMA, the BHA or the ubiquitous 'consultants' may be able to help. A final source of assessment is, of course, guests themselves where a unit has the facility to record guests' comments on their treatment by staff. This is common in many hotels nowadays but is sadly less so in restaurants.

The appraisal interview and target setting

If job performance assessment is the first stage in the appraisal of a new employee (it would be the third stage after evaluation of 'action planning' and 'performance development' with employees who had already participated in an appraisal cycle) then the appraisal interview is the second. Whatever the case, the appraisal interview is, as we have suggested, at the heart of the appraisal process.

The same techniques that lead to good interviewing practice in general apply no less to appraisal interviewing. However, the context of the appraisal interview demands certain extra considerations. These can be identified as follows.

1. Appraisal interviews can be difficult because of mutual suspicion on the part of appraiser and appraisee arising from the appraisal itself or the specific perception of each other held by the parties to the interview. It is thus necessary for both appraisee and appraiser to exercise a large amount of calm objectivity.
2. Appraisal interviews are normally conducted by an appraisee's line manager. Some appraisal systems allow for an appraisee, subject to the approval of senior management, to nominate an alternative appraiser if they can demonstrate that the appraiser who they would normally be involved with is in some way unacceptable for professional or organizational (not usually personal) reasons.
3. The length of appraisal interviews may vary. An Institute of Personnel Management survey in 1986 found that the majority of appraisal interviews (53 per cent) took between one and two hours, with 27 per cent lasting between thirty minutes and an hour (Anderson and Evenden 1992: 252). Clearly, to sustain interviews of any length, a suitable environment is necessary. As with selection interviewing, there should be no interruptions to the interview which should, if possible, be conducted on neutral territory. Unlike the majority of selection interviews, however, a degree of informality can and should be maintained provided this does not descend into 'chumminess'. A crucial aspect of appraisal if the process is to work is avoidance of the temptation to say, as Riley (1996: 126) puts it 'You and I know each other – let's get this form off to Personnel'.
4. At the same time as you are avoiding excessive friendliness it is important that the appraiser does not adopt the attitude of 'What do you want first – the good news or the bad news'. In short, a dichotomous approach to the appraisal interview is unnecessarily antagonistic, especially where most issues of performance *and* development are likely to be perceived, if not by both parties then certainly by the appraisee, as being somewhat grey rather then simply black and white. Similarly, it is important for the appraiser to avoid being both overly negative as well as overly positive, and for the appraisee to avoid aggressiveness in their responses to the appraiser.

5. A key approach to the appraisal interview that will eliminate many of the problems outlined in (4) above is one that emphasizes appropriate **preparation** for the interview. If the interview itself is to be a balanced discussion of the tasks, responsibilities and performance of the employee that encourages the employee to talk freely of their success and problem areas, then it is important that both parties to the interview have confidence in the information gathering that forms the basis for appraisal (i.e. the other three stages of the appraisal process), and that both parties actually examine this information in detail before the interview. Clearly this is easier to do when the appraisal system is development-oriented rather than reward-oriented since in the case of the latter, management tend to reserve the information they might gather in order to deploy it in discussions about rewards. However, even here it should be possible to agree on the evidence base (**what** evidence is collected) and the provenance of any raw data that is collected, even if there is dispute over the data's accuracy or interpretation.

If both parties have adequately prepared for the appraisal interview by reviewing this data and other information then it should be possible to achieve a rational discussion if both parties focus on the information gathered in a reasonably objective way. One way of ensuring that preparation of the interview is adequate is a so far unmentioned aspect of the appraisal interview – the paperwork! Preparation for the appraisal interview is necessarily a paper-based exercise – often a lot of paper is involved. However, the completion of appraisal forms is a useful way of ensuring adequate reflection on the part of the appraisee as well as the appraiser. A typical appraisal form is shown in Box 8.2. Careful management of this aspect of the appraisal process not only ensures adequate preparation for the appraisal interview but commits both appraiser and appraisee to expressing their views formally, ensuring greater openness in the process as a whole.

Target setting

One of the key objectives of the appraisal interview is target setting for the period up until the next appraisal occasion. These targets are primarily targets for the employee/appraisee but may include targets for the organization as represented by the appraiser (for example, in providing more resources for training; in tackling problematic aspects of work-flows in the work environment). In general, the following points should be observed in target setting.

- Target setting is a mutual process, and should be the subject of consensual agreement.
- The targets set should be realistic and attainable. If they are over-ambitious this will ultimately demotivate the employee/appraisee as well as damage their case in subsequent appraisals. If the targets are

Box 8.1

A typical Appraisal Form

Copthorne Glasgow   **Employee Appraisal Report**

Name: ....   Job Title: ....

Department: ....

Date Employed: ....   Time in position: ....

Conducted by: ....   Job Title: ....

Last review date: ....   This review date: ....

1. Job description: Issued/discussed
2. Assessment of performance

Area	Comments
Job Knowledge and Understanding	
Personal Appearance	
Timekeeping and Attendance	
Ability to work on own Initiative	
Communication	
Relationship with Colleagues	
Relationship with Guests	
Quality of Work	
Performance under Pressure	
Consistency and Dependability	
Adaptability	
Overall Performance	

3. Agreed areas for improvement

Area	How	Target Date	Review Date

4. Objectives

Objective	How Achieved	Target Date	Review Date

5. Training and Development

	Undertaken	Proposed
On the job:		
Off the job:		
Corporate:		
External:		

6. Career Development – Comments:

7. Assessor's Additional Comments:

8. Employee: suggestions/ideas:

Employee Signature: ....   Assessor Signature: ....

Date: ....   Next review date: ....

This appraisal report has been reviewed and discussed with the employee

9. Personnel and Training Managers comments:

Signature: ....   Date: ....

This form remains the property of the company and will not be copied to any third party outside the company

too low-level in nature, then the employee will not be stretched or challenged.

- Most important of all, target setting should proceed logically from the appraisal interview's assessment of performance and development needs, building on the issues raised therein and addressing performance gaps and development needs.

Action planning

Once job performance assessment and the appraisal interview is complete, the targets that have been set need to be converted into an action plan which may be agreed at the end of the appraisal interview or very shortly afterwards. The objective of the action plan is to map out how targets will (hopefully) be achieved over the period until the next appraisal. Whether or not these are checked along the route, as it were, or left for review at the next appraisal interview depends on the resources devoted to the appraisal cycle within the organization. Ideally, the action plan should embrace the following elements.

- A statement of targets to be achieved, including how they are to be achieved, by when and in what manner (including the recording of any extra organizational resources that will be required for achieving targets).

- A note of any staging points on the way to achieving targets. This may involve taking each target in turn and seeing if it can be achieved gradually or processually, thus identifying certain points leading up to attainment.
- A statement of any distinction between personal development aims ('what I will do to improve myself') and organizational development aims ('what aspects of performance must I address') – such a distinction may arise in several areas where personal and organizational development are mutually exclusive.

Performance development

Performance development is the most complex of all four stages of the appraisal process as it requires the creation of an organizational culture that is performance driven but not performance-obsessed. Often, performance development is seen as a responsibility of management (indeed, Anderson and Evenden 1992, take this view) and, typical though this may be, the development of manager's performance development skills is not an adequate substitute for involving all an organization's personnel in the process. According to Anderson and Evenden (1992: 217) performance development embraces the process of appraisal; objective and target setting; the management of marginal performance; the development of coaching and counselling skills; and the development of managers as trainers. Few of these functions need be the sole prerogative of management, however. Indeed, given the current emphasis on empowerment in organizations (see Wood 1994 and Chapter 7 in this volume) there are good arguments for the devolution of much decision-making and peer management to work groups such that management assume more of a monitoring, mentoring and facilitative role rather than simply a directive one. If a genuine performance-driven organizational culture is to be developed it cannot be imposed but has to be evolved using all possible inputs from an organization's personnel.

APPRAISAL – HOW OFTEN?

Several references have been made in this chapter to the 'gap' between appraisal interviews. The core question here is how long should the appraisal cycle be? The answer very much depends on whether the form of appraisal is reward- or development-oriented since the former will as likely as not require to be conducted more regularly as remuneration decisions are involved. Clearly, the implication here is that the reward-oriented appraisal cycle should be a year in length in which case, all aspects of the appraisal process have to be realistically tailored to this. A common problem with such a short cycle is that the reward basis to appraisal causes extra pressures and may lead to unrealistic expectations on the part of both the organization (as reported by management) and its employees. With development-oriented appraisal, a longer cycle is possible and two yearly cycles are not uncommon as this allows sufficient time to set and meet realistic performance targets. Obvious disadvantages of a longer cycle include the possibility that necessary performance development is unreasonably delayed. There are no simple rules guiding the length of the appraisal cycle and organizational leaders have to exercise judgement in determining the relevant parameters, mindful as ever of the costs of the processes involved.

APPRAISAL IN SMALL AND MEDIUM-SIZED HOSPITALITY BUSINESSES

We saw in Chapter 1 that many hospitality businesses are small and medium-sized in nature and that, in general, personnel practices were underdeveloped. What merits does the appraisal process therefore have that might benefit the small hospitality business? Surely appraisal is only for large companies with numerous employees? At a practical level it must be conceded that these attitudes are not wholly unreasonable. Given that many small business operations consider themselves to be infallible in most aspects of their behaviour, not least in dealing with their staff, appraisal appears as part of another one of those 'fairy' techniques taught in hotel schools and of little practical use. Furthermore, unlike many aspects of equal opportunities practice, or health and safety policy, appraisal has no legal enforcement or dimension – it really does appear a luxury.

There is a response to this. The first thing to note is that, realistically, appraisal is not going to figure in small family-concern type businesses or single-person operations. Appraisal **is** a technique that has certain minimum requisites or parameters. We suggest these would include:

- the equivalent of at least twenty full-time non-managerial employees;
- a minimum of one layer of professional management between the organization's proprietor and operative staff; and
- some evidence of departmentalization where individual departments have their own heads or supervisors.

Second, and following from this, we know from the substantial body of research literature available that no matter how hard they protest to the contrary, the treatment of employees by the proprietors (and their managers) in small hospitality businesses is often heavy-handed to put it mildly. In the wider context of systematic employee relations therefore, appraisal could be one vehicle for helping overcome these difficulties, at least in medium-sized operations. Any proprietor or manager worth their salt would, given their freedom under employment law, have some form of staff handbook containing the rules and regulations they wished to see observed. Within this handbook there would be scope not only for outlining statutory duties of both employer and employee but a systematic exposition of related 'voluntary' policies of which appraisal might be one. If this seems a little idealistic then it should be noted that there *are* many medium-sized businesses in the hospitality and other sectors which manage to achieve these minimum standards in personnel practice, including the operation of appraisal schemes, which are invariably helpful in building trust in the employment relationship.

In this chapter we have elaborated the key elements of the appraisal process. The core concepts that may be usefully reviewed as a way of mapping the terrain of debates about good practice in appraisal may be summarized as:

- the objectives of appraisal – which are to ensure effective job performance through measurement, counselling and personal development;
- the distinction between reward-oriented and development-oriented appraisal – where the former links appraisal to reward and remuneration and the latter places greater emphasis on overall organizational culture and effectiveness; and
- the concept of the appraisal cycle – appraisal is a continuous process comprising job performance assessment, appraisal interview and target setting, action planning, performance development, and the length of the appraisal cycle.

REVIEW AND DISCUSSION QUESTIONS

1. How would you assess the job performance of
   (a) a chef;
   (b) a waiter;
   (c) a housekeeper?
2. What methods would you employ to support an underperforming member of staff and assist them in improving their performance?
3. Should different categories of employee be appraised at different intervals?
4. Is development-oriented appraisal worth the effort?
5. How would you respond to an employee who complained that their appraiser had treated them unfairly?

Productivity  9

In the previous chapter, on appraisal, we referred on numerous occasions to the question of performance standards. One aspect – a wider aspect – of performance standards that we consider in this short chapter is that of productivity. Productivity is the holy grail of most commercial enterprises – which is to say that higher and higher productivity is a goal often sought by such enterprises. But, though we hear the term bandied around on the television and radio and read about it in our newspapers, what exactly is meant by 'productivity'?

In essence, productivity is a qualitative relationship, a measurement. It is a measurement of the relationship between the quantity of output of a productive system and the quality of inputs entered into the system in order to yield this output. Put in the form of equation, we can say that:

$$\text{Productivity} = \frac{\text{output(s) realized}}{\text{input(s) utilized}}$$

This we may term a 'general' representation of the measurement of productivity and it is immediately apparent that as a calculative device it is very crude indeed. For example, employing the equation tells us nothing about the quality of inputs or outputs – as a raw statement of what productivity is, this representation lacks any context for interpreting those values which may be derived from application of the equation. More pressingly, the equation is not really an equation in the mathematical sense at all, since even in quantitative terms the insertion of values for inputs and outputs into the equation will be in different dimensions (i.e. on different scales of value).

The generic representation of what productivity **is**, therefore, constitutes an essential sketch of the crucial relationship between inputs and outputs and nothing more. However, it is an expression of a relationship that can yield more specific, actual, mathematical formulae for computing certain specific aspects of productivity. In this book we are concerned with human resources and thus labour productivity (as opposed to materials or overheads productivity) is the area of interest. Indeed, there is a very good case for arguing, as Riley (1996: 70) does, that the study of productivity in the hospitality industry is *de facto* the study of labour productivity. This is because whilst the hospitality industry is capital intensive, it is also labour intensive relative to many other industries, and labour 'inputs' are extremely variable and unpredictable in nature. If we accept this view of Riley's we must also accept its corrollary, namely that the origin of demand for labour in hospitality organizations is sales, or forecast sales, and the management of productivity in hospitality services is the management of (a) job design to ensure efficient working practices that best utilizes technology and human resources; and (b) the relationship between the forecast demand for labour and the actual supply of human resources. In respect of (b) Riley asserts, productivity is therefore about efficiently matching labour demand and supply.

This is a useful approach but it does have certain limitations, the key limitation also being the key strength. This is that Riley's prognosis clearly places labour at the centre of the productivity equation, and emphasizes the responsibility of management for the effective utilization of labour. This managerial approach precisely locates the obligation of management to manage, rather than abandoning responsibility for human resources on the grounds that much of the variability that is often imputed to the work-force in the hospitality industry defies effective managerial control of employee performance. The 'downside' of this approach lies in the submerged inference that management has, on managing productivity, access to perfect knowledge about demand (sales) and supply (of labour), an inference belied by Riley's quite proper assertion that a key management technique in managing productivity is forecasting. Forecasting is a valid and useful technique in this context but by definition is tentative – it can be used in such a way as to yield 'wrong' results. Given that productivity **can** and **should** be managed – on this point Riley is surely correct in terms of both the actual and moral imperative (managers have an obligation to their ultimate stakeholders to manage as efficiently as possible and labour is costly) – then forecasting is as good a technique as any, but it is fallible.

Running parallel with this reservation is another, namely that while Riley is undoubtedly right in arguing that labour productivity is the most important expression of the overall productivity equation in hospitality services, this does not mean that it necessarily has the most significant affect on the **overall** performance of a particular organization. Labour is a variable cost and one, as we have seen, that is relatively easily managed. Other aspects of productivity management – for example, materials management, quality control – may be less easy to manage effectively (in food service or in hotels one must always have some food and some available accommodation; to attract custom the quality of these 'materials' must match some consumers' expectations) but if an appropriate configuration of resources (inputs) is not in place at the outset, then the amount of productivity management – of labour or anything else – will overcome problems of inappropriate unit location or capacity; inappropriate or insufficient equipment and technology; and control over quality and costs (see Ball 1994, for a discussion of these elements in the specific context of foodservice operations). Accordingly, the traditionally poor productivity of the hospitality sector cannot be attributed to failures in the management of labour productivity alone (but see Box 9.1). Other factors include:

- the large number of small businesses in hospitality each employing few people – this inhibits, for example, the introduction of technology (limited purchasing resources for technology throw operations back on their own or other human resources, often unpaid family labour);
- poor materials management among small and medium-sized businesses – many such businesses have limited bargaining power and are thrown back on relatively costly suppliers;
- poor marketing among small and medium-sized businesses – often, the operators of such units have no formal qualifications in management and may be characterized, broadly, as amateurish in their approach to management, including marketing: this means that strategies are not put in place to utilize capacity to the full; and
- ideology among small and medium-sized units' operators: often, inexperienced operators who enter the industry are not so much interested in 'making millions' but in making a living: this inhibits innovation and investment as operators seek to 'get by' rather than maximize entrepreneurial opportunities.

In all the above examples we have cited small and medium-sized businesses which still make up the bulk of the hospitality industry. Many of these problems can and do apply to chains of whatever size, however, and this is largely attributable to:

- the unpredictability of demand for hospitality services; and
- the perishability of hotel and catering products.

In essence here, the arguments are that (a) even large chain organizations find it difficult to predict demand accurately and thus have to maintain a certain resource base in order to cope with sudden and unexpected increases in demand, thereby rendering them less productive as many such resources will be wasted (food goes off; labour is kept on duty, idle); and (b) hotel and catering products are perishable, not just as is the case with food, often in a literal sense, but in the sense that products and services like rooms, if not let on a given day cannot be let again on that day, nor may a restaurant seat that is not sold during a particular service period be 'let' again – hospitality products cannot be 'stored' for future use. Some caution is necessary in the use of these arguments as large hospitality organizations, especially chains, are probably better at managing these aspects of the productivity process than is generally supposed. Hotels, for example, are not as dependent on individual advance bookings and casual trade as the 'unpredictability' argument would suggest: many hotels diminish this problem by accepting block tour bookings, ensuring that spare capacity is let even at a marginal price. Technological advances and more accurate marketing planning mean that in the case of food and restaurant management respectively, wastage can be substantially reduced and the possibility

Box 9.1

Productivity in British and German Hotels

Prais *et al.* (1989) compared similarly matched hotels in Britain and Germany. They found that for the British sample there was an average of 2.06 guest nights per employee compared to 4.01 in Germany or, put another way, German hotels employed 0.25 persons per guest night whereas in Britain the figure was 0.49: thus the German hotels apparently required only around half (51 per cent) of the labour per guest night as British hotels. Distinguishing two sub-categories of employee – housekeeping and reception workers – the authors found German hotels to be substantially more efficient than their British counterparts, requiring around only 60 per cent of the full-time equivalent personnel employed in British units. Indeed, German hotels were able to function with some 70 per cent of the labour force of London hotels and with around one-half of the labour force of British provincial hotels. Productivity in German hotels was around 150–200 per cent of that of the British hotels sampled.

In what they concede is an impressionistic comment, Prais *et al.* note that there seemed to be less cost consciousness in the British hotels; less pressure on the use of room-cleaners' time; less purchasing expertise (vacuum cleaners used in British hotels were mainly of the domestic type while in Germany they were of the more robust industrial kind); and less likelihood that the choice of furniture, fittings and equipment had been made with a view to the most effective use of maintenance and labour.

In studying the formal qualifications of hotel workers, the authors observed that in German hotels, 30 per cent had vocational qualifications in hotel work and a further five per cent had qualified in office work, maintenance and other, related, trades. In British hotels comparable figures were 12 per cent and two per cent. Some nine per cent of the full-time equipment workforce in German hotels were on approved apprenticeship schemes whereas in Britain, the figure was under two per cent including those on the Youth Training Scheme (YTS). In respect of the target occupational groups, 75 per cent of German Housekeepers had vocational qualifications compared to only one British Housekeeper (about seven per cent of the sample) and 55 per cent of reception staff were vocationally qualified compared to 17 per cent in Britain. German housekeepers were more likely to spend time on organizational and administrative tasks than British housekeepers who, in turn, spent more time checking the work of their staff and finishing off unsatisfactory cleaning jobs themselves. Greater economy in the staffing of reception areas was also noted in Germany – German hotels had an average of four full-time staff compared to 6.6 in Britain: German receptionists engaged flexibly in a much wider range of tasks than their British cousins. In examining the quality of management in German hotels, the authors note that over 90 per cent of managers had vocational qualifications in Germany whereas just under half did so in Britain. German managers spent more time on strategic management issues (notably marketing) than the British managers who tended to engage in routine day-to-day duties.

Source:

Prais, S. J., Jarvis, V. and Wagner, K. (1989) Productivity and national skills in services in Britain and Germany: hotels. in *National Institute Economic Review*, November, pp. 52–74.

of filling restaurant capacity can, probabilistically speaking, be increased by matching locational choice to the volume of passing pedestrians.

LABOUR PRODUCTIVITY: PERFORMANCE STANDARDS

Despite reservations about certain conventional academic explanations of low productivity in hospitality services it remains a fact that operations do face a greater or lesser degree of certainty in their relationship with the markets for their products and services. As we have already suggested, perhaps the greatest potential for variation is the variation of labour inputs. Paradoxically, labour is one of the easiest 'resources' that management can control but this is not the same as saying that, typically, management manages labour 'inputs' well. Human resources may be easy to control in terms of varying employee inputs, but they are difficult to manage effectively.

A first step on the road to the effective management of labour productivity is the setting of performance standards which are, in essence, measures of desired and possible output set against a specified time period. The key word here is 'possible' since performance standards must be realistic and attainable by the majority of employees required to meet a given performance standard in terms of available technology, ascertained work routines and the ability of the unit or organization to sustain the standard through training. Many performance standards are in fact industry norms. For example, it is generally accepted that a bedroom cleaner in a single (usually eight-hour) shift will clean between 12–15 rooms depending on the type of hotel (see Box 9.2). Variations according to sector or type of business are important to setting performance standards, as are the criteria by which the standards themselves are set. In particular, there is a temptation to set performance standards according to some measurement of sales or capacity – i.e. according to variations in level of business. There are two problems of which the manager should be aware in employing such criteria, however. The first is whether the quality and quantity of historical data exists to produce an accurate picture of variations in business activity and, if it does, what it says about the regularity with which performance standards should be revised: business levels change and it is important where possible to take note of any regularities in such changes in historical data (e.g. daily variations by time; seasonal variations).

The second problem relates to the issues of averaging. Simply put, the question here is whether a performance standard should reflect the supposed performance of an average worker. Riley (1996: 70) is of the view that the above average worker (not the best) is the employee to which the performance standard should be addressed but there is a danger in this approach that the overall standard will be skewed. The purpose of a performance standard is to give some form to what can be achieved, but by the very nature of being a numerical measure, this elides the possible sources of variation that inhibit performance. Consider the bedroom cleaner whose fifteen rooms have been occupied by a drunken rock band and their entourage whose care of the facilities has been far from that of the 'typical' hotel guest. These rooms will probably take longer to clean. In fact, we can predict that there will always be some rooms that are more difficult to clean than others and, given some attached probability of occurrence (say a 30 per cent chance that each day four of 15 rooms will be so affected), we can build such considerations into the performance standard. However, because performance standards are fairly blunt instruments, our options for building in these considerations are practically limited. There is some merit, however, with due deference to Riley (1996) in erring on the side of caution and setting performance standards to match some idealized concept of the 'just below average' worker. The disadvantage of this approach is that in seeking to match labour supply to demand forecasts, there will be a tendency to err on the side of having too many workers available, especially if the forecast demand has a high level of 'negative' uncertainty associated with it (i.e. is too optimistic). This could mean having the additional expense of labour on duty which cannot be fully utilized but must be paid for. One way round this problem is utilization of casual labour at the margins of the labour forecast. Demand levels are likely to form a pattern over time and, if the historical data is available and analysed correctly, this may reveal the core of staff routinely required plus levels of variance according to factors such as season. Some of this variance might be met by the use of regular part-time workers but at periods of extreme variance in (high) demand, additional workers might be employed from a casual pool of the unit's own creation, or from agency staff.

MATCHING SUPPLY AND DEMAND

We have spoken of performance standards for jobs in the hospitality industry (see Johns 1996 for further discussion). We have also discussed in the most general terms the matching of labour supply to demand. In this section we examine the latter process in a little more detail.

Box 9.2

Establishing room-cleaning performance standards at Gleneagles Hotel

Sheila Perera, then Chair of the UK Housekeepers' Association and Executive Housekeeper at Gleneagles Hotel investigated how long it took her staff to clean rooms. She compared her experience with other housekeepers. Of interest are the constraints and problems Perera identifies as routinely facing room cleaners. These included:

- what is required to be cleaned (Perera's checklists for Gleneagles specify not only items in a room but parts of these items, e.g. the water supply pipes to the lavatory in the bathroom);
- access to rooms, which is not always immediate or at times that suits the cleaner's routine because of guest occupation;
- use of in-room facilities varies considerably (for example, at Gleneagles only around 35 per cent of guests use the tea trays and 25 per cent the mini-bars) as does general use of the room by guests, thus affecting the severity of cleaning required;
- whether or not cleaning schedules allow for regular cleaning of awkward areas or rooms are instead taken out of service periodically for 'deep' cleaning (at Gleneagles the former applies so deep cleaning is an ongoing process); and
- at what point of the daily routine the cleaner is at – cleaners do tire, like everyone else, the more they do.

Perera's responsibility for housekeeping in one of the world's most prestigious hotels has led her to develop performance standards for room cleaning. These are 'ideal world' times when cleaners would not be under pressure: in reality, some ten minutes would be deducted from the totals which are:

- for bathrooms 22–32 minutes (depending on size)
- for bedrooms   23–41 minutes (depending on size)

Accordingly, full room service times range from 35–63 minutes allowing for a ten minute 'pressure' deduction. Further, non-use and general guest care of the room may reduce cleaning times further – Perera reckons on a band of 25–60 minutes and believes that regardless of the hotel type it must take around 23 minutes to service a single room with bathroom.

Source:
Konopka, C. (1995) Between the time sheets. *Caterer and Hotelkeeper*, 31 August, pp. 42–3.

In doing so, let us return to our room cleaners. The generally accepted industry standard of 12–15 rooms per cleaner per eight-hour shift is employed in what we will decide is our mythical four-star hotel, which has 300 rooms. Now, if all the rooms are full, then, on a performance standard of 15 rooms per cleaner per eight-hour shift we would require $300 \div 15 = 20$ cleaners. This might be necessary if the hotel is full, given the implied quality of the establishment. We might, however, consider that 20 cleaners is excessive, especially if we have additional and separate job categories of floor housekeepers/supervisors who are normally expected to become involved in cleaning in cases where the number of room cleaners is perceived as insufficient to complete designated tasks within a set time period. Accordingly, our performance standard might rise to, say, 17 rooms per cleaner which would yield 17 or 18 cleaners ($300 \div 17 = 17.6$). Now this kind of variability is taking a chance, not only in moving away from widely accepted industry norms but in displacing work to a category of employee (supervisors) whose main role might be expected to monitor the quality of cleaners' work. If we go the other way and, say, decide on 13 as our performance standard then we find that 23 workers are necessary ($300 \div 13$). Here, we are moving towards the lower end of the industry norm and perhaps also towards the view that we should take our calculations to the just-below average worker as described in the last section. In this case we might decide that given a forecast of 300 room occupancy, and a performance standard of 13, that some of the workers (say three) might be drawn from our pool of casual employees.

Of course, while it is not unusual for hotels to enjoy full occupancy, there are occasions when forecast and actual demand is less than capacity. Furthermore, in other departments – the restaurant, the bar – capacity is more difficult to determine as is, accordingly, a performance standard. Thus, while there is a broadly accepted **industry** performance standard for room cleaning, this is not generally the case for other hotel or restaurant departments. Again, the nature of the market and the quality of the products and services intervene to produce sectoral varieties in sensible performance standards. For example, Riley (1996: 73) suggests that for waiting staff, 20 covers every four hours is a possible performance standard and for cooks 90 covers per eight-hour shift is reasonable. If the fixed capacity of our hotel restaurant is 100 covers and the restaurant is fully booked for luncheon, then five waiting staff should cover our needs. Here we encounter some of the problems of performance standards. First, if the restaurant is also four-star in standard then five waiting staff may be insufficient to meet the quality standards expected. Second, if we have 100 guests for luncheon, this does not mean they will all arrive at the same time – although they might! In other words, performance standards generally do not take account in these circumstances of the flow of trade over a given time period. There can be hardly any restaurant-user who has not encountered slow and inadequate service in a full restaurant to be told upon remonstrating with the staff that 'we didn't expect it to be this busy' or 'we've had an unexpected rush'. A third problem comes when fixed capacity is treated as variable capacity. In the case of restaurants, this occurs when sales are accepted into 'second sittings' (more precisely, tables are sold more than once in a given trading period). For the sake of argument, assume that our hotel books 150 guests for luncheon on a given day. Does this mean we should increase our staff? The answer is 'probably not' but it depends on how the performance standard has been set relative to the quality of the operation and, in our case, the performance standard is probably too conservative.

Matching supply of labour to forecast demand is not, therefore, an easy task, and the concept of performance standards can lull us into a false sense of security. In managing performance standards, the construction of the standard itself is typically conceived of as a means of providing firm answers to the practical problem of 'how much should a waiter do?' The emphasis here has been on the importance of managing the margins of the performance standard – the difference between the absolutely necessary number of staff required and the total reasonable number of staff that could be required. In other words, despite their appearance, performance standards are not true quantitative methods – they are qualitative methods. Recognition of this fact and the context in which performance standards are applied (the context of relative demand variability) is reflected in innovative methods employers have utilized to cope with demand variability. Always an employer of relatively large numbers of part-time and casual workers, the hospitality industry has seen recent developments including flexible and annual hours agreements (see Goss-Turner 1992: 89–90).

Flexible hours arrangements come in various forms. At one level, employees are contracted to work a different number of hours per day each week or month by agreement with management at the start of the rota schedule. This means that on days where demand is predicted to be leaner, adequate labour resources are available and labour supply is scaled down on quieter days. An alternative arrangement is the 'shift menu' where employees are allowed to select their own shifts up to the maximum number of hours for which they are contracted. Now that Wages Councils no longer govern pay (see Chapter 10) there is no legally enforceable rate for overtime so if employees volunteer for shifts, normal hourly pay can be applied and employees cannot complain about the hours they are expected to work, having chosen them themselves (interestingly, Goss-Turner 1992: 89, observed this phenomenon at a time when the non-application of overtime rates may have been construed as illegal: Wages Councils were not abolished until 1993). In October 1993, Forte introduced flexible rostering contracts, removing time-and-a-half pay for overtime and double-time pay for working bank holidays. Staff were paid their normal hourly rate under the new contracts for all hours worked, being rostered on a monthly base to reflect forecast demand (management, however, retuned the rostas at short notice if business required it) and, if necessary, moved between neighbouring hotels if circumstances demanded (Bartlett

1993). The new contracts were justified by management in terms of cost savings, the human resources director of the company being quoted as saying that the changes merely reflected what had been practice for some time, with overtime having been steadily phased out in favour of time off in lieu. The new contracts meant that, depending on demand, employees could work 60 hours one week and 20 the next. In Lancashire, the GMB union organizer was less than happy noting that Forte was using a monthly base figure of 156 hours, such that hours worked in a week in excess of what would have been the overtime cut-off under the Wages Councils (which were abolished in August 1993) were not paid at an enhanced rate but 'counted' in the total.

Annual hours agreements are simply where employees are contracted to work a certain number of hours in a year and when these hours are worked is largely at the discretion of management. In some cases, this can mean that for certain periods at least, employees do not work at all, being utilized only when management faces peaks in business demand.

FROM PERFORMANCE STANDARDS TO PRODUCTIVITY

Performance standards are, in essence, physical measures of labour productivity, for example: rooms cleaned ÷ number of room cleaners; restaurant covers ÷ number of waiting staff. More than this, given a time period element they indicate how many staff should be utilized to meet a performance standard. By comparing forecast demand for services with actual demand and forecast labour demand with actual labour employed, a measure of productivity can be derived – simply put how many extra (unnecessary) staff were employed (or to what extent the target was undershot). Physical measures of productivity tell us nothing about **costs** however and it is common to use either financial measures of combined physical/financial measures to derive commercially useful measures of productivity. In the area of labour productivity, a variety of useful measures include (see Ball 1994: 189), for example:

- restaurant revenue for a time period ÷ time worked in restaurant (a physical/financial measure); and
- restaurant sales ÷ restaurant payroll (a financial measure).

Productivity remains very much a grey area in human resource management for the hospitality sector but, in conclusion, the following points can be made:

- human resource productivity in hospitality services is generally low and provides considerable opportunities for improvement;
- labour productivity can be managed though, traditionally, management's approach to labour resourcing has been reactive rather than directive and systematic;
- concepts of productivity and productivity measures may vary accord-

ing to the type of operation, the technology employed and the market in which the unit operates;
- the essence of effective labour productivity is effective forecasting of demand needs and human resourcing to meet these needs based on occupational performance standards; and
- occupational performance standards need to be understood relative to different, broader, measures of productivity, notably financial measures that relate labour utilization to the cost thereof relative to sales.

REVIEW AND DISCUSSION QUESTIONS

1. Suggest reasons why productivity in hospitality services is generally low.
2. In respect of productivity performance, are there lazy workers, or only lazy managers?
3. Identify ways in which productivity in selected hospitality industry jobs could be improved by choice and deployment of technology.
4. Should productivity measures be linked to enhanced rewards?
5. 'If you want a job doing properly, do it yourself'. How fair is this view relative to team versus individual performance in respect of productivity?

10 Pay and reward systems

We begin this chapter with a somewhat negative observation, namely that, relative to other industries, the majority of jobs and occupations within the commercial hospitality industry have always been poorly paid. That this is the case is testified to by the body of research literature on hotel and catering (see Wood 1992 for a review) but in the 1990s is it still true?

Until 1993, wages for operative workers in certain industries regarded as being vulnerable to low pay were regulated by Wages Councils, statutory bodies comprising employer, employee and neutral representatives whose principle job was to set, each year, a rate of (usually hourly) remuneration. Three Wages Councils covered different sub-sections of the commercial hospitality industry and, at abolition in 1993, the mean hourly rate of pay set by these councils was £2.97 per hour which is £115.83 for a 39 hour week or £6,023.16 per annum. This is not a prince's ransom. However, operative workers are not the only group of industry employees who have traditionally been regarded as 'low paid'. Managers too have generally been believed to earn less than their counterparts in other industries. In respect of operative workers, Wages Councils set minimum rates and those cited above could, of course, be regarded as an underestimate of real earnings. However, hospitality industry researchers have shown that the Wages Council rates tended to be the going rates – i.e. employers paid at or slightly above the relevant hourly rates (where they were not breaking the law and paying less) (Lucas 1995). So what is the truth?

Table 10.1 shows data derived from the Government's 1994 New Earnings Survey (NTC/Bacon and Woodrow 1995). Here we can see that compared to all occupations, both operative and managerial positions in the hospitality industry are less well paid. At the same time, however, both hourly and annual rates of pay appear to be much higher than would be suggested by the last minimum rates set by the Wages Councils before their abolition in 1993. Here, we must be cautious, for these figures do not tell us how much of the weekly gross pay is derived from overtime working. Clearly, if relatively large sums are earned from overtime payments (even where these are paid at the basic, rather than 'special' overtime rate) then the basic pay in the industry is lower than these crude average figures suggest. Table 10.2 addresses this issue. This evidence suggests that

Table 10.1 Hospitality industry pay rates 1994

Job	Average gross weekly pay (£)	Per annum (£)	Hourly rate (39-hour week) (£)	Comment
Hotel and accommodation managers	299.30	15,563.60	–	56% earned less than £300
Restaurant and catering managers	281.60	14,643.20	–	64.2% earned less than £300
Chefs/cooks	203.90	10,602.80	5.22	68.5% earned less than £220
Waiting staff	157.10	8,169.20	4.02	87.8% earned less than £220
Bar staff	165.20	8,590.40	4.23	81.4% earned less than £220
Catering occupations	183.00	9,516.00	4.69	76.3% earned less than £220
All non-manual occupations	359.50	18,694.00	9.21	47.1% earned less than £300
All manual occupations	262.70	13,660.40	6.73	39.5% earned less than £220 70.0% earned less than £300
All occupations	325.70	16,936.40	8.35	55.2% earned less than £300

Source: derived from NTC/Bacon and Woodrow 1995

relatively little of the weekly wage is made up of overtime payment but this is not the same as saying that the basic wage is sound relative to other pay.

The Wages Councils used to set a basic hourly rate (for the first 39

Table 10.2 Hospitality industry pay rates and the contribution of overtime 1994

Job	Average gross weekly pay (£)	Of which overtime (£ %)
Hotel and accommodation managers	299.30	2.80 (1%)
Restaurant and catering managagers	281.60	6.50 (2.3%)
Chefs and cooks	203.90	8.90 (4.3%)
Waiting staff	157.10	4.30 (2.7%)
Bar staff	165.20	11.70 (7%)
Catering occupations	183.00	8.70 (4.75%)
All non-manual occupations	359.50	9.30 (2.6%)
All manual occupations	262.70	35.20 (13.3%)
All occupations	325.70	18.30 (5.6%)

Source: NTC/Bacon and Woodrow 1995

hours in a week) and an overtime rate (for subsequent hours) but evidence suggests that employers rarely paid overtime rates. Instead, for extra time worked they either continued to pay the basic rate or nothing at all. The crucial factor here, then, is the number of hours an employee works. For example, referring to Table 10.1, the average gross weekly pay of waiting staff in 1994 can be seen to be £157.10 which yields an average annual salary of £8,169.20 and an average hourly rate of £4.02 for an assumed 39 hour week. We do not know, however, what the length of the average working week is for this category of staff although again, research literature suggests that many operative and managerial staff work much longer weeks than their counterparts in other industries. If overtime is not paid and the number of hours worked is greater than 39 per week, then the average hourly rate will naturally fall. For example, if a waiter or waitress works 45, 50 or 55 hours under such circumstances then the average hourly rate would be £3.49, £3.14 and £2.85 respectively.

At the time of writing a combination of impressionistic evidence and verified data suggests that for operative workers, hourly rates lie on average between £3.00 and £3.35 an hour. A report in the trade magazine *Caterer and Hotelkeeper* of 2 March 1995 ('Minimum wage rate returns', p.7) suggested that Holiday Inn Worldwide offered £3.00 an hour as its basic minimum while Bass Taverns, involved primarily in public house management, were offering £3.05 an hour. More recently yet, a further *Caterer and Hotelkeeper* report ('Hospitality firms race to raise pay', 27 June 1996, p.7) recorded the hourly rates of eleven leading hospitality firms culled from a report by the independent Industrial Relations Services organization, suggesting that rises in hourly rates were indicative of employers' expectations of a Labour government being elected in 1997 and enforcing a minimum wage rate of around £4.15 an hour (see Table 10.3). In the companies listed at least, weekly basic rate (for 39 hours) appears a little better than in 1994. If the £3.00–£3.35 band is indeed typical, it might suggest that our hypothetical waiter/waitress was probably working around 47–52 hours a week in 1994 order to make their £157.10 average. But even if this is not the case, and the figures presented in Table 10.1 are wholly accurate, they indicate that hospitality industry employees are better paid than the industry's reputation might suggest but that these earnings are still below the norm. For example, managers' salaries at £299.30 and £281.60 per week are still 17 per cent and 22 per cent respectively below the average for non-manual occupations whereas for operative positions the deficit ranges from 40 per cent less than the average (waiters and waitresses) to 33 per cent less than the average (chefs and cooks). It would appear, therefore, that low pay remains a problem in the commercial hospitality sectors and this must be kept in mind in considering the discussion that follows.

Table 10.3 Minimum hourly rates in selected UK
hospitality firms 1996

	£
Accor UK	3.50
Bass Taverns	3.05
DeVere Hotels	3.42
Granada Road Services	3.60
Greenall's Hotel & Leisure	3.42
Holiday Inn (South)	3.90
Jarvis Hotels	3.20
Pizza Hut	2.92
Stakis	3.35
Swallow Hotels	3.25
Traveller's Fare	3.05
Whitbread Inns	3.25

Source: derived from Sangster, A. (1996) Hospitality firms
race to raise pay. *Caterer and Hotelkeeper*, 27 June, p. 7.

PAY STRUCTURES

Most organizations have, by accident or design, some kind of pay
structure. According to Riley (1991: 109–10) an efficiently functioning
pay structure performs four tasks:

1. it ensures sufficient number of people are attracted to work in the
   organization from the external labour market;
2. it encourages the internal labour market to function effectively so
   that promotion and training incentives exist to motivate staff;
3. it ensures that feelings of inequity are not engendered; and
4. it allows for the development of new jobs evolved through reorganization or the introduction of new technology (and, of course,
   facilitates the scope for removing old jobs no longer of relevance
   to the organization).

The whole concept of a pay structure of course implies a hierarchical
structuring of pay such that some people are paid more than others. The
pay structure thus embraces those criteria that an organization considers
important in this hierarchy. Strictly speaking, the various levels of pay
according to these criteria may be termed 'differentials' although the
latter term is also routinely employed to describe differences in pay
within already structured grades or categories, especially in organizations that employ many different occupational and skill groups.

  This last statement is important because the hierarchical nature of pay
structures is usually predicated on distinctions between occupations and
skill. Other differentiators typically include level of responsibility, prior
educational qualifications and/or those obtained 'on the job', and working conditions (for example, special allowances may be paid for working shifts and unsociable hours). Taken together, these elements should
be fused into a structure that possesses the qualities identified by Riley

(1991) and listed above. Of course, this is somewhat idealistic. Many organizational pay structures have not been, as it were, formally 'installed' but have grown up haphazardly according to custom and practice. Furthermore, in some cases, organizational pay structures have been distorted as a result of government intervention. To a degree this is true of the hospitality industry where, as we saw in the last section, rates set by Wages Councils were often treated by employees as the 'going rate'. This convenient mechanism offered employers little motivation to engage in developing even simple formalised pay structures. To this observation we can add two others, namely (a) that hospitality industry organizations are notorious for failing to develop internal labour markets, relying instead for recruitment on the external labour market; and (b) the perceived level of available internal rewards, notably tips, often leads employers to claim that low financial rewards (wages) are justified. All these elements give rise to distinctive 'structures' of pay in the hospitality industry and are further complicated in some cases by the informal individual contracts that employers strike with certain employees. Although generally believed to be on the wane, research evidence has suggested that in the past at least, these informal contracts, whereby certain individuals' pay rates are set secretly and informally, have been fairly widespread. The employees who have benefited from informal contracts have traditionally been those who have some special skill that is of value to employers. It is indicative of the nature of pay structures in hospitality services that at least in some cases in the past, such rewards have been informal rather than related to formal grading or differentials.

Indeed, we can go further than this and note that in many (but by no means all) hospitality organizations informality is the defining feature of pay structures. In noting this, we can translate Riley's four (ideal) features of a pay structure into four explicit statements about pay structures in the hospitality industry as follows.

1. Low pay in the industry (in the past supported by adherence to relatively low hourly rates of pay set by Wages Councils) has not been generally effective in attracting the quantity and quality of employees from the external labour market. Further evidence to support this view comes from the Department of Employment whose evidence suggests that hotel and catering employers are among those with the highest number of 'hard to fill' job vacancies (Lucas 1995; see also Chapter 2 in this volume).
2. Hospitality industry employers have a poor (though perhaps improving) track record on training, although the industry is traditionally associated with the availability of many opportunities for relatively fast advancement (promotion). However, to a very large extent these aspects of the industry's operating practices are linked only weakly to pay such that internal labour markets themselves are weak and relatively unstructured.
3. A wealth of research evidence suggests that many hospitality indus-

try workers consider themselves to be poorly paid. However, this general feeling of inequity is not the same as perceptions of inequity that arise within organizations when employees, having gone at least some way to reconciling their employment position, perceive themselves as being treated unfairly in remuneration terms relative to their colleagues in the immediate employment environment. Interestingly, and in confirmation of the arguments outlined in this section, one of the prime sources of disaffection is the perceived unequal distribution of gratuities rather than formal pay differentials, at least partially confirming the extent of the absence of formal pay structures in hospitality services and the visibility of informally struck pay differentials through the medium of individual contracts.

4. Job structures have, superficially at least remained remarkably stable in hotel and catering services. Underneath the surface of formal job structures, however, there has always been a good deal of flexibility in the way work is performed although evidence suggests that this flexibility occurs more within departments than between them. The tendency for operative workers to be paid roughly similar 'going' hourly rates has not conventionally posed a problem to employers who have been able to absorb changes in technology within existing job and occupational structures.

Following from the above, then, it is possible to cautiously assert that the reality of hospitality industry pay structures differs somewhat from the idealized HRM model of what such structures should do. The usual caveats apply here. Many small businesses have no obvious need for a formal pay structure, and this is unlikely to change in the near future. Furthermore, recent research evidence is suggestive of the possibility that many traditional remuneration practices associated with the hospitality industry, several of which have been discussed in this section, are in retreat and in corporate organizations at least, greater emphasis is being placed on formal pay structures more akin to the 'ideal' model outlined earlier. It is too early to tell whether this is a widespread or established trend but in any case, it is unlikely to detract from the persistence of (relatively) low pay in the industry and the general feeling among industry employees that they are undervalued. It has been frequently suggested that hotel and catering jobs are taken by those who are unable to obtain alternative employment (the reference is to those who are 'regular' members of the labour market, not, for example, students seeking a job to help them pay their way through college). This in itself implies that among operative workers at least, expectations of pay in the industry are not great.

For managerial employees, as noted earlier, low starting pay after graduation from college has often been offset by the belief that relatively rapid career and financial progress in the industry is possible. In point of fact, the figures considered in Table 10.1 above are suggestive of the fact that hospitality managers fare slightly worse on average than managers as a whole, although of course such figures do not take account of non-monetary and other benefits that may make up a total remuneration package (we will return to this later in the chapter). Attitudes may also be changing here. A survey in *Food Service Management* (Gary Crossley, 'Youthful Aspirations', April 1995: 18–20), a constituent part of the *Caterer and Hotelkeeper* trade magazine, found that final year college students expected to earn an average of £11,205 per annum in their first job, higher than students intending to enter hotels (£10, 800) or restaurants (£10, 250). Further, 17 per cent of those going into the food service sector (defined as the cost sector and contract catering) expected a starting salary of £15,000 per annum or more. In this section we have talked about pay structure and related conditions of employment. Interestingly, this small survey in *Food Service Management* (of 176 final year students) also found that:

- the factor most likely to put any student off working in the hospitality industry in general was poor salary (29 per cent) followed by poor working environment (22 per cent);
- salary was only the fifth most important factor overall considered very important when looking for a job behind 'on the job training'. 'working environment', 'speed of career progression' and 'the sector of the industry'; and
- of those who had decided not to work in the hospitality industry, the most significant deterrent was poor pay (53 per cent) followed by long hours (47 per cent).

JOB EVALUATION

Job evaluation is the name given to the process and techniques whereby individual jobs and groups of jobs are assessed and placed within a pay structure. Given that most pay structures are, by definition, hierarchical in nature, job evaluation is the process of establishing the relative worth of jobs in an organization. Depending on which source is consulted, job evaluation techniques can be broadly classified into the quantitative and qualitative (McKenna and Beech 1995) or the non-analytic, analytic and competency based (NTC/Bacon and Woodrow 1995) or several other headings depending on authors' personal predilections. In the end, such systems of classification are perhaps less important than the techniques themselves, the most common of which are as follows.

Job ranking

Also sometimes known as the 'factor comparison' method, job ranking involves:

- establishing a set of characteristics associated with task performance – for example, minimum level of education required, level of task complexity, level of responsibility; and

- using agreed job descriptions, ranking all jobs on a scale (usually 1–5) on a whole job basis.

This last point is important, for those involved in the job evaluation process are being asked to consider the absolute value of a job, on its own merits, without recourse to analysis of the actual constituent elements of the job but with reference to a set of general job characteristics.

Paired comparisons

The paired comparison method of job evaluation is a refinement of job ranking and involves comparing each job (description) with each other job. In this manner each job is scored as more important (2 points), less important (0 points) or equally important (1 point). For each paired comparison, the total number of points is summed to produce a rank order of jobs.

Job classification

Job classification systems are in essence a reverse job ranking exercise, in that a number of job grades are determined by reference to clearly defined factors such as skill level or responsibility and then jobs are compared with these grade definitions and allocated accordingly.

In the case of all of job ranking, paired comparisons and job classification the aim is to produce a satisfactory grading system for jobs within an organization. In the case of the first two methods, the grade system is derived from a process of ranking and comparison where in the case of job classification, the evaluation process begins with an already determined grade system. The main advantages of all three methods are that:

- they are relatively easy to understand;
- the methods employed are generally easy to perform (although where many jobs are involved, the paired comparisons method can be cumbersome without a computer applications system); and
- they are usually inexpensive to perform and install.

Disadvantages of these three methods of job evaluation include:

- the possibility that, as 'whole job' methods, important differences between jobs are ignored and jobs may be inappropriately classified;
- an over-reliance, following from the above point, on the collective knowledge of the job evaluators involved in the evaluation process – evaluators are unlikely to be familiar with the details of all the jobs to be classified; and
- a tendency to rigidity and inflexibility such that subsequent grading systems predicated on job evaluation are 'set in stone', risking the possibility that they come to be regarded as unfair by job holders as well as giving rise to ambiguities where certain jobs appear to straddle particular grades.

Points ranking systems

Generally accepted as the most widely used method of job evaluation, points ranking systems rely on the identification of job characteristics or factors which are believed to be (a) applicable to the analysis of most or all jobs in the organization; and (b) differentiate between such jobs. These characteristics or factors can be broken down into various sub-factors and then degrees or levels. Typically, such factors/sub-factors include skill, knowledge, responsibility, degree of decision-making, job complexity and requirement for problem solving. Points are awarded to each degree/level and the factors/sub-factors are weighted in terms of their predetermined overall importance. Each job description is scored against each factor and a total points score calculated for each such job description. Grades (and thus the remuneration structure) are generated from a comparative analysis of all job descriptions as scored.

Some issues in job evaluation

Invariably, even the most apparently scientific systems of job evaluation (for example, points ranking systems) are fundamentally subjectively-based. This can be a crucial factor in issues relating to discrimination, as job evaluation often lies at the heart of equal value claims – that is, where legal redress is sought because a woman (it is usually a woman) believes herself to be discriminated against by an employer because of her gender, in that she performs work of equal value to a man but is paid less. It is thus important that job evaluation schemes are free of gender bias in their construction. If this is one issue that must always be at the forefront of a manager's application of job evaluation system, a second is the growing significance of so-called 'benchmark' jobs.

A benchmark job is a job that is taken as typical of several other jobs that are perceived as being similar in nature. The benchmark job is then the one subject to the techniques of evaluation. The attraction of this approach is clear. In organizations where there are many different types of job, job evaluation (especially where analytic in nature – i.e. points ranking systems in the list enumerated above) can be time- and resource-consuming, often bureaucratic and necessarily rigid. The use of benchmark jobs as the basis for evaluation is likely to be quicker, less bureaucratic and perhaps lead to greater interpretative flexibility. However, as Riley (1991) notes this 'shortcut' approach has dangers, not least in that it discourages a balanced and comprehensive approach to job evaluation. To this we might add that a major limitation of all the more unwieldy techniques of job evaluation is that in dynamic organizations job content can change rather quickly, rendering pay schemes based on evaluation rather redundant within relatively short periods of time. The use of benchmark jobs can seduce those involved in job evaluation into prolonging the life of an outdated evaluation structure and pay scheme because such jobs take on a life of their own and tend to be focused upon to the exclusion of the jobs of which they are meant to be typical, and which may have changed or be changing.

A third issue to derive from this discussion of job evaluation relates to the observation of many commentators (e.g. Goss 1994; McKenna and Beech 1995) that there may be an emerging tendency towards simplified pay grade structures as a result of organizational 'delayering'. This latter trend has been noted as a feature of industrial relations in the new HRM-era that started in the 1980s. Job titles are as general as possible and embrace flexibility in the work that job holders are expected to perform. This not only erodes grade differentials but may lead to salary bands within grades. Sometimes, the adoption of a 'flatter' job grade structure may be linked directly to a single, unified pay scheme where every employee is covered by one salary structure and pay salary progression is determined by performance appraisal. One likely consequence of such a trend is that job evaluation techniques will become increasingly irre-levant to the setting of job grade and salary structures. It would be both foolish and premature, however, to suggest that job evaluation is about to be consigned to the dustbin. A survey by the UK Institute of Personnel and Development conducted in 1994 found that, while it was indeed the case that traditional systems were on the wane, they were being replaced by new, flexible, systems of job evaluation (Armstrong 1996). The key findings of the research, based on a questionnaire survey of some 316 organizations, supported by visits to 35 of these, found that:

- formal job evaluations schemes were operated by 55 per cent and 22 per cent without formal job evaluation systems intended to introduce it;
- traditional, rigid and bureaucratic approaches to job evaluation were not widely regarded as appropriate to modern working practices;
- in organizations with formal job evaluation, 68 per cent used a proprietary scheme; 29 per cent used point-factor rating systems; and 21 per cent used job classification;
- there was an increasing tendency for job evaluation to be integrated with processes such as continuing professional development, career management, succession planning and performance management, rather than being regarded as a stand alone 'personnel' technique; and
- attendant on the preceding point, a tendency to evaluate people as well as jobs.

Armstrong's research is thus suggestive of the earlier noted trend towards a more 'human resource management' approach to job evalua-tion associated with flexibility, and integration of evaluation into over-all human resource strategy within the organization.

REWARD SYSTEMS

Before we examine the principles that are usually presented as under-pinning the effective design and operation of reward systems – princi-ples according to good personnel and human resource management practice – it is crucial to look at how research has uncovered actual practices in the hospitality industry (by which we mean, primarily, the commercial sector of the industry).

The total and informal rewards systems

The main reference points for this discussion are the summaries contained in Wood (1992), Baum (1995) and Lucas (1995).

Research has shown that in commercial hospitality services, the majority of operative workers are paid an hourly rate (however this is delivered – whether in the form of a weekly pay packet or monthly salary) whereas senior supervisory and management staff tend to be salaried. Pay in the industry is, as we have noted, generally low in comparison to other forms of enterprise. It has been frequently supposed that low formal remuneration (pay) has been offset by various forms of 'payment in kind' such that pay is but one element in what Mars and Mitchell (1976) termed a 'total rewards system' which comprises:

> Basic Pay + Subsidized Food + Subsidized Lodging + Tips and/or Service Charges + 'Fiddles' + 'Knock-offs'.

The 'informal' element of this package is constituted by tips, service charge, 'fiddles' and 'knock-offs' which are informal in the sense of not forming part of the calculated elements given to the employee as part of their remuneration package. Each element in the total rewards system can be elaborated as follows.

- **Basic pay**. The rate for the job, usually hourly for the operative worker, paid by the employer to the employee.
- **Subsidized food**. This usually takes the form of meals on duty although in some operations employers extend the benefits of their trade purchasing power to employees such that food can be bought for domestic consumption. Under the Wages Council system of wage protection certain deductible allowances were permitted to employers for the provision of meals on duty. The provision of such food is often cited by employers as an important element in offsetting nominally low basic pay but many commentators have noted that (a) the quality of food offered to employees is often poor and workers rarely have the opportunity to eat at their leisure; and (b) the value of meals on duty is limited for those workers who have family commitments as the financial benefit is reduced because other members of the family still have to be fed.
- **Subsidized lodging**. Again, the provision of live-in (or live-nearby) accommodation at a subsidized or zero cost to the employee is often presented as a key non-financial benefit with a significant 'shadow' cash value by employers. While this may be true, it has again been noted that staff accommodation is often of poor quality. It is also usually only a genuine benefit to single employees. Even here, the

availability of live-in accommodation often means a lack of privacy for employees and the possibility that their close geographical proximity to their place of work will lead employers to treat them as being 'on call'.

- **Tips and service charge**. Tips and other gratuities are a form of reward originating with customers and (usually) given as recognition for an employee's service where this is perceived as in some way exceptional. Again, the extent of tipping in hospitality services is often cited by employers as a means whereby employees' income is supplemented. As a justification for low basic pay however, this argument is at best spurious. If tipping is unregulated, then only staff in customer service roles who have direct access to customers benefit from tipping (Dronfield and Soto 1980, estimated that around 50 per cent of the hospitality work-force has no access to customers and thus no direct access to tips). If tipping is regulated (by employers) then a pool may be established and monies distributed to all workers in a unit or operation on some proportional basis. While this does occur, for motivational reasons many employers when operating a pool or tronc system confine distribution of the proceeds only to staff of the department concerned. Whatever the case, tipping is not always as extensive or as valuable (in cash terms) as is often supposed. Furthermore, there is always some ambiguity as to the use to which tips are put. Employers have been known to use tips to subsidize basic pay and the now common practice of tipping by credit card (whereby the credit card slip is presented without a total, allowing the customer to add a gratuity before signing) also raises problems of ownership. These are illustrated in Box 10.1. The second case noted in Box 10.1 refers to service charges which are unambiguously the property of the employer. However, as can be seen from Mr Saavendra's case, employers have to be careful how they make contractual provision for the distribution of service charges. Again, there is some evidence of the service charge being used to subsidize basic pay.
- **Fiddles and knock-offs**. 'Fiddles' are a form of pilferage usually involving means by which employees secure direct cash benefits for themselves at the expense of either employer or customer (Mars and Nicod 1984; Wood 1992). This can mean basic stealing or, usually, more sophisticated means of siphoning cash from the unit or operation. 'Knock-offs' are a particular form of fiddle involving the purloining of usually small items, normally comestibles but also items such as soap, linen, towels and so on. While many hospitality organizations have become increasingly alert to these aspects of the employment environment and sought to control and eliminate fiddles and knock-offs, there is considerable evidence to suggest that such practices formed (and in many cases continue to form) a normative aspect of hospitality employment cultures, with employers, if not actually encouraging such behaviour, then certainly tolerating it within informal limits as part of an 'understanding' that employees are entitled to reasonable supplements in lieu of limited basic pay.

Box 10.1

The ambiguous ownership of tips

Mr Nerva was a waiter at the Heaven and Hell restaurant. He and some of his colleagues took their employer to court because they believed they had not been paid the (then) minimum rate laid down by the Wages Council for their sector. The employer claimed that the minimum had been paid, once the distribution of tips paid by customers adding sums to their cheques or credit card payment had been taken into account. They did not include cash tips which the employer conceded could not be treated as part of employees' wages. The employer claimed that the tips in question were distributed on a weekly basis, irrespective of whether the card sum/cheque had cleared, and ignoring the commission to the credit card company (i.e. the employer was effectively underwriting that percentage). Mr Nerva argued that the customers did not intend their tips to go to make up basic pay. Mr Justice Mance ruled in the employer's favour, saying that customers who tipped by cheque or credit card could not know how the money was distributed and, as far as the law is concerned, they are leaving it to the employer to decide how the sum should be paid out; it is, in effect, the property of the employer with customers only having a 'general hope and expectation' that the tip be passed on.

Mr Saavendra worked at a London restaurant where his contract said his pay was a standard rate 'plus service'. Each customer had a 15per cent service charge added to their bill and this was distributed to employees according to their position in the staff hierarchy. Because of recessionary pressures, the employer decided to allocate the service charge only partly to staff, reserving some for the restaurant. Mr Saavendra was unhappy both because takings were down (reducing the service charges available for distribution) and because those service charges that were collected were being skimmed by the employer. He claimed unlawful deduction of wages under the terms of the 1986 Wages Act. The Employment Appeal Tribunal agreed that while the employer had the right under the contract to allocate the service charge to the employees, he could not reserve a portion for the restaurant as the contract said that the service charge was for the employees and the latter had not given their agreement to the employer's new action. The employer had therefore unlawfully deducted employees' wages.

Sources:

Nerva and others v RL and G t/a Paradiso E Inferno Restaurant [1995], *Industrial Relations Law Reports*, p. 200.

Saavendra v Acegrand t/a Terrazza Est [1995], *Industrial Relations Law Reports*, p. 198.

Labour Research (1995) A tip for a good meal, June, p. 23.

Critique of the total rewards system

A major criticism of the total rewards systems as defined by Mars and Mitchell (1976) is, of course, that it is not total at all, omitting many other forms of formal and informal remuneration. Henderson (1965) cautions that tips, free meals and subsidized accommodation need to be distinguished from other supplements to wages, specifically pensions, paid vacations and sick pay. Johnson (1983) argues that the concept of the total rewards system excludes important elements such as seasonal bonuses, productivity payments, relocation expenses, free uniforms and free transport to and from work – items which defray workers' costs or enhance their remuneration. Thus, in summary, we can observe that total rewards must at least take account of any or all of the undernoted:

- Basic pay
- Overtime pay
- Bonuses
- Performance related pay
- Shift allowances
- Productivity rewards
- Contributory pensions
- Life assurance
- Sick pay
- Contributions to education costs for personal development
- Health care schemes
- Free or subsidized meals
- Free or subsidized accommodation
- Tips and/or service charge
- Fiddles and knock-offs
- Free uniforms
- Free transport to and from work
- Subsidized use of company facilities and discount performances
- Company car
- Holiday pay
- Contribution to costs of membership of professional organizations
- Contribution to cost of child care

However, at this point it is wise to sound a note of caution. While the hospitality industry has in some respects seemingly always relied to a greater or lesser degree on both formal and informal reward elements there is some evidence that the latter are declining in significance (Walsh 1991) as employers place greater and greater controls on such elements in order to curtail costs. We refer here not simply to tips, fiddles and knock-offs but to other elements which have, in any case, never been especially strong in the industry, such as contributory pension schemes.

PAY SYSTEMS AND ADMINISTRATION

All payment systems are directed towards providing employees with a remuneration package. A remuneration package has three primary elements (NTC/Bacon and Woodrow 1995). These are:

- Compensation – usually comprising basic salary; enhanced salary where appropriate (overtime); and holiday pay and other benefits (examples of the latter would include statutory payments for which the employee may qualify such as maternity and statutory sick pay, and payments permitted as part of an organization's policy – for example, paternity leave pay);

- Security – normally comprised of pension or superannuation and various forms of insurance, including health insurance; and
- Reward – including merit increases, bonuses, profit sharing dividends (performance related pay would be included here but is not strictly either a merit increase or bonus as will be shown below).

Also included within the remuneration package is the national insurance contribution of the employer (see Box 10.2).

Remuneration packages may be delivered in a variety of ways in the form of differing systems or part-systems. The five most common systems are time rates; payment by results; individual and/or group performance-related pay (including performance related pay); skill and/or competency based pay; and cafeteria or flexible benefit systems (McKenna and Beech 1995).

Box 10.2

National insurance and pay

Employers have a legal duty to pay national insurance contributions (NICs) in respect of their employees (excluding self-employed persons working as contractors). The level of NIC payments by both employees and employers depends on whether the parties concerned have contracted out of the State Earnings Related Pension Scheme (SERPS). In 1995–6, employees earning less than £58 a week did not pay NICs. Above £58 per week, an employee contracted out paid two per cent on £58 and thereafter 10 per cent on earnings between £58 and £440. A contracted-in employee paid 8.2 per cent on earnings between £38 and £440. For employers, payment structure was more complex but based on a sliding scale rising from three per cent on £58–£104.99 per week to 10.2 per cent on all earnings above £440 per week (contracted out) and for contracted-in employees, a more complex scale operated band on a percentage of between 3–10.2 per cent on £58 plus a percentage of the balance (from 2–10.2 per cent) on salaries ranging from £58 a week to more than £440 per week.

Sources:
NTC/Bacon and Woodrow (1995) *Pay and Benefits Pocket Book*, Henley: NTC Publications Ltd.
Boella, M. J., Calabrese, M., Goodwin, C. and Goss-Turner, S. (1996) *Catering Questions and Answers: Employment Law*, London: Croner's Catering.

Time rates

Perhaps the most common payment system in the UK, a time rates system rewards people on the basis of hours worked whether these are an hourly rate (£3.30 per hour), a weekly wage (£142 for a 39-hour week), or a monthly salary (this would normally be expressed as a per annum sum which would be paid in twelve equal instalments). In many industries, time rates are allocated to job grades after job evaluation. Within grades it is common to have an incremental scale along which employees move, usually at the rate of one increment per annum. Such schemes reward experience and the value of the task as assessed by job evaluation rather than the individual employee's own skills, competencies or work rate and quality. Advantages of time rate systems are that they (a) encourage retention of human resources through the stability associated with employees' knowledge that they will gradually improve their rewards because of the incremental nature of pay; (b) are easy to administer and allow the employer to accurately predict total labour costs; and (c) ensure quantity of output is not emphasized to the detriment of quality, and cost advantages to the employer accrue over time as employees enhance main skill and efficiency (McKenna and Beech 1995: 135). The principle disadvantage of time-rate systems is their inability to reward more productive workers through the motivation that might come from output-based rewards. The absence of an intrinsic motivational element is evident in the observation that two workers, the first twice as productive as the second, can occupy a similar grade (and an incremental position within that grade) and receive similar rewards.

Within the commercial hospitality industry, job evaluation related to grade is comparatively rare and hourly rates predominate as the principal means of time rate reward. This can be efficient from the employer's point of view because of the very large number of part-time and casual workers employed. This is not to say that weekly wage and monthly salary rates are not paid – they manifestly are, although such payments are often confined to managerial and higher grade workers where pay is very much packaged together with other non-cash elements of the kind discussed earlier. Also common in some companies in the hospitality sector is the four-weekly salary payment whereby, as the term implies, those covered by this mode of pay administration have their salary paid every four weeks rather than monthly – this often gives rise to a thirteen month year for such employees. Certain hospitality industry companies have also experimented with other time-rate derived payment schemes, notably flexible rostering and annual hours contracts (see Chapter 9) and 'zero-hour contracts' (see Box 10.3).

Payment by results

A contemporary version of the piecework system whereby pay is linked to the quality of an individual worker's output, payment by results (PBR) is difficult to combine with time rate systems of reward and

Box 10.3

'Zero-hours' contracts at Burger King – a Christmas carol with a difference

As organizations increasingly recognize the importance of flexibility, there are as we have already noted, a range of strategies to achieve flexible working. The improved responsiveness to market uncertainties and variability of demand can be crucial, although organizations also need to be aware of some potential difficulties and risks in the use of flexibility. This can be seen in issues like a loss of stability, continuity, commitment and quality, as well as creating possible employee resentment.

These issues are nicely illustrated by the case in December 1995 of Burger King, when they attracted opprobrium from a range of politicians, trade unionists and newspapers (for example, they just missed out on the *Observer*'s new Friend of Scrooge Award for businesses in the vanguard of corporate selfishness). The case arose out of the seemingly inappropriate use of 'zero-hours' contracts by a number of Burger King outlets. 'Zero-hours' hours contracts are an extreme form of temporal flexibility, which have been seen in a range of service sector industries, and in particular the hospitality and retail industries. The use of temporal flexibility can be important to organizations in allowing for the adaptability of working-time patterns to reflect work pressures and variability in customer demand. However at its most extreme level, 'zero-hours' contracts mean that there is no formal commitment made by employers regarding the number of hours the contract holder (i.e. the employee) will work. Instead, the employee is effectively 'on-call', working only for those periods that the employer calls upon them to do so. Clearly, while such arrangements provide a very high level of flexibility for the employer, they offer little in return for the employee, other than a lack of continuity and predictability.

The case of Burger King generated a high level of adverse publicity for the company due to the fact that their use of 'zero-hours' contracts resulted in apparent abuse by a number of managers. The example which attracted the most publicity was that of a Glasgow student, who regularly earned £1 for a five hour shift, even though he had been led to believe that he had been hired for £3.10 an hour. The reason behind such low wages was the practice of asking staff to 'clock-off' to take unpaid breaks when business was slack. Immediately business picked up staff were asked to 'clock-on' again, to meet these short-term changes in demand. When these practices were revealed there was a public outcry, and, after a campaign led by the Labour Party and the trade unions, Burger King were forced to pay £106,000 in compensation to 900 workers, who had been affected by these practices. Even though Burger King had argued that this 'misuse of rostering' was not company practice or widespread within the company, they agreed to the compensation. Subsequently, Burger King have told managers in both franchised and company outlets that 'clocking-off' staff during quiet periods is unacceptable and had now become a dismissable offence. Nonetheless the publicity generated by the case reflected badly on Burger King as an employer, especially when it was revealed that global sales for the previous year were £5000 million, and Grand Metropolitan the owners of Burger King had made a profit of £912 million. Burger King were held up as exemplifying the fact that low pay and poor employment practices are not simply found in small organizations – not really the image that any organizaton wants to be portraying to the world. Furthermore, agreeing to the compensation payment did not necessarily rectify the bad publicity. Though the compensation payments were welcomed, Ian McCartney, the Labour Party's Employment spokesman commented, somewhat sardonically, that 'Scrooge has backed down just in time for Christmas' and suggested that under a future Labour government such 'zero-hours' contracts would be made unlawful.

Sources:

Bowcott, O. (1995) Burger King backs down and pays up. *The Guardian*, 6 December, p. 4.

Caterer and Hotelkeeper, (1996) Burger King pays out £106,000 to staff. 4 January, p. 6.

---

must for the most part be seen as an alternative to such systems. The rationale for PBR systems is that they motivate workers to produce more and in so doing increase both output and the employee's reward (most PBR systems reward employees per unit produced). The implementation of such systems requires both careful job and task study and analysis to establish the most effective way of producing the units in question as well as the creation of quality control systems to ensure that in the drive for greater rewards, employees do not take short-cuts that reduce the quality of outputs. The obvious problem with PBR systems is that they are nigh-on-impossible to implement in service industries where outputs are not wholly tangible. In such circumstances, PBR systems are simply absurd but we should not ignore the moral objections to PBR systems. Piece-working is very much alive and well in the UK and is often found in industries where there is a large degree of home working (i.e. where employees operate out of their own home with materials supplied by the employer). Most such jobs are positively Dickensian in nature, being paid at exploitatively low rates.

Performance related pay

Individually-oriented systems of performance related pay (PRP) can add to time-rate systems of reward in that an individual employee's performance is measured against specific prior objectives, usually set and assessed in the context of performance appraisal and performance appraisal techniques (see Chapter 8). PRP assessments are usually conducted by an employee's supervisor(s), sometimes with professional help from outside human resource consultants retained on a systematic basis or from in-house HRM specialists. Subsequent to this, any PRP to be allocated may take one of several forms such as a lump sum; a bonus (often a percentage of basic salary with the percentage increase determined by the level of enhanced performance); and accelerated increment(s) (more rapid than normal movement up the pay scale within grade or, if a person is at the top of a grade, there may be some nominally 'discretionary' points reserved for performance-related reward that do not take the person to the next grade but may pay them at or very near the lowest increments on that grade).

Clearly, the administration of a PRP system requires a relatively sophisticated form of pay management (McKenna and Beech 1995: 137–8) where:

- the measurement of performance must be valid and reliable and amenable to meaningful calculation in order to establish significant differences between individuals;
- pay **grades** (and by extrapolation pay scales) must be of sufficient incremental width to allow meaningful differences in pay among employees; and
- the appraisal system must be carefully and accurately designed and relate closely to the organization's ability to relate performance to pay.

If there are serious faults in the administration of appraisal or there is little culture of trust within the organization, or management lacks the will and the strength to manage, then PRP systems can be divisive. However, PRP can, theoretically, offer many advantages to an organization. It can increase motivation by rewarding performance rather than simply providing cost of living pay increases of an incremental nature to all employees irrespective of the quality of their performance. PRP can attract high performers to an organization, especially at the managerial and supervisory level. Furthermore, 'non-performers' or 'underperformers' in an organization have the opportunity for remediation – that is, through the appraisal process they can be clearly told of the course of action that needs to be taken in order to improve performance and thus have opportunities to do this, thereby achieving the criteria necessary to qualify for PRP.

Disadvantages of PRP systems include the view that good performance is expected from all employees and where poor performance exists it is the job of management to rectify the situation. In this view, if a PRP system adds to the costs of wages and salaries throughout the organization or unit then it is more logical to target poor performance than give extra rewards to people who are being paid in any case to do the (adequate or high performance) job they are being paid for. Furthermore, PRP systems can lead to adversarial relationships between managers and subordinates and between peers and each other, detracting from openness and teamwork – qualities prized by many modern organizations and inherent to an HRM approach to labour relations. Perhaps the most obvious objection to PRP systems is that in effectively punishing non-performers or underperformers, the organization creates motivational problems for this group that are difficult or even impossible to overcome. Some of the objections to PRP in a wider context are to be found in the article in Box 10.4.

Group performance related pay schemes

Group PRP schemes are one method by which organizational disharmony and adversarialism may be avoided. The most common forms of group PRP are profit-related pay and employee share and share option schemes. Profit-related pay schemes are supposed to encourage employee identification with the organization through linking profits to pay, employees sharing in the 'good' times as well as times when organizational performance is not so good. The benefits to be gained from working for anything other than a constantly highly performing organization are therefore variable. Other alleged benefits of profit-related pay include a diminution of the 'them and us' barrier; an encouraged tendency towards co-operation rather than conflict; and an increased sensitivity among all members of the organization to the link between performance and profitability. The variety of employee share option and similar schemes are relatively complex and only the two main types are crudely summarized here (NTC/Bacon and Woodrow 1995: 50–62).

Profit-sharing schemes are where a company gives money to trustees to acquire shares in a company to be distributed free to eligible employees. Eligibility is governed by appropriate legislation and allocation of shares to employees is a matter of agreement between the company and the Inland Revenue. **Savings-related share option schemes** are where employees who are deemed eligible by the appropriate law can choose, if they wish, to join a scheme whereby they can purchase shares in their company via the proceeds of a savings contract.

Another variant of group PRP that has some currency is less structural in character than formal profit-sharing or share-option schemes. It involves the payment of bonuses to defined members of a work team when that team achieves certain productivity or quality criteria. A useful summary of the variety of schemes on offer is given by Armstrong (1996) reporting on an Institute of Personnel and Development (IPD) survey. Some of the schemes uncovered by the IPD survey included bonus payments distributed according to:

- attainment of sales and a measure of customer satisfaction (Norwich Union and Lloyds Bank);

Box 10.4

Some views on the pros and cons of PRP

Just desserts

No sooner has it become general practice than performance-related pay is under attack from management theorists. Does it work?

IN CORPORATE America, performance-related pay (PRP) is now an article of faith. Most American firms use some sort of financial incentives—such as merit pay, bonuses and share options—to reward and motivate their employees. Some have even taken to hiring "compensation consultants", with their performance measures, pay formulae and compensation grids, in a bid to turn remuneration into a science.

Employers introduce PRP—"eat what you kill", to its fans—for three reasons: to tighten their control of overall wage bills, to increase their flexibility and to motivate individual employees. In some forms (such as piecework and merit pay), it rewards individual productivity; in others (such as profit shares and divisional bonuses), it ties pay to group performance. But all PRP schemes try to get away from the idea that employees should advance together, lockstep, regardless of their varying contributions.

That gospel has now spread around the world. In 1979 only 8% of British firms awarded annual bonuses to managers, let alone workers. Today, more than three-quarters of firms use additional financial incentives. As well as being more common, PRP now accounts for a bigger share of pay. A typical senior British manager finds that 40% of his pay depends on performance, compared with less than 10% five years ago. And PRP has even crept into the public sector. Last year the government forced 1½m civil servants to accept PRP. Even the BBC and the Royal Household (the staff, not the family) are introducing the system.

In 1992 Japan's Honda linked 40% of managers' pay to performance; starting next June, performance will determine the entire package. In July another carmaker, Nissan, will increase the merit-based part of managers' pay from 60% to 85% of the total. In performance-paying firms such as Tokyo Gas and Fujitsu salary differentials between managers at similar stages in their careers have increased from 2-3% to 10-20%. In Germany, several organisations, including the newly privatised Post Office, have introduced PRP; many of German industry's current labour battles revolve around incentives to increase productivity.

The trouble with all this, according to a growing number of commentators, is that PRP does not work. In the United States, Alfie Kohn, a management theo-

MANAGEMENT FOCUS

rist, has stirred up an angry debate in the *Harvard Business Review* with an uncompromising article, "Why Incentive Plans Cannot Work". In Britain, a number of academic studies from independent research groups, such as the Institute of Manpower Studies and Incomes Data Services, have insisted that PRP is demotivating the workforce.

The critics advance four basic objections to PRP:

• Performance is notoriously difficult to measure. How do you calculate what each

Why the carrot? Can't you simply appeal to his sense of job satisfaction?

person contributed to the collective effort? If you rely on objective measures, such as a group's output, you sacrifice sensitivity and risk rewarding routine performance. Yet, if you rely on the opinions of supervisors or peers, you sacrifice consistency and risk favouritism. And, in the case of chief executives, the people being measured often rig the indicators.

• Money is not a particularly good motivator. Here the opponents of PRP divide into two opposing groups. The first holds that workers are much more influenced by the opinions of their colleagues and the intrinsic interest of their work than by crass material rewards. Mr Kohn, for instance, argues that financial incentives buy only short-term compliance rather than long-term commitment. A second group argues that money is too alluring: it forces workers—particularly salesmen—to do almost anything to shift their product and harm firms' reputations.

• PRP schemes have become a substitute for good management. At best, this means managers spend more time fiddling with

incentives than bringing out the best in their workers. Now that "flat" organisations are all the rage, with firms devolving decision-making, organising workers into teams and making everyone responsible for customer service, PRP looks decidedly antiquated. Significantly, the late W. Edwards Deming, the father of "total quality mangement", once said bluntly, "pay is not a motivator."

• PRP schemes are expensive. Workers have to be bribed to give up their existing practices, managers have to be retrained, performance measures have to be paid for. Moreover, PRP does not necessarily hold down pay rises. One firm, studied by the Institute of Manpower Studies, found that its wage bill increased by 8.25% in the first year after PRP was introduced, 12% in the second and 14% in the third.

No alternative

Defenders of PRP admit that many of these criticisms are justified, but argue that the fault lies with badly administered PRP schemes, rather than the concept itself. They have a point—not least because few of PRP's critics can suggest anything better. Suitably modified, PRP still looks the best way to recruit and retain scarce talent, to reward good work and send signals to poor performers. Indeed, as the fashion for less hierarchical organisations makes it harder to reward by promotion, pay is becoming more important.

The best managers have already started to reinvent PRP, shifting their attention from individual to group performance and from quantity to quality. Thus 3M, America's sticky-tape and post-it giant, pays its top people bonuses only if they contribute in several ways, including product innovation. As part of its annual pay review, John Lewis Partnership, a British retailer, has introduced open performance reports: these grade employees on personal qualities, such as their ability to get on with people, and then outline objectives for improvement and assess whether these are achieved. At AT&T's Universal Card Services division in Florida, staff pay is linked to the "know how" and "problem solving" involved in each job. It also uses a daily "excellence award" to reward high quality work.

Underneath these individual adaptations lies a more general pattern. Firms are abandoning the rigid formulae of the 1980s (where whole industries used the same method to calculate performance), in favour of tailor-made schemes. It looks as if those compensation consultants have a safe future after all.

© The Economist, London 24 January 1994

- speed of processing, accuracy and customer satisfaction (Pearl Assurance);
- whether local unit managers think a team has made a valuable contribution to performance (Benefits Agency);
- the team meeting both predetermined team *and* organizational goals (Rank Xerox; Portsmouth NHS Helpful Trust); and
- attainment of productivity targets (Finance Division of the Automobile Association in Scotland).

The most common forms of team bonus rewarded by the survey were payment of the same sum to members of the team, and as a percentage of base salary, the latter being the more popular. Armstrong (1996: 23) reports that team-pay appears to work best if teams:

- are 'stand alone' units where it is easier to agree clear performance targets and standards;
- are relatively autonomous with a large degree of self-management;
- have to perform work where tasks are largely interdependent and team work is *de facto* essential to success;
- are socially and structurally stable, mature, with team members sharing esteem and having a familiarity with communal strengths and weaknesses in task skills; and
- are comfortable – i.e. members are flexible and multi-skilled yet still capable of expressing original and sometimes controversial points of view which are treated seriously by other members of the team.

Advantages of this kind of team-pay can include cost effectiveness and cost-savings and the use of peer pressure to improve poorer performers in teams leading to overall improvements in organizational performance. Disadvantages include the possibility that teams can hit a downward spiral, leading to less pay and thus creating difficulties in attracting good quality staff to the team. The opposite trend is possible too, with strong team players gravitating towards highly successful, highly paid teams. Armstrong's analysis of the IPD survey suggests that team pay is not all that widespread but appears to work well in those organizations that have adopted it. A relatively sophisticated form of rewarding people, it remains to be seen whether it will have any general appeal to operators in the hospitality industry.

Skill-based pay

So far the methods of payment discussed have all been 'output' based. Quite simply, skill-based pay rewards 'inputs', specifically the acquisition and deployment of skills. Skill-based pay is, of course, not a new phenomenon, having to a degree co-existed alongside systems of manufacturing mass production for the best part of a century. Mass production systems of course heighten the demand for unskilled labour but in recent years, the drive in some industrial sectors to flatter, 'delayered' organizations has placed a premium on multi-skilling allowing reward systems based on employees' widening of their skill base. Multi-skilling as the term has been strictly understood in industrial relations has been used in the commercial hospitality industry, largely without success (see Wood 1992, for a review). Demand for unskilled or only partially-skilled staff remains high in the industry making it, in the foreseeable future at least, unlikely territory for the introduction of skill-based pay.

Cafeteria or flexible benefit systems

Flexible benefit systems, known as the cafeteria system in the UK, comprise salary and a variety of other benefits, for example company car, additional holiday entitlement, life insurance, private health insurance, membership of social clubs, modified working hours, special pension arrangements, mortgage subsidies, mobile telephones and so on (McKenna and Beech 1995: 144). The cafeteria system is **different** to the system of formal and informal rewards described earlier in the chapter as being a feature of hospitality industry employment. With cafeteria systems, access to elements in the total reward system are generally determined exclusively by management. More importantly, a key aspect of cafeteria pay is that employees are remunerated to the **same** 'cash' value but negotiate with management the value of elements within the total remuneration package such that non-salary elements are usually 'deductions' from basic salary (Goss 1994; NTC/Bacon and Woodrow 1995: 43). To illustrate this point, examine Table 10.4 which shows a hypothetical cafeteria system applicable to senior executives in a hotel company where three such executives have chosen a different mix of benefits.

CONDEMNED TO LOW PAY?

In this chapter, we have examined key aspects of reward as an aspect of human resource management practice, noting existing conventions in the commercial hospitality sectors. The key issues to consider are as follows.

- Pay in hotel and catering services used to be protected by a type of minimum wage legislation but this is no longer the case: though too early to tell categorically, it does appear that the abolition of protection is exerting a downward pressure on wages if only in respect of comparative pay over time rather than a direct 'slashing' of wages.
- Pay structures, by definition, are hierarchical in nature although in the hospitality industry they can assume an informal character in that elements of the remuneration package can be manipulated by management to suit short-term needs. Moreover, progression through the

Table 10.4 A hypothetical cafeteria benefits system for three hotel company senior executives

	Jean (£)	Leslie (£)	Anne (£)
Salary	35,000	32,000	30,000
NI on salary	3,570	3,264	3,060
Childcare	–	–	10,000
Car(s)	3,000	4,000	–
NI on cars	216	576	–
Pension	–	4,800	–
Life Assurance	300	–	–
Medical Insurance	250	500	640
Permanent Health Insurance	–	400	–
Mortgage subsidies	4,270	–	–
Accommodation allowance	–	2,500	2,800
Club subsidies	–	–	500
Extra holidays	–	–	1,500
Company holiday allowance	2,000	–	500
Mobile telephone	394	960	–
Total	49,000	49,000	49,000

Source: adapted from NTC (1995) *Pay and Benefits Pocket Yearbook,* Henley: NYC Publications Ltd.

pay structure can be rapid, even for relatively subordinate members of staff, as promotion opportunities arise regularly as a result of labour turnover.

- Job evaluation is the main means by which jobs are assessed and given a place within the pay structure. Some hospitality organizations, especially in the fast-food sector, have very sophisticated job evaluation schemes and many grades within the pay structure. Other hospitality organizations, notably hotels, often pay lip-service to the concept of job evaluation, at least for operative workers, instead determining pay rates somewhat crudely according to market conditions.

- Within the hospitality industry a distinction must be made between total or informal rewards, the latter being benefits (usually in kind) that the employer grants to selected employees or which come from the customer by virtue of tipping. Again, a large element of informality exists in the structure of formal and informal rewards which does not match 'best practice' in other major industries where, even when flexibility exists, pay systems are designed to ensure careful control over wages.

REVIEW AND DISCUSSION QUESTIONS

1. Should we tolerate low pay in the hospitality industry?
2. Is low pay in the hospitality industry accounted for by employers' meanness or structural inefficiency?
3. Are 'fringe benefits' important to workers in the hospitality industry?
4. Identify key elements of an effective payment scheme.
5. How could you effectively introduce performance related pay in hospitality services?

Disciplinary and grievance procedures 11

Historically, management in most UK industries has adopted a paternalistic attitude towards relations with staff. In such environments punitive disciplinary measures would be used indiscriminately and the threat of discipline would be used as a means of motivating staff. As noted by Farnham and Pimlott (1990), the emergence of trade union representation, statutory rights for employees, contracts of employment and necessary improvements in social conditions at work, forced employers to change their attitudes towards staff discipline. With a decline of the 'master and servant' relationship came a realization that to achieve company objectives managers must gain the respect and co-operation of employees so as to maintain their motivation. The means by which respect can be secured reflect sound human resource management practice and are described in this chapter.

We can list certain peculiarities of the hotel and catering industry that have hindered the development of a progressive management approach to disciplinary matters.

- There is little trade union representation in the hotel and catering industry. Unlike many other industries management has not come under pressure to implement programmes of employee rights. Management have therefore been able to direct staff without the fear of retaliation in the form of collective disputes.
- The heterogeneous nature of the hotel and catering industry makes the effective monitoring of employee relations difficult, if not impossible.
- A large proportion of the hotel and catering work-force is employed on a casual basis. Casual workers have few statutory employment rights.
- A high level of staff turnover is accepted as normal by employers and staff alike. In this type of environment the dismissal of an employee may not be regarded as an unusual or significant event.
- The scope for worker dissatisfaction is high considering the relatively low wages, physically demanding work, occasionally abusive customers, intense relationships with colleagues and the need for consistent standards of service. Management may be inclined to use disciplinary procedures as a reaction to displays of worker dissatisfaction.

At a basic level, disciplinary and grievance procedures are necessary as it is the role of management to maintain control of the work environment. Without rules anarchy may ensue. All human resource management practices that aim to improve worker productivity through the creation of a harmonious work environment can be seen as being, in part at least, conflict avoidance strategies. Even when such strategies are highly successful there will always be instances in which certain workers act in a wilful manner, possibly by refusing the reasonable requests of management, by damaging company property, by drinking on duty, by endangering the safety of others or by stealing. Disciplinary measures are necessary in these and similar circumstances to display to staff that their behaviour is considered unacceptable.

Commentators have suggested that for a variety of reasons the nature of workplace communities and of workplace activities in the hotel and catering industry may encourage deviant behaviour by staff. It is likely that disciplinary procedures will be invoked regularly in environments in which deviance is commonplace. Shamir (1981) and Spradley and Mann (1975) offer the following explanations for this deviance.

- **Opportunity**. There are many opportunities for staff to indulge in theft, whether this be of food and drink from the hotel or restaurant (i.e. the employer) or from guests (stealing from guest bedrooms).
- **Working hours**. It is often the case that hotel and catering employees are often working during other peoples' leisure time. It is therefore difficult for them to form social relationships outside the industry. A sense of difference or even exclusion may exist which staff will seek to reaffirm by indulging in extremes of behaviour, such as drinking heavily.
- **Living arrangements**. Many workers in the hotel and catering industry are provided with live-in accommodation by their employers. This may actually serve to heighten workers' exclusion from the mainstream of society and therefore encourage deviant behaviour.
- **Nature of work**. Those with menial, uninteresting jobs may engage in behaviour regarded as deviant as a means of countering their monotonous existence while at work

The importance of disciplinary rules at work has been recognized by the state. Section 1 (1) of the Employment Rights Act 1996 requires employers to inform staff of company disciplinary procedures through their publication in employees' terms and conditions of employment. Employers must specify:

- disciplinary rules applicable to the employee;
- a person to whom the employee can apply if he is dissatisfied with any disciplinary decision, or if he seeks redress of any grievance relating to his employment;
- how such an application should be made; and
- any steps following from such an application.

If rules are to be enforceable they will have to be understood and accepted by management and staff alike. It is therefore advisable to involve employees and management of all levels in the formation or revision of disciplinary rules.

The nature of disciplinary procedures will vary depending upon the style and size of organizations. However, the Advisory, Conciliation and Arbitration Service (ACAS) provides useful guidelines from which company specific rules could be developed (ACAS 1994:3). These guidelines suggest that disciplinary procedures should:

- be in writing;
- specify to whom they apply;
- provide for matters to be dealt with quickly;
- indicate the disciplinary actions which may be taken;
- specify the levels of management which have the authority to take the various forms of disciplinary action, ensuring that immediate superiors do not formally have the power to dismiss without reference to senior management;
- provide for individuals to be informed of the complaints against them and to be given an opportunity to state their case before decisions are reached;
- give individuals the right to be accompanied by a trade union representative or by a fellow employee of their choice;
- ensure that, except for gross misconduct, no employees are dismissed for a first breach of discipline;
- ensure that disciplinary action is not taken until a case has been carefully investigated;
- ensure that individuals are given an explanation for any penalty imposed; and
- provide a right of appeal and specify the procedure to be followed.

In her study of personnel practice in the UK hotel and catering industry, Price (1994) surveyed 241 establishments. Only 24 per cent of the sample had formal disciplinary procedures which included all the clauses which are recommended in the ACAS Code of Practice. Price noted that 'On the whole, those items intended to protect employees from capricious decisions were included less frequently, while those which underlined management authority were included most frequently' (1994: 50).

As noted in the ACAS guidelines it is essential that each case should be carefully investigated before any disciplinary action is taken. Management will hold little credibility if it is seen to operate disciplinary procedures in an indiscriminate manner. It may be useful to conduct disciplinary interviews during which those involved are given a chance to explain to management their version of events. Employees should also be given the opportunity to present witnesses who may be able to substantiate their claims. If the alleged misbehaviour is of a serious nature then it is advisable to consider suspending the member of staff involved, on full pay, while the facts are established. Only once management is satisfied that it has reached the truth should disciplinary measures be imposed. There is a recognized procedure for disciplining staff that involves four progressive stages. Each stage brings the employee closer to the ultimate sanction of dismissal. These stages are as follows.

- **Stage one: Verbal warning**. If an employee's performance is unsatisfactory in some respect then he or she should be given a formal verbal warning.
- **Stage two: Written warning**. If the offence is of a serious nature, or if an employee has failed to respond to a verbal warning, then he or she should be given a written warning. This should include details of the offence and a plan of what is expected of the employee in light of what has occurred.
- **Stage three: Final written warning**. If an employee's offence is of a particularly serious nature or if he or she has failed to improve their behaviour despite having received a first written warning, then a final written warning should be imposed. This should state that if the employee continues to perform in an unacceptable manner then dismissal will follow. A final written warning is sometimes accompanied by a period of suspension from work.
- **Stage four: Dismissal**. Any employee who fails to improve conduct after receiving a final written warning should be dismissed. Dismissal can also be used for employees who commit a single act of gross misconduct such as stealing or being drunk on duty.

The progressive nature of this approach gives employees the chance to modify their behaviour before being severely disciplined. Demotion as a disciplinary tool should be avoided. It is unlikely that a demoted worker will ever be able to regain motivation and make a significant contribution to the organization. Similarly, employers should avoid overreaction. It is always a matter of perception as to what certifies minor, intermediate and major infractions of discipline but a sensible organization will have at least a rough scale of offences ordered by degree of acceptability/unacceptability. Box 11.1 shows one possible scale of this kind.

It is essential to keep concise records of any disciplinary action that is taken. The nature of each offence, the discipline imposed and any related communication between management and employees should be recorded in case the member of staff involved decides to lodge an appeal. It is usual that following a set period of satisfactory behaviour a continuing employee will have any records of misconduct removed from their personnel file.

GRIEVANCE PROCEDURES

Grievance procedures relate to the right of staff to express dissatisfaction with aspects of their employment. Such problems in no way undermine management authority. They ease communication between staff

Box 11.1

A possible scale of disciplinary offences

TYPE OF PROBLEM AND DISCIPLINE	EXAMPLES
Minor infractions (will result in internal counselling and, if repeated, will lead to formal counselling, verbal warnings and, if continued, more serious action.)	• Regular absenteeism and/or lateness • Poor job performance • Failure to observe health and safety requirements • Improper use of company telephones • Abuse of meal and refreshment breaks • Failure to obey reasonable instructions of a superior
Intermediate infractions	• Refusal to carry out reasonable instructions issued by a supervisor • Discourteous treatment of guests or other employees • Intoxication or incapacity on duty due to the use of alcohol or drugs • Negligence that results in injury to oneself, another employee, or a guest • Sleeping while on duty • Fighting or other physical altercations on company property
Causes for immediate dismissal	• Knowingly falsifying employment records • Unauthorized destruction or removal of company property • Possession, display, or use of dangerous weapons while on company property • Possession of alcohol or drugs while on company premises

and management on difficult topics, and are therefore an aid to the resolution of problems. The nature of the workplace environment has a significant effect on the way in which grievances are presented by staff and received by management. In theory, workers should feel free to bring to the attention of management any grievance which they may have, without fear of reprisal. However, many hotel and catering organizations lack this progressive human resource management approach, and staff may therefore avoid raising grievances as to do so may affect their career prospects (Farnham 1993: 146)

The right of workers to express their grievances in a formal manner, without fear of the consequences, is recognized in law. The Employment Rights Act 1996 obliges employers to include a grievance remedy in workers' terms and conditions of employment (although this is an implied duty). As with disciplinary measures, it is normal for grievance procedures to follow a progressive pattern, as follows.

- **Stage one**. Issues which are raised in an informal manner, without initiating the formal grievance procedure, should be handled sensitively. It is obviously preferable if grievances can be successfully handled in this way.
- **Stage Two**. The aggrieved member of staff should contact their line manager who can make the necessary arrangements for a grievance meeting. An alternative contact should be provided, probably a member of the human resource department where such a department exists, in case an employee feels unable to approach the line manager (in many cases the grievance will relate to the line manager). From this early stage it is essential to treat any grievance from a member of staff as a serious issue – an employee is unlikely to initiate formal proceedings unless he or she feels very strongly about a subject.
- **Stage three**. At a grievance meeting attended by the member of staff involved, a representative of the human resource team and witnesses if necessary, the details of the grievance can be examined and recorded. The grievance meeting should be held in a private room and be free from interruptions. No response should be offered by management at this stage.
- **Stage four**. Management should take some time to fully investigate the circumstances surrounding the grievance. After consideration of the evidence management should decide on an appropriate course of action.
- **Stage five**. Provision must be made for employees to take their grievances to a higher authority should they be dissatisfied with the action that is recommended by management. Employees should be entitled to approach senior management if they remain aggrieved.
- **Stage six**. It is essential to provide written confirmation of the agreement that is reached so as to avoid unnecessary confusion.

By monitoring the nature of staff grievances management can identify and rectify any recurring problems.

In many industries it is normal practice for employees to receive union representation if they have a grievance relating to their work. The lack of union involvement in the hotel and catering industry heightens the importance of implementing effective grievance procedures. Staff must feel empowered to present grievances without the need for external representation.

DISMISSAL

It is possibly the case that dismissal of staff is more common in the hotel and catering industry than in many other sectors. A high level of staff turnover is accepted as normal by employers and staff alike. In this type of environment the dismissal of an employee may not be regarded as an unusual or significant event. In addition, as was noted earlier, there are certain peculiarities of the industry that may have hindered the development of a progressive attitude towards staff discipline.

However, there are some circumstances in which it is necessary for employers to use the ultimate disciplinary sanction of dismissal. Employers must be certain that the grounds for dismissal fall within one of the statutory categories, as detailed in the Employment Rights Act 1996. These are:

- a reason relating to the workers capability or qualification for performing work of the kind he or she was employed to do;
- a reason relating to the conduct of the worker;
- the worker is redundant;
- the worker could not continue to work in the position held without contravention of a duty or restriction imposed by under enactment; and
- for some other substantial reason of a kind such as to justify dismissal of a worker holding the position which the worker held.

By providing these guidelines the Act seeks to encourage reasonable employment practice and to protect employees from unfair dismissal. However, difficulties can arise over the interpretation of these guidelines. Management must hold sufficient evidence to ensure that a decision to dismiss a member of staff is justified. Such a decision can only be taken having carried out a proper investigation and having followed the correct legal procedures.

The Act recognizes three types of dismissal as follows.

1. Direct dismissal, in which a member of staff is presented with a date for the termination of their employment and a full explanation of the reasons for termination.
2. The expiry of a fixed-term contract, without its renewal.
3. Constructive dismissal, in which the employer changes the circumstances of an employee's conditions to such an extent that the employee feels forced to leave. Constructive dismissal is legal if an employer can show that he or she acted in a reasonable manner at all times.

If an employee believes that the grounds for his or her dismissal lie outside the statutory categories, or that they are based on flawed evidence, then he or she is entitled to appeal against the decision to an industrial tribunal. Industrial tribunals have responsibility for various aspects of employment legislation. However, approximately 60 per cent of cases relate to unfair dismissal (Farnham 1993: 53). In most cases it is only those employees who have had two years' continuous service who may bring claims of unfair dismissal. However, if dismissal is on the grounds of trade union activity, race or sex discrimination, pregnancy, or is related to a 'spent' conviction as defined by the Rehabilitation of Offenders Act 1974, then no period of continuous service is required before an unfair dismissal claim can be lodged (see Box 11.2).

Dismissed employees take claims to industrial tribunals by contacting the Central Office of Industrial Tribunals (COIT), of which there is one in London and one in Glasgow. In the case of claims against most forms of direct dismissal, claimants must contact COIT within three months of the termination date. For claims relating to redundancy this period is extended to six months. COIT then informs an industrial tribunal in the appropriate geographical location and also a local representative of the Advisory, Conciliation and Arbitration Service (ACAS). If it is felt that it may be worthwhile, ACAS will arrange a conciliatory meeting between the two parties involved in the dispute in an attempt to settle the matter before formal proceedings begin.

The industrial tribunal panel has three members, one of whom is a person suitably qualified in law, the other two being lay people from employer and worker associations. The proceedings are loosely based on those of a courtroom. Both sides begin by stating their positions in opening speeches. There is then a period of questioning witnesses and cross-examination before closing speeches are made. In due course the panel will provide both parties with a written decision. An industrial tribunal can review any decision that it has made should new witnesses appear or previously undisclosed evidence be presented. No legal aid is available to claimants but advice can be obtained from organizations such as the Citizens' Advice Bureau, the Equal Opportunities Commission and the Commission for Racial Equality.

In cases in which unfair dismissal is proved, it is common for industrial tribunals to grant a cash compensatory award, which must be paid by the former employer. Employers are not compelled to reinstate members of staff, but failure to do so may result in the level of compensation being raised. It is possible for claimants to appeal against the ruling of an industrial tribunal by referring the decision to an employment appeal tribunal (EAT). To be successful at this final stage it is necessary to prove that the decision was flawed on legal grounds or that vital evidence was overlooked. In England and Wales EATs are chaired by High Court judges, whereas in Scotland it is a Court of Session judge who presides.

Box 11.2

Industrial tribunals in the 1990s

During the 1990s, there has been an increasing number of applications to industrial tribunals for redress of perceived injustices in the workplace. In the twelve months to March 1994, some 70,000 claims were submitted, a 30 per cent increase on the previous year which itself measured a 28 per cent increase on the year before that. Most claims centre on unfair dismissal (60–70 per cent). In 1994 30 per cent of such cases were upheld: in 1993–4 this figure was around 40 per cent. The highest success rate of cases however is for those brought under the 1986 Wages Act and concerned with the unlawful deduction of pay from employees' wages by employers. In 1993–94, some 60 per cent of such cases were successful. The majority of successful tribunal applicants receive financial compensation. Again, in 1993–94, some key figures were:

- for unfair dismissal, an average of £2,773;
- for sex and race discrimination, average of £2,999 and £3,499 respectively.

These averages disguise other trends however. Thus, one-third of unfair dismissal claimants received in excess of £5,000. Around one-third of successful sex-discrimination claimants received in excess of £8,000 (in November 1993, the upper limit on compensation for sex discrimination cases was removed, with this being extended to cover racial discrimination from July 1994: in 1993–94 only one-fifteenth of successful racial discrimination applicants received more than £5,000 in compensation). The following chart shows the percentages of cases dealt with by industrial tribunals in 1993–94 in certain categories and how they fared.

	Unfair Dismissal	Equal Pay	Sex Dis- crimination	Wages Act	Race Dis- crimination	All
Total cases completed	100	100	100	100	100	100
Cases heard at IT	35	6	26	32	44	37
Dismissal	60	58	66	43	74	53
Upheld	40	42	34	57	26	47
Cases not going to IT	65	94	74	68	56	63
Withdrawn	45	93	43	73	63	57
Settled	55	7	57	27	37	43

At the time of writing in 1996, the Government has proposed changes to the industrial tribunal system. The key change suggested is the use of alternatives to tribunal hearings in dispute resolution by allowing ACAS to fund and provide an arbitration scheme for unfair dismissal claims (the largest category of submissions to industrial tribunals).

Other proposed changes to the operation of industrial tribunals include allowing decisions on the basis of written submission of evidence; allowing more cases to be heard by tribunal chairpersons on their own; and changing the name of industrial tribunals to employment tribunals.

Sources:
Labour Research (1995) Number of Tribunal Cases Soars. January, pp. 21–2.
Croner (1990) *Caterer's Briefing No 85*, October 15, p. 1.

REDUNDANCY

Under the Employment Rights Act 1996 there are various categories of potentially fair dismissal, one of which is that the need for an employee has become redundant. The statutory definition of redundancy, as taken from s.139 1(b) of the Act, is as follows:

(a) the fact that the employer has ceased, or intends to cease, to carry on the business for the purpose of which the employee was employed by him, or has ceased or intends to cease to carry on that business in the place where the employee was so employed;
(b) the fact that the requirements of that business for employees to carry out work of a particular kind or for employees to carry out work of a particular kind in the place where they were so employed, have ceased or diminished or are expected to cease or diminish.

It can therefore be seen that the need to create redundancies could occur due to a trading crisis, through incompetent human resource planning or through business reorganization after a transfer of company ownership.

Redundancies have not been common in the hotel and catering industry, although this may change as the Government continues to pass publicly owned catering facilities to the private sector and as a result of high profile company take-overs. Before embarking on a programme of compulsory redundancies it is worth considering any alternative options that may exist. If, for example, the planned redundancies are due to a downturn in business activity can management be sure that this downturn will be permanent? If not, it may be possible to implement temporary changes in human resource activity such as reducing working hours, encouraging part-time work or introducing job sharing schemes.

If only a proportion of staff are to be made redundant it can prove difficult to form selection criteria. The most common means of selecting staff for redundancy is on a 'last-in-first-out' basis, whereby the most recently appointed staff will be the first to face redundancy. It is risky to select members of staff for redundancy on the basis of their performance or skill levels as dismissed staff have the right to take employers to industrial tribunals on the grounds of unfair selection.

It is often the case that employers offer 'voluntary redundancy' to their work-force as a means of avoiding the emotive subject of compulsory redundancy. However, this can be a costly option for employers as it is often those employees with the longest periods of service who will apply. Redundancy payments for such members of staff are likely to be substantial.

The Employment Rights Act 1996 makes provision for the payment of statutory redundancy payment to staff by employers. The method of calculating the level of statutory redundancy payments to which employees are entitled centres around the number of years of continuous service that are held. Entitlement may be lost or reduced if staff broke their service for reasons such as strikes, work outside the UK or suspension due to misconduct. Details of the complexities of redundancy payments are available from the Department of Education and Employment.

Very broadly, payments are calculated as follows:

- for each year of continuous service while aged 41–64 years, pay 1.5 weeks' wage;
- for each year of continuous service while aged 22–40 years, pay 1 weeks' wage; and
- for each year of continuous service while aged 18–21 years, pay 0.5 weeks' wage.

There is no entitlement for service under the age of 18, over the age of 64, or for part-time work.

Before carrying out redundancies management are obliged to consult with the Department of Education and Employment. If less than 100 employees are to be made redundant within 30 days, then consultation must take place at least 30 days before the first redundancy. If 100 or more employees are to be made redundant within a 90 day period then consultation must take place at least 90 days before the first redundancy.

Responsible employers recognize that redundancy is a highly sensitive subject. This being the case, effective communication with staff about the need for redundancies to be made and the method staff selection to be used is essential. It is also advisable for employers to offer some form of counselling to those members of staff who are selected for redundancy on areas such as seeking new employment and investment of redundancy money.

REVIEW AND DISCUSSION QUESTIONS

1. What factors contribute towards an effective grievance procedure?
2. Why should we need to 'discipline' workers?
3. How might the rights of the employee be reconciled with the needs of the employer in resolving employee grievances against supervisors?
4. Outline a suitable disciplinary procedure for a small hospitality unit.
5. Does the hospitality sector deserve its description as a 'hire and fire' industry?

References

Adam-Smith, D. and Goss, D. (1993) HIV/AIDS and hotel and catering employment: some implications of perceived risks. *Employee Relations*, **15**(2) pp. 25–33.

Advisory, Conciliation and Arbitration Service (ACAS) (1994) *Code of Practice 1: Disciplinary Practice and Procedures in Employment*, London: ACAS.

Anderson, G. (1992) Selection, in *The Handbook of Human Resource Management*, (ed. B. Towers) Oxford: Blackwell, pp. 167–85.

Anderson, G. and Evenden, R. (1992) *Managing Skills: Making the Most of People*, London: Addison-Wesley.

Arkin, A.(1994) Positive HIV and AIDS policies at work. *Personnel Management*, December, pp. 34–7.

Armstrong, M. (1996) How group efforts can pay dividends. *People Management*, **225**, January, pp. 22–7.

Armstrong, M. (1993) *A Handbook of Personnel Management Practice*, 4th edn, London: Kogan Page.

Aslan, A. and Wood, R. (1993) Trade unions in the hotel and catering industry: the views of hotel managers. *Employee Relations*, **15**(2) pp. 61–70.

Aston, G. (1995) Management must give a lead in protecting workers. *Hospitality*, October/November, pp. 28–9.

Baldacchino, G. (1995) Total quality management in a luxury hotel: a critique of practice. *International Journal of Hospitality Management*, **14**(1) pp. 67–78.

Ball, S. (1994) Improving labour productivity, in *The Management of Foodservice Operations*, (eds P. Jones and P. Merricks) London: Cassell, pp. 188–203.

Bartlett, N. (1993) Forte introduces flexible rates. *Caterer and Hotelkeeper*, 19 August, p. 7.

Baum, T. (1995) *Managing Human Resources in the European Tourism and Hospitality Industry – A Strategic Approach*, London: Chapman and Hall.

Bean, R. (1994) *Comparative Industrial Relations*, 2nd edn, London: Routledge.

Beardwell, I. and Holden, L. (1994) *Human Resource Management – A Contemporary Perspective*, London: Pitman.

Becker, C. (1996) Implementing the intangibles: a total quality approach for hospitality service providers, in *Service Quality in*

Hospitality Organizations, (eds M. Olsen, R. Teare, and E. Gummesson) London: Cassell, pp. 278–298.

Blundy, A. (1995) Buddies of the air fight for their rights. *Independent on Sunday*, 26 February, p. 24.

Blyton, P. and Turnbull, P. (1994) *Dynamics of Employee Relations*, Basingstoke: Macmillan.

Boella, M. (1993) *The New Health and Safety Regulations*, Kingston-upon-Thames: Croner Publications.

Boella, M. (1994) *Croner's Catering*, Kingston-upon-Thames: Croner Publications.

Boella, M. J., Calabrese, M., Goodwin, C. and Goss-Turner, S. (1996) *Catering Questions and Answers: Employment Law*, Kingston upon Thames: Croner Publications.

Bratton, J. and Gold, J. (1994) *Human Resource Management – Theory and Practice*, Basingstoke: Macmillan.

Brymer, R. (1991) Employee empowerment: a guest-driven leadership strategy. *Cornell Hotel and Restaurant Administration Quarterly*, **32**(1) pp. 55–68.

Bunker, J. (1990) HIV and the workplace – the American experience, in *HIV/AIDS in Employment*, (eds M. Kapila and D. Williams) London: Health Education Authority, pp. 8–14.

Chell, E. (1983) Political perspectives and worker participation at board level: the British experience, in *Organizational Democracy and Political Processes*, (eds C. Crouch and F. Heller) New York: John Wiley, 142–64.

Clutterbuck, D. and Kernaghan, S. (1994) *The Power of Empowerment – Release the Hidden Talents of Your Employees*, London: Kogan Page.

Collier, R. (1995) *Combating Sexual Harassment in the Workplace*, Buckingham: Open University Press.

Commission on Industrial Relations (1971) *The Hotel and Catering Industry Part 1: Hotels and Restaurants*, London: HMSO.

Commission for Racial Equality (1989) *Racial Discrimination and Grievance Procedures*, London: Commission for Racial Equality.

Commission for Racial Equality (1991) *Working in Hotels*, London: Commission for Racial Equality.

Commission for Racial Equality (1995) *Large Companies and Racial Equality*, London: Commission for Racial Equality.

Confederation of British Industry (1994) Implementation of health and safety Directives in member states. *CBI News*, February p. 17.

Cressey, P. (1993) Employee participation, in *The Social Dimension – Employment Policy in the European Community*, (ed. M. Gold) Basingstoke: Macmillan, pp. 85–104.

Croner (1996) Disability Act Codes of Practice. *Croner's Catering Briefing*, **85**, 15 October, p. 1.

Croney, P. (1988) An investigation into the management of labour in the hotel industry. University of Warwick, MA thesis.

Crouch, C. (1977) *Class Conflict and Industrial Relations Crisis*, London: Heinemann.

Cunningham, I., Hyman, J. and Baldry, C. (1996) Empowerment: the power to do what? *Industrial Relations Journal*, **27**(2) pp. 143–54.

Dickenson, F. (1988) *Drink & Drugs at Work – A Consuming Problem*, London: Institute of Personnel Management.

Dronfield, L. and Soto, P. (1980) *Hardship Hotel*, London: Counter Information Services.

Drummond, G. (1994) Danger at work. *Caterer and Hotelkeeper*, 14 April pp. 38–40.

EIRR (1994a) The UK and 'European Works Councils'. *European Industrial Relations, Review*, **246**, July pp. 14–21.

EIRR (1994b) European Works Councils: the action begins. *European Industrial Relations Review*, **250**, November, pp. 14–17.

EIRR (1995a) Direct communications in European multinationals, *European Industrial Relations Review*, **253**, February, pp. 25–6.

Evans, D.T. (1993) *Sexual Citizenship: The Material Construction of Sexualities*, London: Routledge.

Farnham, D. (1993) *Employee Relations*, London: Institute of Personnel Management.

Farnham, D. and Pimlott, J. (1990) *Understanding Industrial Relations*, London: Cassell.

Forte, C. (1987) *Forte – The Autobiography of Charles Forte*, London: Pan.

Fuersternberg, F. (1993) Industrial relations in Germany, in *International and Comparative Industrial Relations – A Study of Industrialised Market Economies*, 2nd edn, (eds G. Bamber and R. Lansbury) London: Routledge, pp. 175–96.

Gaymer, J. (1990) Legal aspects of AIDS in the workplace, in *HIV/ AIDS in Employment*, (eds M. Kapila and D. Williams) London: Health Education Authority, pp. 15–26.

Gold, M. and Hall, M. (1994) Statutory European Works Councils: the final countdown? *Industrial Relations Journal*, **25**(3) pp. 177–86.

Gospel, H. and Palmer, G. (1993) *British Industrial Relations*, 2nd edn London: Routledge.

Goss, D. (1994) *Principles of Human Resource Management*, London: Routledge.

Goss-Turner, S. (1992) *Managing People in the Hotel and Catering Industry*, Kingston-upon-Thames: Croner Publications.

Grummitt, J. (1983) *Team Briefing*, London: Industrial Society.

Guest, D. (1992) HRM in the United Kingdom, in *The Handbook of Human Resource Management*, (ed. B. Towers) Oxford: Blackwell, pp. 3–26.

Guest, D. (1995) Human resource management, trade unions and industrial relations, in *Human Resource Management – A Critical Text*, (ed. J. Storey) London: Routledge, pp. 110–41.

Hawkins, K. (1994) Taking action on harassment. *Personnel Management*, March, pp. 26–9.

Health and Safety Executive (1993) *HSE Information Sheet, Food Sheet No 1*: *Safety Pays in the Catering Industry*, London: HSE.

Health and Safety Executive (1994) Inspectors call for improved safety in food industry. *Health and Safety at Work*, April, p. 11.

Health and Safety Executive (1996) *Catering Information Sheet No 6: Slips and Trips: Summary Guidance for the Catering Industry*, London: HSE.

Henderson, J.P. (1965) *Labour Market Institutions and Wages in the Lodging Industry*, Michigan: Michigan State University, MSU Business Studies.

Hendry, C. (1995) *Human Resource Management – A Strategic Approach to Employment*, Oxford: Butterworth-Heinemann.

Hofstede, G. (1984) *Culture's Consequences – International Differences in Work-Related Values*, London: Sage.

Hosking, P. (1994) Labour drives for worker directors. *Independent on Sunday*, 25 September, p. 11.

Hotel and Catering Training Board (HCTB) (1987) *Women in the Hotel and Catering Industry*, Wembley: HCTB.

Howells, R. and Barrett, B. (1982) *The Health and Safety at Work Act: A Guide for Managers*, London: Institute of Personnel Management.

Hubrecht, J. and Teare, R. (1994) A strategy for partnership for total quality service. *International Journal of Contemporary Hospitality Management*, **6**(2) pp. i–v.

Hyman, J. and Mason, B. (1995) *Managing Employee Involvement and Participation*, London: Sage.

Institute of Personnel and Development (IPD) (1994) *Personnel Management and Europe*, IPD Brief, July.

Ishak, N.K. and Murrmann, S.K. (1990) An exploratory study of human resource management practices and business strategy in multi-unit restaurant firms. *Hospitality Research Journal*, **14**, pp. 143–55.

James, P. (1990) Holding managers to account on safety. *Personnel Management*, April, pp. 55–8.

James, P. (1992) Reforming British health and safety law: a framework for discussion. *Industrial Law Journal*, **21**(2) pp. 83–105.

Janner, G. (1982) *Janner's Guide to the Law on Sick Pay and Absenteeism*, London: Business Books.

Johns, N. (ed.) (1996) *Productivity Management in Hospitality and Tourism*, London: Cassell.

Johnson, K. (1978) Personnel matters: an overview or an oversight? *Hotel, Catering and Institutional Management Association Journal*, January, pp. 21–3.

Johnson, K. (1983) Trade unions and total rewards. *International Journal of Hospitality Management*, **2**(1) p. 31–35.

Kandola, R. and Fullerton, J. (1994) Diversity: more than just an empty slogan. *Personnel Management*, November, pp. 46–9.

Kapila, M. and Williams, D. (eds) (1990) *HIV/AIDS in Employment*, London: Health Education Authority.

Kelliher, C. and Johnson, K. (1987) Personnel management in hotels:

some empirical observations. *International Journal of Hospitality Management*, **6**(2) pp. 103–8.

Kibling, T. and Lewis, T. (1996) *Employment Law: An Advisers Handbook*, London: Legal Advice Group.

Labour Research (1996) Avoiding the pitfalls of psychometric tests. Labour Research, September, 30.

Lashley, C. (1994) Is there any power in empowerment? Paper presented to the Third Annual Council for Hospitality Management Education (CHME) Research Conference, Napier University, April.

Lashley, C. (1994a) Empowerment: meanings and myths. *Hospitality*, August, p. 17.

Lashley, C. (1995) Towards an understanding of employee empowerment in hospitality services. *International Journal of Contemporary Hospitality Management*, **7**(1) pp. 27–32.

Lashley, C. and McGoldrick, J. (1994) Barriers to employee empowerment. Paper presented to the Third Annual Conference on Human Resource Management in the Hospitality Industry, 'Quality and Human Resources', London, February.

Little, A. (1996) New disability legislation will affect all employers. *Hospitality*, October/November, pp. 26–7.

Lockwood, A. and Ghillyer, A. (1996) Empowerment: the key to service quality, in *Fifth Annual Council for Hospitality Management Education (CHME) Research Conference, Conference Papers*, (ed. C. Lashley) Nottingham: Nottingham Trent University Commercial Centre.

Lord, W. (1994) The face behind the figures. *Personnel Management*, December, 30–33.

Lucas, R. (1993) Ageism and the UK hospitality industry. *Employee Relations*, **15**(2) pp. 33–41.

Lucas, R. (1994) Industrial relations discourse, theory and practice in service industries: are hotels and catering merely a case of oversight? Paper presented to the British Universities Industrial Relations Association (BUIRA) Conference, Worcester College, Oxford, July.

Lucas, R. (1995) *Managing Employee Relations in the Hotel and Catering Industry*, London: Cassell.

Lucas, R. and Jeffries, L. (1991) The 'demographic time bomb' and how some hospitality industry employers are responding to the challenge. *International Journal of Hospitality Management*, **10**(4) pp. 323–7.

Macaulay, I.R. and Wood, R.C. (1992) Hotel and catering industry employees' attitudes towards trade unions. *Employee Relations*, **14**(2) pp. 20–8.

Macaulay, I.R. and Wood, R.C. (1992a) *Hard Cheese: A Study of Hotel and Catering Employment in Scotland*, Glasgow: Scottish Low Pay Unit.

McDermid, K. (1993) Safety first. *Hospitality*, February, pp. 14–15.

McDermid, K. (1994) A question of quality. *Hospitality*, February, pp. 17–18.

McIlroy, J. (1991) *The Permanent Revolution? Conservative Law and the Trade Unions*, Nottingham: Spokesmen for the Society of Industrial Tutors.

McKenna, S. and Beech, N. (1995) *The Essence of Human Resource Management*, London: Prentice-Hall.

MacLachlan, R. (1996) Ageism hits one-third of workers. *People Management*, 25 January, p. 11.

Marchington, M. (1988) The four faces of employee consultation. *Personnel Management*, May, pp. 44–7.

Marchington, M. (1992) Employee participation, in *A Handbook of Industrial Relations Practice*, 3rd edn (ed. B. Towers) London: Kogan Page, pp. 208–25.

Marchington, M. (1995) Involvement and participation, in *Human Resource Management – A Critical Text*, (ed. J. Storey) London: Routledge, pp. 280–305.

Mars, G and Nicod, M. (1984) *The World of Waiters*, London: Allen & Unwin.

Mars, G. and Mitchell, P. (1976) *Room for Reform*, Milton Keynes: Open University Press.

Messenger, S. and Makinson, A. (1992) Managing new national education and training initiatives in the hospitality industry (DeVere Hotels), in *Managing Projects in Hospitality Organizations*, (eds R. Teare, D. Adams and S. Messenger) London: Cassell, pp. 241–62.

Mullins, L. J. (1992) *Hospitality Management: A Human Resources Approach*, London: Pitman.

Newby, T. (1992) *Cost-Effective Training: A Managers Guide*, London: Kogan Page.

Nichols, T. (1975) The sociology of accidents and the social production of industrial injury, in *People and Work*, (eds G. Esland, G. Salaman, and M. Speakman) Edinburgh: Holmes MacDougall/Open University Press, pp. 217–29.

NTC/Bacon and Woodrow (1995) *Pay and Benefits Pocket Yearbook*, Henley on Thames: NTC Publications.

Ollerearnshaw, S. and Waldeck, R. (1995) Taking action to promote equality. *People Management*, 23 February, pp. 24–9.

Orwell, G. (1995) *Pages From a Scullion's Diary – An Extract from Down and Out in Paris and London*, London: Penguin.

Pendleton, A., Robinson, A. and Wilson, N. (1993) Influencing strategic decisions: worker directors in UK bus companies. Paper presented at Employment Research Unit Annual Conference, 'Unions on the brink: the future of the trade union movement', Cardiff, September.

Peters, R. (1993) Making work a place of safety. *Hospitality*, February, pp. 12–13.

Peters, R. (1995) Danger! Discrimination at work. *Hospitality*, February/March, pp. 28–9.

Pickard, J. (1996) The wrong turns to avoid with tests. *People Management*, 8 August, pp. 20–23.

Preston, P. and Scott-Parker, S. (1995) Improving access to the workplace. *People Management*, 16 November, pp. 18–24.

Price, L (1993) The limitations of the law in influencing employment practices in UK hotels and restaurants. *Employee Relations*, **15**(2) pp. 16–25.

Price, L. (1994) Poor personnel practice in the hotel and catering industry: Does it matter? *Human Resource Management Journal*, **4**(4) pp. 44–62.

Ramsay, H. (1991) Reinventing the wheel? A review of the development and performance of employee involvement. *Human Resource Management*, **1**(4) pp. 1–22.

Reiter, E. (1991) *Making Fast Food – From the Frying Pan to the Fryer*, London: McGill-Queens University Press.

Riley, M. (1991) *Human Resource Management: A Guide to Personnel Practice in the Hotel and Catering Industry*, Oxford: Butterworth-Heinemann.

Riley, M. (1996) *Human Resource Management in the Hospitality and Tourism Industry*, 2nd edn, Oxford: Butterworth-Heinemann.

Riley, M. (1993) Back to the future: lessons from free market experience. *Employee Relations*, **15**(2) pp. 8–16.

Roberts, J. (1995) *Human Resource Practice in the Hospitality Industry*, London: Hodder and Stoughton.

Royle, T. (1995) Corporate versus societal culture: a comparative study of McDonald's in Europe. *International Journal of Contemporary Hospitality Management*, **7**(2/3) pp. 52–6.

Royle, T. (1995a) Corporate versus societal culture: a comparative study of human resource strategies in two European Countries, Germany and the UK. Paper presented to the Labour Process Conference, Blackpool, April.

Royle, T. (1996) Avoiding the German system of co-determination: the McDonald's corporation, in *Fifth Annual Council for Hospitality Management Education (CHME) Research Conference, Conference Papers*, (ed. C. Lashley) Nottingham: Nottingham Trent University Commercial Centre.

Salamon, M. (1992) *Industrial Relations: Theory and Practice*, 2nd edn, London: Prentice Hall.

Sangster, A. (1994) Large firms face Works Councils. *Caterer and Hotelkeeper*, 17 November, p. 10.

Shamir, B. (1981) The workplace as a community: the case of British hotels. *Industrial Relations Journal*, **12**, pp. 45–56.

Singh, R. (1992) Human resource management: a sceptical look, in *The Handbook of Human Resource Management*, (ed. B. Towers) Oxford: Blackwell, pp. 127–43.

Spradley, J.P. and Mann, B.J. (1975) *The Cocktail Waitress: Women's Work in a Man's World*, New York: John Wiley and Sons.

Storey, J. (1992) *Developments in the Management of Human Resources*, Oxford: Blackwell.

Streeck, W. (1984) Co-determination: the fourth decade, in *Interna-

tional Perspectives on Organisational Democracy, (eds B. Wilpert and A. Sorge) Chichester: John Wiley and Sons, pp. 391–421.

Thomas, R. (1996) Cheap labourers pawns in the take-over game. *The Guardian*, 10 January, p. 16.

Torrington, D. and Hall, L. (1995) *Personnel Management – HRM in Action*, 3rd edn, London: Prentice Hall.

Towers, B. (1992) Introduction to *The Handbook of Human Resource Management*, (ed B. Towers) Oxford: Blackwell, pp. xvi–xxi.

Tse, E. (1996) Towards a strategic quality framework for hospitality firms, in *Service Quality in Hospitality Organizations*, (eds M. Olsen, R. Teare and E. Gummesson) London: Cassell: pp. 299–313.

Umbreit, W.T. (1987) When will the hospitality industry pay attention to effective personnel practices? *Hospitality Education and Research Journal*, **11**, pp. 3–14.

Walsh, T. (1991) 'Flexible' employment in the retail and hotel trades, in *Farewell to Flexibility*, (ed. A. Pollert) Oxford: Basil Blackwell, pp. 104–15.

Weeks, J. (1989) *Sex, Politics and Society: The Regulation of Sexuality Since 1800*, London: Longman.

Williams, M. (1993) Computer tracking is key to curbing staff absenteeism. *Caterer and Hotelkeeper*, 20 May, p. 14.

Williams, M. (1994) No ill feelings. *Caterer and Hotelkeeper*, 7 July, pp. 52–4.

Williams, M. (1994) Baring the Soul. *Caterer and Hotelkeeper*, 6 October, 68–9.

Wood, R.C. (1992) *Working in Hotels and Catering*, London: Routledge.

Wood, R.C. (1994) *Organizational Behaviour for Hospitality Management*, Oxford: Butterworth-Heinemann.

Further reading

Audit Commission for Local Authorities and the NHS in England and Wales (1990) *Managing Sickness Absence in London*, London: Audit Commission.

Bagguley, P. (1987) *Flexibility, Restructuring and Gender: Changing Employment in Britain's Hotels*, University of Lancaster: Lancaster Regionalism Group.

Brown, R. (1992) *Understanding Industrial Organizations – Theoretical Perspectives on Industrial Sociology*, London: Routledge.

Butler, S.R. and Skipper, J. (1981) Working for tips. *The Sociological Quarterly*, **22**, Winter pp. 15–27.

Butler, S.R. and Snizek, W.E. (1976) The waitress–diner relationship. *Sociology of Work and Occupations*, **3**(2) pp. 209–22.

Collins, H. (1993) *Human Resource Management, Personnel Policies and Procedures*, London: Hodder and Stoughton.

Courtier, D. (1994) What is the role of a safety representative at work? *Caterer and Hotelkeeper*, 1 September p. 57.

Critten, P. (1993) *Investing in People: Towards Corporate Capability*, Oxford: Butterworth-Heinemann.

Department of Trade and Industry (1985) *Quality Circles*, National Quality Campaign, London: DTI.

Donovan Report (1968) *Royal Commission on Trade Unions and Employers' Associations 1965–1968*, Cmnd 3623, London: HMSO.

Equal Opportunities Review (1995) Opportunity 2000 reports mixed progress, **59**, January/February. pp. 4–5.

EIRR (1994c) The first UK European Works Council. *European Industrial Relations Review*, **251**, December, pp. 20–2.

EIRR (1995b) European Works Councils: trends and issues. *European Industrial Relations Review*, **256**, May, pp. 14–22.

Fairhall, D. and Beavis, S. (1995) Nuclear firm to get huge fine. *The Guardian*, 14 April, p. 3.

Ford, V. (1996) Partnership is the secret of progress. *People Management*, 8 February, pp. 34–36.

Gabriel, Y. (1988) *Working Lives in Catering*, London: Routledge & Kegan Paul.

Hall, I. (1993) Equal opportunities: making it happen. *Voice*, July/August, pp. 28–9.

Hiemstra, S.J. (1990) Employment policies and practices in the lodging industry. *International Journal of Hospitality Management*, **9**(3) pp. 207–21.

Hotel and Catering International Management Association (HCIMA) (1996) TUC warns on industry safety standards. *Hospitality*, August/September, p. 7.

Hyman, J. (1992) *Training at Work: A Critical Analysis of Policy and Practice*, London: Routledge.

Hyman, J. (1992a) Training and development, in *The Handbook of Human Resource Management*, (ed. B. Towers) Oxford: Blackwell, pp. 257–76.

Jefferies, D. R., Evans, B. and Reynolds, P. (1992) *Training for Total Quality Management*, London: Kogan Page.

Jenkins, M., McEwen, J., Moreton, W., East, R., Seymour, L. and Goodwin, M. (1989) *Smoking Policies at Work*, London: Health Education Authority.

Labour Research Department (1995) Disabled workers' jobs threat. *Labour Research*, November, pp. 19–21.

Merrick, N. (1995) Firms pushed to address gay rights at work. *People Management*, 23 March, pp. 9–10.

Moorby, E. (1991) *How to Succeed in Employee Development: Moving from Vision to Results*, London: McGraw-Hill.

Moss, G. (1991) *The Trainer's Desk Reference*, London: Kogan Page.

Mullins, L. J. (1995) *Hospitality Management: A Human Resources Approach*, 2nd edn, London: Pitman.

Newby, T. (1992a) *How to Design and Deliver Quality Service Training*, London: Kogan Page.

Nichols, T. (1986) Industrial injuries in British manufacturing in the 1980s. *Sociological Review*, **34**(2) pp. 290–306.

Personnel Management (1994) Companies carry out audit on workers with disabilities, August, p. 5.

Pratt, K. J. and Bennet, S. G. (1982) *How to Pass Exams in Personnel Management*, London: Cassell.

Ridley, A. (1995) The human cost of discrimination. *People Management*, 23 February, p. 30.

Sisson. K. and Storey, J. (1993) *Managing Human Resources and Industrial Relations*, Buckingham: Open University Press.

Skills and Enterprise Network (1994) Employers' attitudes towards people with disabilities. *Skills and Enterprise Briefing*, 4/94, February.

Smith, M. and Robertson, I. (1993) *Advances in Selection and Assessment*, Chichester: John Wiley and Sons.

Stout, S. (1993) *Managing Training*, London: Kogan Page.

Van der Wagen, L. (1994) *Building Quality Service with Competency-based Human Resource Management*, Oxford: Butterworth-Heinemann.

Voice (1993) Safety pays HSE's message to caterers, July/August, pp. 27.

Williams, A. (1995) Giving disabled people equal protection in the workplace. *People Management*, 9 March, p. 45.

Index